THE GREATEST TREASON

The Untold Story of Munich

By the same author
1940

T H E
Greatest Treason

THE UNTOLD
STORY OF MUNICH

by Laurence Thompson

WILLIAM MORROW & COMPANY, INC.

New York 1968

*For Alison
and
Lesley*

Contents

Foreword

THIS is not only the story of an international crisis, but of men under the strain of deciding between peace and a war which they believed would end civilization, and of the different ways in which they reacted to that strain. Because its protagonists are of our common human kind, the colours I have found appropriate are not black and white, but, more realistically, varying shades of grey. Life, particularly political life, is never as clear-cut or as simple as black and white.

The story I have told is that of the Munich Crisis of 1938. To many readers this will be a part of remote history. To me it is part of experience, because I was then aged 23, living in London, and as the crisis mounted, not expecting to go on living for very long.

I therefore began with certain preconceptions. The arch-villain of the piece to me was Hitler, the secondary villain Neville Chamberlain, and the hero Eduard Benes, President of Czechoslovakia. In the course of my research, I have had to revise these over-simple judgments. Hitler remains the villain, though with reservations. Benes comes out rather worse, Chamberlain rather better, than I had expected. Benes was placed in an intolerable position and his downfall was probably inevitable, but reluctant though I have been to judge him, it seems to me that he contributed to his fate by being, in a famous phrase, too clever by half.

I have not tried to whitewash Chamberlain, but have presented him as I found him, an honest but vain man, obsessed with the importance of his chosen role as peacemaker. His dilemma may strike a chord of sympathy in an American generation faced with its own rather similar problems over Vietnam.

It is in reference to Chamberlain that I have chosen my title from T. S. Eliot's play about Thomas à Becket, another vain man facing a dilemma of conscience.

Since I have found myself obliged to challenge a number of accepted legends about the Munich Crisis, it may be worth setting out briefly the processes of thought by which I reached my conclusions.

The commonly accepted story of Munich affirms that, in the early weeks of September, 1938, the Sudeten Germany Party in Czechoslovakia led by Konrad Henlein deliberately broke off negotiations with the Czechoslovak Government, and staged an insurrection which was to give Hitler the opportunity for precipitating a crisis.

When I reached this point in my research, I became both puzzled and intrigued, because much of the available evidence points in quite another direction. In the first place, it seems clear that whether or not Hitler wanted to invade Czechoslovakia, or threaten to invade it, he was in no position to do so until after the end of September. In the second place, the Henleinists had already forced concessions from the Czechoslovak Government which would have presented them with a quite unexpected political triumph and which, if implemented, would probably have led in the course of time to the disintegration of the Czechoslovak state.

Why, in those circumstances and *at that particular time*, should either Hitler or the Henleinists want to break off negotiations which were going much as they had planned? The breakdown, indeed, caught Hitler badly on the wrong foot, and might well have finished him altogether.

It seemed to me that at least part of the answer might be found among the surviving leaders of the Henleinists. I therefore went to some trouble to track them down, and ask them to tell me their versions of events. I have emphasized elsewhere in the book the obvious fact that they cannot be accepted as impartial witnesses. But their story, fragmentary though it is, does seem to me to make sense in the context of what is now known about Hitler's military plans. It led me to the conclusion that, though Hitler had indeed arranged with the Henleinist leaders for an "incident" which would provide him with an excuse for forcing a crisis over Czechoslovakia, this was to have been after the end of September. The events of September 12 and 13 were not it.

I next asked myself who did have a motive for breaking off negotiations at that time—for it is the date, in mid-September, which is the essential point. The answer to which I incline is that it was somebody, or some group, on the Czech side, possibly including Benes. I cannot, of course, prove this. Nobody left full confession in left boot. But I have set out the circumstantial evidence for my conclusions as clearly as I can.

The second legend of Munich which I found puzzling concerns the Czechoslovak Army. This has been described by Sir Winston Churchill as having a strength of forty divisions, and by President Benes as being one of the best in Europe. It was dug in behind fortifications which contemporary reporters called a Czech Maginot Line. Yet it surrendered to Hitler without firing a shot. Why? The accepted answer is that the Czechoslovaks wanted to fight, but were prevented from doing so by the pusillanimity of Britain and France. This, too, is an over-simplification. The Czechoslovak Army consisted, not of forty divisions, but fourteen, with another fourteen reserve divisions of varying effectiveness. The fortifications were nothing like as strong as the Maginot Line. And neither the Czechoslovak military leaders nor the politicians had any intention of fighting, because they knew that whatever Britain, France and Russia did, it meant annihilation for them. Certainly they were "betrayed" by Britain and France— but they were most grateful for the betrayal.

I have also been able to throw some new light on British policy during the crisis, which contradicts another Munich legend of Chamberlain as a weak, bumbling old fool with an umbrella who was completely taken in by Hitler. He was not taken in. He was walking the knife-edge of a deliberate policy and he well knew the risks. But he would never go as far to appease Germany as Sir

Nevile Henderson, the British Ambassador in Berlin, wanted him to go. Just how far that was, the hitherto unpublished extracts from Henderson's memorandum on page 270 make clear.

There are a few more legends of Munich which I have trampled underfoot on my way through the tangled undergrowth of this very complex story, but these are the main ones. And of course I have not said the last word. That is likely to be found, if it ever is, in Prague or in Moscow.

But even though no Western writer at the present time can hope to be definitive, the Munich Crisis seems certain to go on exercising its fascination. It is a classic example of how not to conduct international negotiations, and as such should be compulsory study for all would-be politicians, and indeed for every democratic—with a small d—electorate.

More important, the miscalculations engendered by these events of 1938 led the world into a war which changed civilization. Neither we, nor the generations that follow us, can afford to ignore any lessons we can learn from that.

List of Illustrations

Acknowledgments

THIS INTERPRETATION of events leading up to the Munich Agreement of 1938 differs in some important respects from that hitherto accepted by historians. In particular, it puts forward a new account of what happened in the Sudeten German areas of Czechoslovakia following Hitler's speech at Nuremberg on September 12.

In reaching my conclusions, I have been greatly helped by a series of interviews with the surviving leaders of Konrad Henlein's Sudeten German Party: Dr. Hans Neuwirth, Dr. Franz Köllner, Dr. Wilhelm Sebekovsky, Dr. Walter Brand, and Herr Franz May. I am of course aware that the testimony of these witnesses cannot be considered impartial. But as a working journalist I have been interviewing people for over thirty years, during which one does acquire certain characteristics of a lie detector, and these people were able to convince me that, allowing for inevitable lapses of memory caused by time, they were speaking the truth.

I have also benefitted from eye-witness accounts of events in Prague and the Sudetenland given me by the late Wenzel Jaksch, Herr Ernst Paul, Herr Karl Simon, and Mr. Harry Hochfelder, who has helped me in many other ways. Dr. A. Domes, director of the *Deutsche Stiftung für Europäische Friedensfragen,* and Herr Hans D. Wenders greatly facilitated my inquiries. The director and staff of the Collegium Carolinum in Munich brought to my attention a number of books, pamphlets and documents not readily accessible in Britain and the United States, including Kurt Rabl's German translation of extracts from the official minutes of meetings of the Czechoslovak Cabinet.

Mr. Robert J. Stopford, a member of the Runciman Mission to Czechoslovakia, and Sir John Troutbeck, former First Secretary of the British Legation in Prague, have read and commented on my chapters dealing with events in Czechoslovakia. I have benefitted greatly from their advice, but they are not, of course, to be taken as agreeing with my interpretation of the facts.

On the British side, I am most grateful to Sir Alexander Cadogan for his guidance and for permitting me to quote from his unpublished diary. The Earl of Halifax has allowed me to see his father's papers and to quote an unpublished letter from them. I must express my thanks also to Major T.L. Ingram and the City Librarian of York for facilitating my access to the late Lord Halifax's papers.

M. Edouard Daladier, former President of the French Council of Ministers, has kindly answered a number of questions put to him on my behalf by Lieutenant-Colonel Ferdinand Otto Miksche. I am also indebted to Colonel Miksche for an enlightening appreciation of the strengths and weaknesses of the Czechoslovak Army, in which he served.

Among many other people to whom I am grateful for information and guidance are Mr. Frank Ashton-Gwatkin; Mr. Frank Barlow; Mr. Vernon Bartlett; Lord Brooke of Cumnor; Lord Butler of Saffron Walden; Mr. David Clarke; Group Captain M.G. Christie; Mr. W.N. Ewer; Sir Roy Fedden; Mr. G.E.R. Gedye; Mrs. Geoffrey Goodman; Sir Charles Harris; Dr. Fritz Hesse; Mr. J. Kosina; Sir Reginald Leeper, the Librarian of the British Broadcasting Corporation; Dame Marjorie Maxse; Mr. C.F. Melville; Dr. Paul Schmidt; Dr. Otto Strasser; Major-General Sir Kenneth Strong; the Earl of Swinton; and Sir Horace Wilson.

I must also express my indebtedness to the Clerk of the Records, House of Lords Record Office; the Librarian of the Foreign Office and Mr. G. Hiscock; the Office of the Chief of Military History, United States Army, Washington; and the director and staff of the British Museum Reading Room and Newspaper Library.

Mrs. Ray Wolf made my translations from the German. Mr. John Hartley of Visnews enabled me to see again the contemporary British newsreel films. Mr. L.R. England of Mass-Observation Ltd. has allowed me to quote freely from "Britain; by Mass-Observation." The Controller of Her Majesty's Stationery Office has allowed me to quote from official documents, copyright of which is vested in the Crown. The late Dr. John Masefield's verse on page 152 is quoted by permission of the Society of Authors and *The Times*.

Finally, I owe more than I can easily express to my long-suffering editor, Hillel Black. Is not every able editor, as Thomas Carlyle once asked, a ruler of the world? Hillel is.

The last temptation is the greatest treason:
To do the right deed for the wrong reason.
T. S. ELIOT: *Murder in the Cathedral*

CHAPTER 1

The Shadow of General Douhet

WHAT BROUGHT the crisis suddenly home to thousands of Londoners, the one thing most of them remember thirty years later, was the sight of sweaty men digging up the sacred turf of the Royal parks.

In hot summer weather like that of September, 1938, secretaries in flowered, sleeveless dresses, men in shirtsleeves with their jackets slung over their arms, would stroll in the parks at lunch time, sit on the grass or in deckchairs, flirting, gossiping, eating sandwiches, throwing crumbs to the sparrows and pigeons or to the multicoloured waterfowl on the lake which runs the length of St. James's Park from the center of government in Whitehall almost to Buckingham Palace.

Watching the pelicans on the lake in St. James's Park, one might find oneself standing beside the Prime Minister and Mrs. Chamberlain, the Prime Minister's guardian detective lingering discreetly a few yards away; or see Winston Churchill and Anthony Eden crossing the gravelled expanse of Horseguards Parade—Eden dark, good-looking, well-groomed, the embodiment of every woman's ideal of the British diplomat; Churchill thickset, talking volubly, flourishing his stick to emphasize points which, in his case, were always numerous and forceful. One went home that night and said importantly, "I saw Mr. Chamberlain today. He looked ever so worried," or "I saw Winston Churchill in the park. He looked as if he wouldn't half give that old Hitler socks," and felt that one had somehow made a contribution to the governance of that great Empire on which the sun had not yet set.

1

Overnight, this familiar summer scene changed. Men came, marking out long lines on the grass with wooden pegs. More men, hundreds of men, appeared with picks and shovels, since there was little mechanical equipment available for the task set by the Government, which was to dig within three days enough air raid trenches to shelter a tenth of the population of every great city. Two thousand of the men came up from Hammersmith, in West London, where the immigrant Irish labourers lived in seedy doss-houses. Thousands of others were signed on from among the long queues of unemployed outside the Labour Exchanges. The crisis was a godsend for some of them, at least.

The men trampled and muddied the grass where pretty secretaries were accustomed to sunbathe, ripped off the turf, raised above each trench ugly yellow mounds of raw London clay. During the night of September 27, it rained heavily, and lunchtime strollers on what came to be known as Black Wednesday, September 28, glumly contemplated the pools of water at the bottom of the trenches and wondered whether it might not be better to risk German bombs than to die of pneumonia.

Most of those watching the trench-diggers on that day carried small cardboard boxes. These contained the gas masks—they were urged to call them "respirators"—which had been issued since the previous weekend. In spite of the war-talk all through the summer and the expensive Government publicity campaigns appealing for volunteers for the Air Raid Precautions Service, fewer than half the required number had come forward to be trained. Although thirty-eight million respirators were available in depots all over the country, there were not enough people trained in fitting the public with them, and a number of the depots had to remain closed. As late as mid-September, an A.R.P. worker in a prosperous London suburb complained, "We're treated generally as though we're selling something, told to call at some other time as 'the wife doesn't feel like trying gas masks on.'"

But when posters went up announcing "Air Raid Precautions. Distribution of Gas Masks," there came the smell of fear. There were ugly scenes outside some of the undermanned depots distributing gas masks, as queues clamoured to get what was now seen as a life saver. From a number of places it was reported that invalids, given precedence at the head of the queue, had recovered their health with astonishing celerity once the little cardboard boxes were in their possession. The British Communist Party found a useful source of propaganda in the difference between the civilian gas mask and the more elaborate respirator issued to the armed forces and to A.R.P. workers, promising "We will get you real gas masks, which only the rich are getting."

Some people, fitting on for the first time the rubber mask with its snout and staring goggle-eyes which made them look like pigs, were physically sick into it. From all over the country, doctors reported an increase in cases of diarrhoea and nervous indigestion, of people living for days on nothing more solid than that inevitable British standby, a nice hot cup of tea. There were "scares": A rumor circulated that a squadron of planes flying over East London had sprayed chlorine gas, and a number of people became genuinely ill. Some, mostly mothers with children, found themselves unable to face the prospect of war. A 42-year-old woman recorded, "I have been collecting poisons for some time with guile and cunning. I have sufficient to give self, husband, and all the children a lethal dose. I can remember the last war. I don't want to live through another, or the children either. I shan't tell them, I shall just do it."

Because of the panic which the Government expected to follow the outbreak of war, plans had been made to parcel out a major part of Britain's field army of two understrength and under-equipped divisions to control the crowds. There were Government plans for evacuating women and children from the big cities, but it was feared that publication of the plans would of itself cause day, however, following the Prime Minister's grave broadcast panic, and they had therefore been kept secret. On Black Wednes-of the evening before and the news that the Fleet was mobiliz-ing, Londoners began to evacuate themselves. The evacuees were mostly the well-to-do. Lines of taxicabs filled with luggage drew up at the main railway stations; there were queues at the booking offices, particularly those serving Scotland and Ireland; and it was later officially estimated that some 150,000 people had left London and other big cities for Wales alone. Estate agents reported a rush of inquiries from businessmen for properties in the country near London, and "practically every available cottage in rural Sussex is taken."

A few silver barrage balloons floated above the capital, and anti-aircraft guns raised their muzzles comfortingly from sand-bagged emplacements. Hitler's friend, Miss Unity Mitford, after-wards told the Fuehrer that there were only three, but she was, as usual, misinformed. To cover the country, Anti-Aircraft Com-mand had some 400 heavy guns, out of an establishment of 1,264, and of these 400, 350 were out-of-date. Manchester, Britain's fourth largest city, was given one new gun for a few days to hearten its 700,000 people, but the gun was then taken away for display elsewhere.

Contrary to these appearances, British plans for defense against air attack were at this time the most advanced in the world. French air raid precautions consisted principally of piles of sand stored on the top floors of buildings for use in dealing with incen-diary bombs. In Prague there was a shortage of gas masks, and the two ministries concerned with air raid precautions had been engaged in a series of quarrels about who was responsible for what. Even Germany had no plans as elaborate as those of the British, though care had been taken to mount anti-aircraft guns in ostentatious proximity to the British and French embassies in Berlin.

What had been lacking in Britain until this September crisis was any willingness to pay for the implementation of the Govern-ment's plans, or any real belief that they were necessary. The view expressed by a letter-writer to a paper in the East End of London was widely held: "The A.R.P. nonsense is only a gigantic national bunkum parade organised to fool the great British public and to lower their morale . . . All the money today is in armaments. It is a shameful waste and could be better spent to eliminate poverty and disease in Britain." Nor was this opinion confined to the pacifist Left Wing. In July, the President of the Society of Motor Manufacturers and Traders, Lord Kenilworth, told a public lun-cheon: "I do not know how anybody can expect the country to set-tle down to normal occupations when people's minds are so dis-tracted by foolish talk and propaganda about air raid precautions and such things, which lead the man-in-the-street to believe that they are going to be bombed out of their house tomorrow. A more foolish idea I cannot possibly conceive, if one has an eye to keeping the workpeople employed and making the public settle down to their normal avocations."

Another view was that air raid precautions were necessary, but that Neville Chamberlain's largely Conservative Government was not prepared to make them available to the mass of the people. On September 11, when the Munich Crisis was no more than a small cloud on a remote horizon for a majority of the British, an enterprising London publisher advertised a popular book on Air Raid Precautions with the heartening statement: "Professor Haldane in his sensational book 'ARP' (out tomorrow) exposes the futility of official A.R.P. measures and details a scheme for 100 percent protection. Second edition before publication." By the end of the crisis, three weeks later, the publisher was happily able to announce that Professor Haldane's book was in its fifth edition.

The book thus publicized was not unduly alarmist by the standards of the time. Haldane was a large, cantankerous, woolly rhinoceros of a man, a distinguished scientist of strong Communist sympathies and great personal courage. He had exposed himself to air bombardment in the Spanish Civil War and studied its effects at first hand. He suggested that an air attack might take two forms: a knockout blow or an attempt to wear down resistance. "The former would be directed against London, the latter against ports and munition centers . . . [The Germans] would be prepared to lose half their air force to lay London in ruins . . . The 'knockout blow' might kill 50,000 to 100,000 Londoners." This was well below the official estimate of the Committee of Imperial Defence that the opening air attack on London, lasting two months, would kill 600,000 people and injure twice that number. A quarter of the bombs dropped, it was expected, would contain gas, hence the elaborate preparations for manufacturing and distributing gas masks. Another Government committee of psychiatrists had reported that mental casualties might be three times as many as physical casualties, which would mean that, in addition to nearly two million dead and wounded, the authorities would have to cope with between five and six million cases of acute panic and hysteria.

This was the threat which in late September underlay the

tension of Londoners watching trenches being dug, the scramble for gas masks, and the panic evacuation. It was not confined to London, but hung over the whole of Europe. In Prague, there was a blackout more stringent than any enforced in London after the outbreak of war a year later, and a series of rumors that German planes had already crossed the Czechoslovak frontier. The head of the French Intelligence Service had put on record his belief that his country was powerless to deal with the German air threat. Even in Geneva, headquarters of the League of Nations, that sad monument to mankind's desire for peace without the inconvenience of doing anything about it, there had been a trial blackout, and the professionally neutral Swiss had deemed it wise to hold anti-aircraft exercises.

In so far as this state of mind could be attributed to the influence of any single person, that person was a comparatively unknown general of the Italian Air Force, Giulio Douhet, principal propagator of the theory of the knockout blow from the air. Douhet had elaborated his ideas in a series of papers published between 1921 and 1929. They had percolated through the military specialists to whom they were primarily addressed, into books, articles and speeches by publicists in a score of languages, until by September 28, 1938, it could be said that Douhet's shadow hung over the civilized world.

At the heart of Douhet's theory lay the belief that there was no defense against the bombing plane, since it could choose its own route to its target and could not be found or intercepted in the wide open spaces of the air. When the bomber reached its destination, "within a few minutes some twenty tons of high explosive, incendiary and gas bombs would rain down. First would come explosions, then fires, then deadly gases floating on the surface and preventing any approach to the stricken area. As the hours passed and night advanced, the fires would spread while the poison gas paralyzed all life . . . A complete breakdown of the social structure cannot but take place in a country subjected to this kind of merciless pounding from the air. The time would soon come when, to put an end to horror and suffering, the people themselves, driven by the instinct of self-preservation, would rise up and demand an end to war."

The tightly-packed island of Britain, according to Douhet, was particularly vulnerable to air attack. "Dominated from the air, England would be lost," he wrote. "Her magnificent fleet, her naval predominance, would be of no avail. Even if her merchant marine could bring supplies to her ports, they could not be unloaded and forwarded. Hunger, desolation and terror would stalk the country."

A government-employed scientist, Robert Watson-Watt, backed by Air Chief Marshal Sir Hugh Dowding and the former Air Minister, Lord Swinton, was at this moment engaged in proving Douhet wrong by providing radar detection of approaching bombers. But in 1938, the official doctrine of the British Air Staff was that the only answer to the bomber was more bombers to strike even harder at the enemy. As for the knockout blow, the Chief of Air Staff, Sir Cyril Newall, reported to Swinton in April, 1938: "No one can say with absolute certainty that a nation can be knocked out from the air, because no one has yet attempted it. There can be no doubt, however, that Germany and Italy believe it possible, as there can be no other explanation for their piling up armaments to a level which they could not hope to maintain in a long war."

At half-past two on the afternoon of Black Wednesday, the House of Commons met in special session to hear a report from the Prime Minister on his negotiations with the German Chancellor, Adolf Hitler, over the future of the Sudeten German districts of Czechoslovakia.

Most members of Parliament were as ill-informed as the public about what had passed between Chamberlain and Hitler, first at Obersalzberg, in the Bavarian mountains, then at a second meeting a week later at Godesberg, on the Rhine. One Labour M.P. complained during the long drawn-out crisis: "Here I am, a member of parliament, a representative of the people, and I'm impotent. There's *nothing* I can do." A prominent Conservative M.P., whose services were much in demand as a speaker and writer explaining the background to public events, was reduced to getting his information from the B.B.C. radio news. In such a situation, rumours proliferated, and the presence of a microphone on the dispatch box in front of the Prime Minister's place in the Commons led to reports that, for the first time in history, the speech of a British Prime Minister in the House of Commons was to be broadcast to the nation. Such a speech, it was widely assumed, must be of major importance, perhaps a declaration of war.

The microphone in the Commons symbolizes many of the legends which have grown up about the Munich Crisis. There was never any question of the Prime Minister's speech being broadcast. What had happened was that a great many members of the House of Lords had applied for the limited number of seats in the Peers' Gallery of the Commons. The Leader of the House of Lords had therefore asked the Speaker's permission to install a microphone, which would relay the Prime Minister's speech to the Library of the House of Lords and to another gallery of the Commons where, among a distinguished audience, sat Queen Mary, the Queen Mother.

Nor was the Prime Minister's speech going to end in a declaration of war. Its ending would have been an appeal for further negotiations, which would have exposed Chamberlain not only to the criticism of the leaders of the Labour and Liberal Opposition, but to a devastating assault from the principal opponent in his own party, Churchill, who would have been expressing an uneasiness fairly widely felt among Government supporters and might even have succeeded in bringing the Government down.

The Commons was packed and tense when the Prime Minister entered from behind the Speaker's chair, looking white-faced and drawn. His supporters rose and waved their order papers, mumbling the words "Hear! Hear!" which pass in the sedate British House of Commons for wild and enthusiastic applause. Labour and Liberal M.P.'s, and some Government members, including Churchill, remained stonily seated.

Shortly before three o'clock Chamberlain rose, spread the notes of his speech on the dispatch box in front of him, and in calm and measured tones began his narrative of events. The situation facing Britain, he said at an early stage of his speech, had no parallel since 1914—and this increased the expectation of those listening to him that the end could only be war.

About twenty minutes after Chamberlain had begun his speech, Sir Alexander Cadogan, Permanent Under-Secretary at the Foreign Office, received an urgent telephone message from Sir Nevile Henderson, the British Ambassador in Berlin. Cadogan took down the message, which was a short one, and gave it to a secretary to type on a single sheet of Foreign Office paper. Then, carrying two copies of the message and not forgetting his black hat and rolled umbrella, Cadogan ran out of the Foreign Office courtyard into Downing Street, along Whitehall, across the busy intersection of Bridge Street and Parliament Square, to the St. Stephens entrance of the House of Commons nearly half a mile away. The Civil Service head of the Foreign Office was a short man in his fifties, not in the best of condition, and it is not surprising that he arrived at the Commons somewhat out of breath. He was then faced with a long walk—it would have been improper to run—through the Parliament building itself, until he reached the Members' Lobby, immediately outside the Commons Chamber. There he asked for Lord Halifax, the Foreign Secretary, who was sitting in the Peers' Gallery, listening to the Prime Minister's speech.

A messenger was dispatched up the stairs to the Peers' Gallery, while Cadogan waited below, and Halifax was seen to smile as he read the slip of paper the official had passed to him along the crowded bench. Halifax showed it to the former Prime Minister, Lord Baldwin, sitting beside him. A few minutes later Halifax himself appeared in the Members' Lobby. As a peer, he could not enter the House of Commons, but he took Cadogan along with him to the corridor behind the Speaker's chair, whence the message could be passed to the Prime Minister.

It was now about ten minutes past four, and Chamberlain had been speaking for over an hour. During his speech there had been a constant, quiet, coming-and-going of Commons messengers, passing along the benches telegrams and pink telephone slips to the tensely listening members, and no one thought much, if they noticed it at all, of the single sheet of paper being handed along the Government Front Bench to Chamberlain.

It reached the Chancellor of the Exchequer, Sir John Simon, sitting close to the Prime Minister. Simon read it, slid along the bench and tugged at the standing Prime Minister's coattails. At first he got no response, and tugged again. At the second tug, Chamberlain stopped speaking, looked round, had a brief whispered conversation with Simon, read the paper once . . . a second time. . . .

There was a silence of perhaps half a minute which, such was the tension that had been built up, seemed to one observer like half an hour.

As the dramatic hush lengthened, Chamberlain was heard over his microphone to whisper to Simon, "Shall I tell them now?" Simon nodded, and when the Prime Minister turned again to the silent Commons, he was smiling.

"I have now been informed by Herr Hitler," he said, "that he has invited me to meet him at Munich tomorrow morning. He has also invited Signor Mussolini and Monsieur Daladier. Signor Mussolini has accepted, and I have no doubt Monsieur Daladier will also accept. I need not say what my answer will be . . . I am sure that the House will be ready to release me now to go and see what I can make of this last effort."

For a second there was absolute silence, then pandemonium. An unknown Conservative member shouted, "Thank God for the Prime Minister!" In the Peers' Gallery the Archbishop of Canterbury was seen to be striking the rail in front of him with both hands while Lord Baldwin banged the floor with his stick. Queen Mary, sitting in the Ladies' Gallery between Mrs. Chamberlain and the Duchess of Kent, was crying. Attendants in the Distinguished Strangers' Gallery made a quickly-abandoned attempt to control the clapping of the assembled members of the diplomatic corps.

It was, Chamberlain wrote afterwards, "a piece of drama that no fiction ever surpassed." He himself stood alone by the dispatch box while the cheers of his supporters rose and fell and rose again. According to one observer, his face appeared white and tightly set, as if he were making an effort, almost too great, to control himself. According to another watcher, hostile to Chamberlain, the Prime Minister appeared ten years younger and exhibited a somewhat complacent air of triumph.

The applause for the Prime Minister lasted for perhaps five

minutes, during which most of the Opposition members sat glum and silent. Then Clement Attlee, Leader of the Labour Party, scrapping the speech he had been prepared to make, wished the Prime Minister good fortune on his journey, and with this blessing, most of the Opposition members joined in the cheering, some of them sheepishly.

Members of all parties crowded round Chamberlain, eager to shake his hand. Churchill growled, "I congratulate you on your good fortune. You were very lucky." A single Government member, Harold Nicolson, stayed stolidly seated throughout the hysterical scene. A Conservative member behind him hissed, "Stand up, you brute!" Nicolson remained seated.

A young Conservative member capered out of the Chamber and into the Central Lobby, waving his hands and shouting to a waiting party of his constituents, "You're not going to be called up now, you needn't worry." Half a dozen other members followed him, laughing and calling out the news which quickly spread to the crowds outside, to the people waiting in Whitehall, to offices and factories.

As the news spread, the face of London changed. The people in the streets no longer looked strained and glum, but smiled at each other, and even spoke. A small procession of poorly dressed demonstrators carrying banners with the slogan, "Stand up for Czechoslovakia," walked up Lower Regent Street, but it was now they who looked tired and dejected, ignored by the smiling crowd.

One of Chamberlain's ministers, Ernest Brown, had already expressed the opinion of Londoners, suddenly released from the valley of the shadow of the knockout blow: "God has sent him a peroration, and it is in time."

CHAPTER 2

A Faraway Country

ON SEPTEMBER 27, the evening before Chamberlain addressed the Commons, Britons sitting by their radio sets had heard the sad, flat tones of their Prime Minister telling them: "How horrible, fantastic, incredible it is that we should be digging trenches and trying on gas masks here because of a quarrel in a faraway country between people of whom we know nothing."

The Prime Minister was perhaps being unusually modest about his own knowledge of the faraway country; but of a majority of his audience, who were inclined to lump all these unknown people together as "Them Sizzeks," it was certainly true. The ostensible cause of the crisis was the fact that "them Sizzeks" comprised not only some 7½ million Czechs, but also 2¼ million Slovaks, three-quarters of a million Hungarians, half-a-million Ukrainians and some thousands of Poles, together with just over three million Sudeten Germans, most of whom lived in self-contained communities along the borders adjoining Germany and Austria.

The hostility of Czech and German goes back at least to the religious wars of the fifteenth century, and it is almost impossible even now to discuss the Sudeten question among the contending parties without being involved in a dispute about John Hus and the Holy Roman Empire. It is like trying to discuss the Irish question with a Boston Irishman: at the end of three hours of increasingly acrimonious debate, one has got as far as Oliver Cromwell and the massacre of Drogheda. This is the kind of situation which the British are peculiarly unfitted to understand. Centuries of isolation and comparative security have given them a habit of lazy tolerance, and as all political issues seem to them capable of a compromise solution, they continue to be taken by surprise when this comfortable belief proves to be unfounded.

During the previous half-century, they had been subjected to a barrage of liberal propaganda about the rights of minorities, and to many of those who in 1938 had managed to grasp that there was a difference between Czechs and Sudeten Germans, it seemed eminently reasonable that what was represented to them as a repressed minority should be given its independence. To put these years of propaganda into reverse proved as difficult as it would be today if, for instance, it suddenly became politically expedient to prove that South African apartheid policies were justified.

Czechoslovakia to the outside world meant Bohemian glassware, Pilsen beer, the great Skoda armament works. The majority of its inhabitants, the Czechs, are a practical, hard-headed, industrious race, not much given to the romantic extravagances of their Polish and Hungarian neighbors. A Czech literary hero, the good soldier Schweik, very popular internationally between the wars, survived Austrian domination not by fighting, but by exercising the evasive tactics of Brer Rabbit. Among both Czechs and Slovaks were many small peasant farmers, who tend to be pacifists of an extremely practical kind, since it is their land which is fought over and devastated in any war. Their party, the Agrarians, was the largest in Czechoslovak politics.

Czechoslovakia itself was one of those European states which had been formed after the First World War from the wreck of the Austro-Hungarian Empire. Its godfather was President Wilson, who was persuaded by two remarkable men, Thomas Masaryk, son of a Slovak coachman, and Eduard Benes, son of a Czech farmer, to include the establishment of a Czechoslovak Republic among the Allied war aims.

As the republic emerged from the peace treaties reluctantly signed by Austria and Hungary, it was shaped like a tadpole, with Bohemia at its western head, Moravia its middle, and Slovakia the tail. The tadpole was surrounded on three sides by three countries—Austria, Hungary and Poland—from which it had taken territory, and Germany held the tadpole's Bohemian head between as yet open jaws. If any combination of these neighbours should prove hostile, Czechoslovakia had something like 1300 miles of frontier to defend against them. In order to give the new republic a defensible frontier, as well as for other reasons, a higher proportion of the Sudeten German population was included in Czechoslovakia than was strictly desirable under the Wilsonian ideal of self-determination. Lansing, the American Secretary of State, protested against "the fixing of frontier lines with a view to their military strength and in contemplation of war." American experts made a laborious survey and proposed a frontier between Czechoslovakia and Germany which did not differ greatly from that achieved under the Munich Agreement nearly twenty years later. American idealism laboured in vain. The wicked Europeans, particularly the French, continued to believe that wars were most likely to be prevented by having frontiers which could be defended against predatory neighbours, and Czechoslovakia was given the frontier of the Ancient Kingdom of Bohemia, swallowed up by the Hapsburg Empire in the sixteenth century.

This political horsetrading played its part in providing the United States with an excuse to withdraw from a bickering and war-minded Europe. It also left Czechoslovakia with a large population of Sudeten Germans who had belonged to the ruling population under the Austrian Empire and were now ruled by the Czechs. In an effort to placate American opinion, a promise had been given during the peace negotiations that this multi-national state would in the course of time become a federation of self-governing nationalities on the lines of Switzerland. The time never proved convenient. The Czechs, having sat under the Austrian table for three hundred years, were now on top of it, and had no intention of inviting anybody else to join them. The harder the other nationalities tried, the stronger became the spirit of Czech nationalism and patriotism, and even the most enlightened of Czechoslovak politicians found it more convenient to swim with this tide than against it.

The most influential of these politicians after Masaryk was Benes, a man who in many ways represented in his own person the strengths and weaknesses of Europe between the wars. Physically a small man, by education the cosmopolitan product of the universities of Prague, Paris, London and Berlin, by profession a professor of political economy, it was he—the civilized politician, the man of peace—who had emerged on top from the cataclysm of war and the crash of empires. A genuine idealist, he had not scrupled to lie for his country. A genuine democrat, he had achieved his international position by his mastery of those arts of intrigue, lobbying, the friendly grip on the arm and the casual word in the ear which turned a decision in his favour. There was not a great deal about political "fixing" which he did not know. If the gift of a sinecure directorship could influence a politician's vote in the cause of righteousness, Benes was not the man to hesitate to serve the right. It was inevitable that he should become a foremost protagonist of the League of Nations, a master-manipulator with those Committees of Ten and Committees of Fourteen which seemed to hold the future of the world in their hands until an explosion at Mukden, in far-distant Manchuria, blew down the pack of cards.

To the outside world, Benes was an international statesman of preeminent renown; domestically, like Roosevelt in the United States, he was a controversial party politician with a reputation for trickiness, whose National Socialist Party was responsible for a great deal of unenlightened Czech chauvinism. He was not a man to lead or dominate. He could manipulate, persuade, cajole. If people could not be manipulated and would not be persuaded, he had no resources left. He was also a Czech, to the Sudeten Germans a symbol of the Czech nationalism which they detested and sought to replace by that superior brand of nationalism which is made in Germany.

Until 1933, Czech domination of Czechoslovakia's minorities had been a situation which European liberals widely and vocally deplored. Even Czechoslovak Communist spokesmen proclaimed a fight "against the peace treaties on which is founded the imperialist domination of the Czechoslovak bourgeoisie and the submission of the oppressed minorities of Czechoslovakia." Until the thirties, there were well-founded hopes that Germany would eventually become Communist, and while that was possible, international Communist policy favoured the cession of the Sudeten German areas from Czechoslovakia to Germany. Instead, Germany went Nazi, and Czechoslovak Communists, in common with those of other countries, suddenly discovered the virtues of patriotism. Liberals, less habituated to such lightning changes of mind, continued to advocate some form of self-determination for the Sudeten Germans; or, if they wished it, secession. As Chamberlain bluntly put it: "My personal opinion was that on principle I didn't care two hoots whether the Sudetens were in the Reich or out of it, according to their own wishes."

The world economic crisis of the early thirties, besides helping the Nazis to power in Germany, had a particular effect on the Sudeten German areas. Parts of them were heavily industrialized, their trade ties were with an Austria that no longer existed, and unemployment in the Sudetenland, already heavy, was made worse by the slump. Out of some 600,000 unemployed in Czechoslovakia, over half were concentrated in the German areas. Sudeten Germans looking for jobs found them across the frontier in Germany, and began to contrast the stagnant villages of the Sudetenland with the economic miracle apparently being achieved in Germany under Hitler.

They had other grievances. Although in theory there was no barrier to the advancement of Czechs, Germans, Slovaks, Poles and Hungarians within the Czechoslovak republic, this theoretical equality of opportunity was in practice more equal for some than for others. In the Sudetenland, most of the principal officials were Czech. There were Sudeten Germans in the Czechoslovak Army, but few held a rank above that of captain unless they had adopted Czech names. There were German schools, but the most modern and well-equipped schools were Czech, and German parents received the impression that if they wanted their children to get on in the world, they would be well-advised to send them to Czech schools.

There is no doubt that these grievances were genuine and deeply felt. But one must put them into perspective. A Sudeten German politician of those days was telling me with burning indignation of three Sudeten German students sent to prison for three years under the tyrant Benes for political agitation. He paused, smiled, and added wryly, "Under the Czechs, we thought three years in prison was a long time. When we joined the Reich, we found it was twenty years."

Political agitation built up in the Sudetenland until, in the elections of 1935, it found a focus in the Sudeten German Party, headed by the thirty-seven-year-old Konrad Henlein. In appearance, Henlein was tall, athletic, with a hearty, somewhat school-masterly manner. He wore rimless glasses and badly-fitting suits which caused one observer to describe him as looking like a caricature of a pre-First World War professor; but he possessed considerable charm and a kind of open bluffness which impressed even sophisticated people with his honesty. He was so obviously not very clever.

Henlein's mother was a Czech. He volunteered at the age of seventeen for the Austrian Army in World War I, became an officer, was captured on the Italian front, and, although one of the youngest officers in his prisoner-of-war camp, made a name for himself by organizing gymnastic activities. After the war, his relatives wanted him to continue an army career. He passed the entrance examination for the Czechoslovak Military Academy but changed his mind and became a bank clerk.

Gymnastics was the key to Henlein's political success. In Central Europe, gymnastics occupy the place in the national life held elsewhere by baseball or football, but with political overtones. The Czech Sokol movement not only organized spectacular displays by thousands of young men and women working together in perfect rhythm, it also had nationalist tendencies described by a Czechoslovak writer during the Second World War as "to prepare our nation as well as other Slav nations for a victorious struggle with their age-old enemy, the Germans." Henlein organized a gymnastic movement among the Sudeten Germans, became a paid official of the movement, then founded a school in Asch for training gymnastics instructors. As a gymnast, and organizer and trainer of gymnasts, he was a popular figure before he became a politician.

The Sudeten German Party, like all political parties, was a coalition of often conflicting ideas, united by agreement on the one point that Sudeten Germans must be liberated from Czech tyranny. There was always disagreement on what would happen afterwards. The "moderates" would have been content to go on living in a Czechoslovak republic, which perhaps they hoped to dominate. The "radicals" wanted secession and union with Germany, whose Nazi Party they greatly admired. Until the advent of Henlein, the party had been led by intellectuals, mostly lawyers, given to making speeches six hours long, and to that extent, even among Germans, who are a serious race, lacking mass appeal. Henlein made no long speeches. The intellectuals drafted one for him, but he threw most of it away. He went from town to town and village to village, pouring out in simple language the thoughts his audiences would have liked to express if they had been able to. He talked about men out of work and children who could not rise in the world unless they became Czechs, the always popular subject in any language of the tyranny of petty bureaucrats, who in the Sudetenland were Czechs.

Henlein, one of his intellectual associates said scornfully, was no politician—he was like a man who rides, and doesn't know where he's going. Maybe. But in the 1935 election he swept the Sudetenland, his party won 43 seats, and became the second largest party in the Czechoslovak Parliament.

The leaders of the Agrarian Party, the most powerful in Czechoslovak politics, were always opposed to the more rabid forms of Czech nationalism and in favour of reaching some accommodation with the growing power of Germany under Hitler. Both the Agrarians and the Czech nationalists surrounding Benes saw which way the wind was blowing in the Sudetenland. The nationalists did their best to sabotage Henlein. The Agrarians took the initiative in approaching him before the 1935 election, and offered to form a coalition government with the Henleinists if the latter won a minimum of 25 seats. The Henleinist leaders were mostly young, fiery, ambitious, and elated at their unexpected electoral triumph. They had got as far as discussing among themselves who should have what ministry in the new coalition government, when the Agrarians went back on their agreement. To the natural disappointment of politicians thus suddenly deprived of the fruits of office was added the suspicion that the detested Benes had played a principal part in torpedoing the agreed coalition. A few months after the election, Thomas Masaryk resigned the presidency of the republic, recommending Benes as his successor. Once again the Agrarians agreed with the Henleinists to support a rival candidate for the presidency, and again they broke their agreement, a great deal of subterranean French influence being brought to bear in Benes's interest. There was a certain resulting disillusionment among the "moderates" of the Henleinist Party about what could be achieved by constitutional means and an increase in the influence of admirers of the Nazis beyond the frontier. The most important of these extremists was the forty-year-old Karl Hermann Frank, a man of a very different stamp from the bluff and unpolitical Henlein. Frank's father was a teacher. He himself had studied law, but gave up before taking his degree because, according to some accounts, he was too poor to finish the course, according to others because he could not stick at anything for long. He became a bookseller, and although he was no intellectual, he had a reputation for having read the books he sold. His favorite writer is said to have been Rilke. He had lost one eye in a schoolboy fight, and his glass eye gave him a slightly sinister appearance of inscrutability which he carefully cultivated.

Frank was Henlein's Cassius, a lean, ambitious man, unsure of himself, what the Communists call an *apparatchik*, with no talent for organizing a mass movement but a great deal of talent for organizing those small activist cells through which mass movements are manipulated. He had no influence in the Henleinist Party until 1934, when the Czechoslovak Government had unwisely arrested three of the moderate leaders. When they returned from four months in prison, they found Frank in Henlein's confidence, and he was never thereafter dislodged.

Henlein and his Sudeten German nationalists would have been no more, or no less, important than nationalists elsewhere, but for Czechoslovakia's neighbour, Germany. Sudeten German nationalists had been in touch with Berlin as early as 1933, but so had other nationalist leaders—Indian, Palestinian, Ukrainian—who were supported or not according to the use which the German Government thought might be made of their services. This is no doubt very wicked, but it is something which all govern-

ments, or at any rate their intelligence agencies, are in the habit
of doing at all times. In that respect, the German Government
was no worse than anybody else, and the Sudeten German nationalists who approached it were at least as respectable as Sir
Roger Casement, hanged as a traitor by the British in 1916, but
to the Irish a patriot and martyr.

It was not until the election year of 1935, in fact, that the
German Government showed much interest in the Sudeten German nationalists. That was also the year in which pacts of mutual
assistance were signed between Russia and France, and Czechoslovakia and Russia. There was already a treaty between
Czechoslovakia and France, committing each to go to the assistance of the other if it were attacked. The effect of the three pacts
was that, in the event of war between France and Germany,
Czechoslovak airfields could be used by French and Russian
bombers.

The heart of the German Foreign Ministry may or may not
have been wrung by the grievances of the Sudeten Germans. It
was certainly wrung by the thought of "aircraft carrier Czechoslovakia," those Czechoslovak bases now available to French and
Russian bombers which were less than an hour's flight from Berlin
and within easy range of the German industrial complex about
Dresden and Leipzig.

Hitler had come to power in Germany pledged to return his
country to the position in Europe she had occupied before the
Treaty of Versailles. He expected the French and Russians to
fight to stop him, possibly by waging a preventive war. In such
circumstances, Czechoslovakia appeared to Germany much as a
Cuba harbouring Russian missile bases appeared more recently to
the United States. Czechoslovakia had to be eliminated or neu-
tralized by one means or another. The grievances of the Sudeten
Germans provided a convenient way of doing so, and one can
safely say that if the grievances had not existed, Hitler would
have had to invent them, instead of merely painting the lily with
the bold touch of Dr. Goebbels' art.

In 1935, the German Foreign Ministry took a hand in healing
feuds between rival leaders in the Sudetenland, concentrating
support behind the popular demagogue Henlein. The German

press, which up to that point had been favouring more "radical" leaders, received a direct order from Hess, deputy leader of the Nazi Party, to stop attacks on Henlein. Substantial German funds, some 330,000 marks (about 140,000 dollars), were made available for the Sudeten German Party's election expenses.

According to one of the intellectuals of the party, Dr. Hans Neuwirth, this money did not come either from the Nazi Party or the German Government, but from private German subscribers who included General Karl Haushofer and his son, Dr. Albrecht Haushofer. The Haushofers played a somewhat enigmatic role in Nazi Germany. They had links with Hess, who had been General Haushofer's adjutant during the First World War, and with General Niedermayer, who as German military attaché in Moscow maintained the unofficial connections between the Russian and German General Staffs which certainly continued for some time after Hitler's rise to power. The elder Haushofer tried to influence Hess, and through Hess, Hitler, in favour of an alliance with Russia. The younger Haushofer was shortly to be engaged in secret negotiations with Benes, supposedly on Hitler's behalf. He was always a doubtful supporter of the Nazi regime and was eventually hanged for his part in the unsuccessful attempt to assassinate Hitler in July, 1944. The Haushofers and their circle, like almost everybody else in Germany, believed that "aircraft carrier Czechoslovakia" had to be dealt with. Their method, however, was that later described by Baron Ernst von Weizsaecker, Secretary of State at the German Foreign Ministry, as bringing about Czechoslovakia's "chemical dissolution" by discreet encouragement of its German, Slovak and other national separatists. After the Henleinist success in the 1935 election, the German Foreign Ministry thought the party worth supporting to the tune of 15,000 marks (about 6,250 dollars) a month. The Henleinists had a nuisance value as a means of putting pressure on Benes, but they were not valued much more highly than that.

The relationship between Hitler and Henlein was never a close one. Before the Austrian *Anschluss*, they apparently met only once, when Henlein attended the Olympic Games in Berlin in August, 1936. There were a number of meetings between them after the *Anschluss,* but the Fuehrer was to find Henlein on the whole more of a hindrance than a help. The German Foreign Ministry did maintain touch with the Henleinists. It seems to have found them touchy, always quarrelling with each other, running to Berlin with petty complaints. It was not a particularly rewarding association on either side.

It was in Britain, curiously enough, that Henlein acquired his most effective influence. At the beginning of his rise to power, Henlein had been taken up by the anti-Czech Sudeten German aristocracy, one of whom, Count Kuehn-Luetzow, introduced him to a former British air attaché in Berlin, Group Captain M.G. Christie. Christie proposed Henlein as a suitable speaker on Sudeten German problems to the Royal Institute of International Affairs in London. He gave a dinner party for him before the meeting at Chatham House in December, 1935, and introduced him to, among others, Sir Robert Vansittart, then Permanent Under-Secretary at the Foreign Office. This link with Vansittart was to have important consequences during the 1938 crisis.

The invitation to Henlein to lecture at the Royal Institute of International Affairs had repercussions inside the Sudetenland. The Institute, of which Dr. Arnold Toynbee was then the distinguished Director of Studies, had great prestige, though in fact it is less official than its title makes it sound. The Prince of Wales, soon to be King Edward VIII, was thought in Germany to have pro-German sympathies—Hitler professed to believe that he was forced to abdicate because of them—and it was not difficult, among the simple people of the Sudetenland, to represent Henlein's invitation from a Royal Institute as a summons to London to present their grievances at the very highest level. Henlein's prestige among his own people rose considerably. That of his political rivals in the Sudetenland, the Sudeten German Social Democrats, who were almost totally ignored in Britain, consequently fell.

On March 7, 1936, a few days after the French Chamber of Deputies had ratified the Franco-Russian Pact and a few months after Benes became President of Czechoslovakia, four brigades of German troops marched across the Rhine bridges and reoccupied the strip of German territory along the French and

Belgian borders which had been demilitarized under the Versailles Treaty. Goering later described how he and the German Air Minister, General Milch, spent a night sleepless with terror at the thought of the reprisals France and Britain were likely to launch against Germany, and from which they were quite unable to defend their country. Hitler himself regarded the Rhineland operation as the most dangerous moment in the development of his plans for breaking, one by one, the conditions of the Versailles Treaty. But he had chosen the moment with his accustomed skill. Italy's war with Abyssinia was approaching its climax, and French and British eyes were on the Mediterranean. The British Government, with that mixture of conscience and cowardice which was characteristic of the time, found it inopportune to prevent Germany from reoccupying her own territory. The French would not move without British support. The last moment passed at which Hitler might have been stopped without the danger of a major war.

The reoccupation of the Rhineland weakened France, and so weakened France's distant ally, Czechoslovakia. In the autumn of 1936, Albrecht Haushofer appeared in Prague as one of two emissaries apparently sent by Hitler to ascertain whether Benes would now like to change his mind about his French and Russian alliances. The mission was so secret that it was not known even to the German Foreign Ministry, which was highly indignant when it found out. Benes never undervalued his skill as a manufacturer of formulas, and in his own account of these negotiations there is a trace of his besetting weakness, admiration for his cleverness as a negotiator: "During the talks I frequently gained the impression that they [the German emissaries] were astonished by my arguments, my outspokenness, my frankness and my categorical statement of opinion." He also noted that Haushofer showed an increasingly critical attitude towards the Nazi regime and towards the Fuehrer himself.

According to Benes, he was asked, not to abrogate publicly his French and Russian treaties, but in case of war between Germany and France and Russia, simply to ignore his obligations to his allies. Benes professed himself astonished and shocked by the cynicism of this proposal. Perhaps he was. But he kept the negotiations going secretly for some months, thus convincing the Germans of his fundamental insincerity, and went so far as to draft a treaty between Germany and Czechoslovakia under which they would have agreed to strengthen their economic ties and settle all disputes peacefully, but which did nothing to assuage German concern about "aircraft carrier Czechoslovakia." The negotiations then faded out in peculiar circumstances. Benes afterwards told Churchill that towards the end of them, he received a message from "a high military source" in Germany, informing him that if he wished to take advantage of Hitler's offer he had better be quick, because events would shortly take place in Russia which would render insignificant any help he could give Germany. While he was pondering over this hint, he became aware that messages were passing through the Soviet Embassy in Prague between "important personages in Russia" and the German Government.

Benes was not the only man to receive such hints. In January, 1937, the new American Ambassador to Moscow, Joseph E. Davies, travelling by way of Berlin, had a talk at the German Foreign Ministry with the head of the department dealing with Russian affairs, who told him that there was much revolutionary activity in Russia, which might shortly break out into the open.

In June, it became known that the Russian Government had arrested its former Vice Commissar of Defense, Marshal Mikhail Tukhachevsky, together with seven other generals. Three days after the marshal's arrest, he was taken out and shot.

The Tukhachevsky affair will probably always remain a mystery, but one can perhaps make an intelligent guess at what happened. Tukhachevsky was one of those Russian generals who had had particularly close connections with the German General Staff in the years immediately following the First World War. The Russians helped the Germans train an illegal army. The Germans helped the Russians with technical advice. These links continued after Hitler came to power, and this freemasonry of generals was certainly distrusted by the ideological zealots of both the Nazi and the Russian Communist parties. There is nothing inherently improbable in the Russian accusation that Tukhachevsky was plotting against Stalin with the connivance of the German General Staff. There would be nothing improbable, either, in a plot by the

German General Staff, with the connivance of Tukhachevsky, against its particular enemy in the Nazi hierarchy, Himmler.

According to Walter Schellenberg, then a junior member of Himmler's Intelligence staff, Heydrich, Himmler's chief assistant, received information at the beginning of 1937 of a plot between Tukhachevsky and the German General Staff against Stalin. Heydrich added to this information some fictional material implicating German generals—Schellenberg adds that very little was necessary—and with considerable cunning used the Czechoslovaks as a channel for passing this on to Stalin.

The choice of the Czechoslovaks was a master stroke. According to Walter Duranty, the most experienced American correspondent in Russia at the time, the current rumor in Moscow was that the GPU had been informed by the Czechoslovak Intelligence Service of treasonable conversations between the German General Staff and Tukhachevsky, in which Tukhachevsky had revealed Czechoslovak defense plans to the Germans.

If Heydrich did pass on, or fabricate, the evidence that led to Tukhachevsky's death, he certainly struck a powerful blow on behalf of his masters. In the first place, he sabotaged for the time being any plans there may have been for a Russo-German alliance. He also temporarily wrecked Russia as a military power. In the purge that followed Tukhachevsky's arrest, almost half the total Russian officer corps lost either their lives or their commands. Russia ceased to be regarded by the rest of Europe either as a desirable ally or an enemy to be feared.

There was a particular effect on Russia's ally, Czechoslovakia. In March of 1938, the German Foreign Ministry heard from "a reliable source" that the Czechoslovak General Staff was still reluctant to entrust too many of its defense secrets to the Russians, because it continued to believe that Tukhachevsky had been in touch with the German General Staff. The Czechoslovak military attaché in Moscow told his British colleague in April that he was "anxiously awaiting the moment when he can telegraph to his Ministry that the purge is over." Although Benes wrote in his memoirs that he had instructed the Czechoslovak General Staff to cooperate fully with the Russians, their relations with their Russian opposite numbers seem to have been no more than formal.

By the end of 1937, Czechoslovakia stood in a dangerously weak position, isolated from allies who had themselves been weakened, surrounded by potential enemies, with a coalition government that spanned the political spectrum from pro-Russian Left Wing Social Democrats to Right Wing Agrarians anxious to reach agreement with Germany, and housing in Henlein's Sudeten German Party a potentially dangerous Trojan horse.

CHAPTER 3

The Gentle Art of Sleepwalking

ON APRIL 20, 1937, Hitler celebrated his forty-eighth birthday. He already showed signs of what became an almost obsessive belief that he would not live long enough to complete all that he had to do. He was a hypochondriac and a crank, worrying about his health, careful of his diet, eating no meat, avoiding alcohol, tobacco, and even such mild stimulants as tea and coffee; but mad he certainly was not.

He liked to see himself not as a politician, but as an artist; and indeed it is not too difficult to imagine him, born thirty years later on the sunny shores of California, as an unpublished and unpublishable disciple of Jack Kerouac. The thwarted artistic ambition, the resentment of any authority except his own, the early preoccupation with Eastern religions, the torrents of undisciplined verbiage which he was too arrogant to make lucid for an audience he at once despised and was eager to dominate: all these things are to be found in the record of his extraordinary progress from the underworld of prewar Vienna to the dictatorship of Germany. Californian affluence, even the crumbs of it, would have tamed him and left him grumbling and contentedly rotting in the sunshine. Poverty, the horrors of the First World War, the degradation of postwar Germany and the insight it had given him into the debasement of which human beings are all too easily capable, had sharpened him into a shrewd and calculating opportunist with a passion for power.

But a bad artist he remained. He disliked the discipline of regular work, preferring to trust to his intuition, going, as he said after the reoccupation of the Rhineland, the way that Providence dictates with the assurance of a sleepwalker. The working conditions he perhaps deliberately created around himself were chaotic. Long periods of apathy alternated with bursts of feverish activity, when the Chancellery in Berlin or the Berghof at Obersalzberg came to resemble the domestic establishment of some great barbarian chieftain, with party functionaries, generals, senior civil servants running in and out to be barked at or charmed, according to which method their master thought most likely to achieve results.

Colonel Friedrich Hossbach, the Wehrmacht's liaison officer at Hitler's headquarters until 1937, never saw the Fuehrer completely lose self-control, nor heard of any such case from an eyewitness. Dr. Paul Schmidt, Hitler's official interpreter, tells much the same story. Sir Nevile Henderson, the British Ambassador, complained that he never seemed to see the Fuehrer except when he was in a bad temper. Henderson does not seem to have suspected that on one occasion at least, after the door had closed behind him, the Fuehrer burst into roars of laughter, exclaiming, "That ought to put the wind up Chamberlain!" The legendary bursts of apparently hysterical fury were the assumptions of an actor who used them as a weapon, and who had the actor's power to convince himself momentarily that he believed what he was saying. Another weapon was the charm exerted through piercing, almost hypnotic eyes. Or upon occasion he would mesmerize some wondering general by reeling off without notes a long and complicated military dissertation. The facts, upon closer examination, generally turned out to be wrong; but the immediate effect of mastery had been achieved.

Hitler came to power because the German people were in desperate straits. He intensified his hold over them by all the resources of radio, a controlled press, the sumptuously theatrical settings in which he delivered his major speeches. But his power rested essentially on the contrast between the degradation they had experienced during the depression, and the new, thriving, bustling Germany in which there were jobs for all, houses and roads were being built, and the humiliating conditions of Versailles were kicked over one by one. Hitler had restored the self-respect of a dynamic, industrious and inventive people. No matter for the moment if it was all done by a confidence trick, if somebody one knew mysteriously disappeared, if the Jews seemed to be having rather a rough time—the Jews probably deserved it anyway, they were always either Communists or had far too much money. So for the time being the confidence trick worked, and as long as it continued working, the majority of the German people were not inclined to quarrel with their Fuehrer.

An observer a little later in Hitler's career noted a common scene: "I saw at close quarters crowds of men and women of all ages at the railway stations pressing towards the carriage. They yelled till their voices broke, and with flushed faces and outstretched arms seemed in the throes of St. Vitus dance. . . . Some women, as it were, flattening their noses against the side of the carriage, held up their children. Hitler would for a moment hold the child's little arms with both hands, and shake them somewhat mechanically, without any change of expression. . . . A middle-aged Berlin woman often came to my mind, who told me that she went to all manner of demonstrations lining the streets through which the Fuehrer passed, but had never yet properly seen him, for whenever he approached, her eyes would fill with tears." With growing confidence and pride, these people proclaimed: "Our Fuehrer always gets his way, and he gets it without going to war."

That was the point: how far could he go without involving Germany in war?

Hitler's main political ideas are set out principally in *Mein Kampf*. That excessively ill-written book is so unreadable that the greater part of the world may be forgiven for not having read it, but since the legend persists that *Mein Kampf* contains detailed plans and a timetable for world conquest, to which Hitler was working and which Western statesmen blindly ignored, it may be as well to consider its contents briefly. The book is a ragbag of thoughts about religion, the supremacy of certain racial groups and the inferiority of others, the art of communication, the disruptive genius of international Jewry: anything, in fact, coming into the author's mind which would help to establish him in his chosen role as an intellectual. Stalin, who clumsily shared a number of traits with Hitler, also longed to be regarded as an intellectual. Mussolini, who was one, regarded intellectuals with a proper disdain.

Mein Kampf does contain, however, a number of second-hand ideas about a Greater Germany created out of a union of Germany and Austria and about seeking in Poland, the Ukraine and Russia an outlet for its expansion and development. A prerequisite to the fulfillment of this program was the avoidance of war on two fronts, and therefore the neutralization of France, either through war or through an agreement with Britain.

Very few Western statesmen doubted that Hitler would put these ideas into practice if he could. It was again Henderson who complained that, while Hitler had told everybody in *Mein Kampf* what he proposed to do, he had inconsiderately omitted to tell them how he proposed to do it. The answer was that Hitler did not know himself. A skilled games-player knows that he wants to beat his opponent, the opponent knows that the object is to beat him, but neither knows what unexpected exploitation of which opening will lead to victory. The question always was whether, and at what point, Hitler could be stopped without the risk of a devastating war. That point was probably passed with the reoccupation of the Rhineland. And some of Hitler's opponents not only had a bad conscience about Versailles, they were also increasingly haunted by the terror of the knockout blow.

By 1937, a number of Hitler's former supporters had become increasingly uneasy about the Fuehrer's brinkmanship. They included Hjalmar Schacht, the financial genius whose jugglery had made German economic recovery possible; Neurath, the Foreign Minister; a substantial number of professional diplomats like Weizsaecker, who was then head of the Political Department at the Foreign Ministry, and later became its chief permanent official; and large sections of the German Officer Corps.

There was a split in the Army between older members of the Officer Corps and those younger ones who owed their rapid promotion to the Army's expansion under the Nazis. The split grew, in a sense, out of a technical disagreement between the followers of Beck, Chief of the General Staff, who like their British and French opposite numbers saw no more in the tank than a mobile gun to support the infantry, and younger generals such as Guderian, who were fashioning about the tank and the close-support divebomber the tactics of the *Blitzkrieg,* the quick and limited war which Hitler had eagerly seized upon as ideal for his purposes. Superimposed upon this difference between the Officer Corps itself was a quarrel between the Army and the Nazi Party over the role of the blackshirted *Schutz Staffeln* or S.S. units, originally formed as Hitler's personal bodyguard, then conceived as a national élite and expanded under Himmler until by 1937 they formed a powerful rival to the Army itself. One can faintly discern traces of this quarrel in the Tukhachevsky affair.

It is important to note that none of these emerging opponents questioned what Hitler was doing; only the method and speed. Weizsaecker worked industriously for the "chemical dissolution" of Czechoslovakia. Von Hassell, the former German Ambassador in Rome, who was one of the dissidents, tried to persuade the British to discuss peace terms in 1940 which would have left Germany with Austria, the Sudetenland, and a large slice of Poland.

The difference between these critics of Hitler and Hitler himself was that they were afraid of a war they were likely to lose. Hitler took immense pains to get his way without having to fight, but he believed that sooner or later he would have to do so and he was prepared to take the risk if he had to. In the meantime, these critics, like a lot of nerveless old women, kept jogging his elbow at important moments, and it would certainly have been convenient to him to get them out of the way.

On the afternoon of November 5, 1937, there arrived at the Chancellery in Berlin the three service chiefs, Goering of the Luftwaffe, Raeder of the Navy, and Fritsch of the Army, together with the Minister for War, Blomberg, and the Foreign Minister, Neurath.

The Fuehrer told them portentously that he wished to place before them the fruit of thorough deliberation and the experiences of his four and a half years of power. Hitler enjoyed these occasional canters round the universe before a captive and distinguished audience. He may, however, have had other motives for calling this meeting, one of which was to smoke out the opposition he knew to be building up against him. According to the postwar testimony of Raeder, on trial for his life at Nuremberg, at least part of the object of the conference was to break Neurath's nerve. According to Goering, in similar uncomfortable circumstances, Hitler told him beforehand that the intention was to put pressure on Fritsch to speed up rearmament. After the conference, Blomberg heard that the French Ambassador in Berlin, François-Poncet, had obtained a report of the proceedings. That may have been intended also as an incidental move in the European war of nerves, for as Ribbentrop noted on another occasion, "A certain intimidation of the other side also has its advantages."

Hitler opened the meeting with a politico-economic lecture about the tightly-packed racial community of 85 million Germans and its right to living space. This could only be achieved by force, with its attendant risk. If his audience accepted that premise, there remained to be answered the questions "When" and "How." The "When" Hitler put in the remote period 1943–45, when German rearmament would be completed, but before the weapons had become obsolete. There might, however, be earlier opportunities of gaining substantial advantages: for instance, if civil war in France occupied the attention of the French Army, or if France and Britain became involved in war with Italy in the Mediterranean. In such circumstances, the time for action against Austria and Czechoslovakia would have come. He asserted that almost certainly Britain, and probably France as well, had already tacitly written off the Czechs.

Hitler, if a brilliant opportunist, was a poor prophet, and none of the events which he foretold at the Chancellery that afternoon ever happened. There was no civil war in France. The British and French avoided war with Italy over Spain. The fruit of Hitler's thorough deliberation, in fact, would have been condemned by any competent young staff officer as "distinctly viewy," and one may perhaps surmise that at its conclusion there was a pregnant silence.

What did happen, however, was that Blomberg, Fritsch and Neurath all expressed doubt and disagreement at the conference and afterwards, and that less than three months later, none of them remained in office. Blomberg had been encouraged by Goering to marry a girl who was conveniently discovered to have a police record as a prostitute, and the War Minister was required to resign. A homosexual named Schmidt was found to swear that Fritsch had been one of his clients, which disposed of the Commander-in-Chief of the Army. Neurath was kicked upstairs, to become president of a Cabinet Council that rarely met, and was replaced by the devoted Nazi Ribbentrop. It was virtually the end of the old order. They whispered in corners, in Guderian's contemptuous phrase, and sometimes more actively, if unskillfully, conspired; but never again had they a chance of control. Thenceforward, Hitler was his own War Minister, Commander-in-Chief, and virtual Foreign Secretary.

A fortnight after the Berlin conference, Hitler received distinguished confirmation that, in certain circumstances, the British at least had written off Czechoslovakia. Lord Halifax, Master of the Middleton Foxhounds, visited Germany to attend a hunting exhibition in Berlin and afterwards to shoot foxes at Karinhall, Goering's country estate. Lord Halifax was Lord President of the Council in Neville Chamberlain's Government. However, it was feared that a visit to Germany by the Lord President might stir up opposition in Britain, not least in Halifax's own party, so the Lord President stayed at home and the Master of the Middleton Foxhounds went in his place.

A meeting between Halifax and Hitler took place at Hitler's retreat at Obersalzberg, in that big room so soon to become depressingly familiar to European statesmen, with the vast north window opening on to sky and mountain and a distant prospect of Hitler's native Austria. It got off to an almost disastrous start. Halifax, alighting from the car, observed a pair of black-clad legs which he took to be those of a footman. They turned out upon investigation to be those of the Fuehrer in person.

Hitler was not only a teetotaller, a vegetarian, and opposed to blood sports—all that Halifax would have classified in England as a cranky "progressive"—but also an old-fashioned nineteenth century rationalist to whom Christianity was a religion fit only for slaves. Halifax was a devout Christian who sought guidance on his knees for the problems of this world. He was also a sporting squire, who much preferred to be hunting or shooting at Garrowby, his country estate on the Yorkshire moors.

Hitler found Halifax "a hypocrite of the worst type, a liar," and spoke of him afterwards with detestation as "the English parson." Halifax, after this, his only meeting with Hitler, wrote that the Fuehrer, although perfectly friendly and courteous, showed a certain reserve, "which may have been due partly to tiredness, but was I think mainly attributable to a feeling that we had a different sense of values and were speaking a different language. It was not only the difference of outlook between a totalitarian and a democratic State. He gave the impression of feeling that, whilst he had attained power only after a hard struggle with present-day realities, the British Government was still living comfortably in a world of its own making, a make-believe land of strange, if respectable illusions." In private conversation afterwards, Halifax is said to have expressed himself more forcibly. In Hitler's presence, he said, he felt as if the devil himself had come upon the earth.

Halifax had been extensively briefed for the encounter. He had received from Sir Nevile Henderson, the British Ambassador in Berlin, an extraordinary memorandum bluntly advocating an understanding with Germany, to be achieved at the expense of what Henderson called "*peaceful* expansion and evolution in the East,"* and a Foreign Office antidote in the form of "certain significant extracts" from Hitler's *Mein Kampf*, in which the principles of the Fuehrer's foreign policy "had been set out with brutal clarity." The outlines of what Halifax was to tell Hitler had been agreed at a meeting before he left, with Chamberlain and Anthony Eden, the Foreign Secretary.

Towards the end of his three hours with Hitler, Halifax came to that vital part of his agreed brief which dealt with Danzig, Austria and Czechoslovakia. On all these matters, he said, the British Government was not necessarily concerned to preserve the *status quo*, but they were concerned to avoid such treatment of them as would be likely to cause trouble. In short, Hitler might negotiate a revision of the map of Europe if he could, but if he tried to alter it by force, there might be trouble.

Halifax's summing up of the meeting was not free from that skepticism which was present in his contemplation of all merely

---

*The principal points of this important and hitherto unpublished memorandum, and the British Foreign Office's comments on it, are included in Appendix.

mortal affairs. He reported his belief in Hitler's sincerity, but added, "As to the political value of the talk, I am not disposed to rate this very high. I should think it was all to the good making contact—but I definitely got the impression that apart from colonies there was little or nothing he wanted from us and that he felt time to be on his side as regards European problems."

In the matter of Austria and Czechoslovakia, "I formed the impression that Germany believes time to be on her side, in the sense that the strong magnet will sooner or later attract the steel filings lying within reach of its attraction, and intends to assist this process as far as possible. They are irritated with the attempts of France—and to a less degree of Great Britain—to check what they conceive to be a legitimate and natural development of their influence, but I should suppose have no immediate, or even perhaps ultimate, intention of so acting as to give anybody a great deal to lay hold of. I am sure Hitler was sincere when he said he did not want war: Goering too. But equally I have no doubt that they all feel that strong armaments are very valuable in making other people a good deal more reluctant to interfere with what they deem primarily their business."

Could Britain, Halifax wondered, extract from Hitler an agreement that so long as Germany did not resort to force, Britain would not do so, either? "However much we may dislike the idea of Nazi beaver-like propaganda etc. in Central Europe, neither we nor the French are going to be able to stop it, and it would therefore seem shortsighted to forego the chance of a German settlement by holding out for something which we are almost certainly going to find ourselves in the last resort powerless to secure . . ."

These were dangerous waters, for from Halifax's admission to Hitler that changes could be brought about by negotiation, it was a short step to a German demand that the British must make it clear to the Czechoslovak Government that they were not going to encourage Czechoslovak resistance to Sudeten German demands; and from Halifax's warning about the use of force, it was not far to an insidious German suggestion that, since the British Government had said the postwar treaties might be amended by negotiation, but must not be amended by force, it was up to the British Government to compel the Czechoslovak Government to prove the point by making the necessary concessions.

On the German side, the skepticism hinted at by Halifax was more strongly expressed by the future German Foreign Minister. The forty-five-year-old Joachim von Ribbentrop had been a devoted member of the Nazi Party since 1930. His greatest claim to fame before that date had been as a highly successful salesman of champagne. In 1936, Hitler decided to use Ribbentrop's talents as a salesman by sending him to London as Ambassador to sell to the British Government that agreement with Germany which the Fuehrer always believed to be possible, disconcertingly though the British behaved.

Ribbentrop's effect on the British was almost as disastrous as that of Halifax upon Hitler. He was not stupid, but he was humourless, priggish, pompous, earnest, the Teutonic elephant— in the Italian Ambassador Grandi's phrase, "tripping it among the crockery." Tom Jones, Baldwin's confidant, quoted about Ribbentrop Pitt's dictum, "I know he can talk sense, but can he sometimes talk nonsense?" and foretold for him many strained moments in conversation with casual and allusive British politicians.

Ribbentrop's influence with Hitler was never as decisive as the British believed, but he did return to Berlin from his Ambassadorship with certain strong impressions which were a curious mixture of sense and nonsense, and which, since he was supposed to know about the British, played their part in shaping Hitler's thinking on the problem of Czechoslovakia.

Ribbentrop presented his conclusions in two long confidential reports written for Hitler at the end of 1937 and the beginning of 1938. Halifax's visit to Germany, he wrote, had been undertaken only because Chamberlain wanted to explore the possibility of an agreement with Germany on a basis acceptable to the British. If agreement were not possible on British terms, Chamberlain would at least have demonstrated how hard he was trying.

Ribbentrop reported his opinion that there were men in the British Government who still believed in the possibility of an amicable arrangement with Germany, but Chamberlain and Halifax were not among them. The only "conditional" friends of Germany he thought worth naming in these secret reports were

Lord Monsell and Lord Londonderry, both former Conservative ministers, but both now out of office; King Edward VIII, who had abdicated; "the Astor group and *Times*"; a seventy-nine-year-old retired diplomat, Lord Rennell, "as well as a number of not insignificant Liberals (Lothian, etc.) and a few representatives of the Left groups who hold pacifist ideals—Lord Allen of Hurtwood, Lord Arnold, Lord Noel-Buxton. Besides these, there is also the influence of City businessmen." This does not seem a very impressive collection, and even these, Ribbentrop added, took a skeptical view of German assurances of peace.

He noted with considerable shrewdness that the British ruling class were as determined to keep power as ever they had been. "I firmly believe that labels like 'nation of shopkeepers' never applied to the English ruling class. The ruling class is now as much as ever prepared to intervene for the promotion of strong material interests as also for a position of world power, up to the point of war. Britain will never lightly risk war. She will always be careful to weigh the balance of power, and if necessary delay a decision. If the better chances are on England's side, she will fight."

The British people, on the other hand, were in the main ready for an agreement with Germany, but they could be conditioned by propaganda to change their minds. "The people would not easily accept a war unless vital British interests were threatened. Yet even in such cases the government can succeed by suitable threatening propaganda in achieving its ends. It would not be impossible for the British Government to present both the British people and the Dominions with the idea of a development leading to war which would threaten vital British interests. Naturally it takes a certain time for this type of propaganda to take effect."

For some time, Ribbentrop wrote, England had been considering the possibility that sooner or later Germany would be compelled by the situation in Czechoslovakia to use force. England would certainly be drawn in if the French intervened, but if war could not be avoided altogether, the British would try to delay it until their defenses had reached a certain level. "People here," Ribbentrop noted, "often speak and write about 1939 as the year when Britain can take a stronger part, but my feeling is that it will be later. Earlier than this, such a conflict would be just as inconvenient for England as the Italian conflict in Abyssinia was last year."

Ribbentrop's final advice to Hitler was that Britain would fight sooner or later, but she was behind with her armaments and was therefore playing for time. "England believes that in a race with Germany time is on England's side—exploitation of her greater economic resources for armament—time for extending her alliances (e.g., the United States). The visit of Halifax, therefore, is to be considered as a maneuver to obtain information and as a camouflage."

The implication of these two reports was that, since Hitler was going to have to fight sooner or later, he would be well-advised to fight sooner, before Britain was ready. Ribbentrop pressed this advice strongly on the Fuehrer in the months ahead. It was resisted by Hitler's generals and by the professionals of the German Foreign Ministry. The sleepwalker's intuition kept Hitler balancing between the two schools of thought throughout 1938, and brought him down finally on the side of caution. Late in his career, when total defeat was almost upon him, Hitler came to believe that Ribbentrop had been right after all, that he should have forced war on France and Britain over Czechoslovakia in 1938, and that he lost the war when he signed the Munich Agreement.

CHAPTER 4

Anschluss

ON FRIDAY, March 11, the British Prime Minister gave a formal luncheon party to bid farewell to Herr von Ribbentrop and Frau von Ribbentrop upon their return to Germany. Most of the guests were senior members of the Government and their wives: Halifax, now Foreign Secretary; Sir John Simon, Chancellor of the Exchequer; Sir Samuel Hoare, Home Secretary; and Sir Thomas Inskip, Minister of Defence. Sir Alexander Cadogan was there, as Civil Service head of the Foreign Office. But to a foreigner like Ribbentrop, who never wholly understood how British politics work, his suspicion of Chamberlain's sincerity may have been strengthened by the presence of that stout advocate of a preventive war against Germany, Winston Churchill—though Churchill was neatly balanced by another outsider, the pro-German Lord Londonderry.

The occasion of the luncheon was not happily chosen. All morning, news had been coming into the Foreign Office of German troop concentrations on the Austrian frontier. More telegrams were handed in to Cadogan during luncheon, which greatly disturbed the usual calm of Lord Halifax and even faintly ruffled the Prime Minister. After the meal, Chamberlain invited Ribbentrop to his study and spoke to him more in sorrow than in anger about his sincere wish for an understanding with Germany, and the unfortunate effect of yet another German coup. More telegrams arrived, each more alarming than the last. The Austrian Chancellor, it appeared, had been given an ultimatum expiring at half-past four that afternoon, under threat of a German invasion.

The situation in Austria had developed so quickly and unexpectedly that Ribbentrop was caught without information or instructions. He could only bluster that the news of the ultimatum was probably untrue; or alternatively that, if it was true, it was all the Austrian Chancellor's fault. Chamberlain, he reported, appeared outwardly calm and cool-headed. Halifax, however, seemed somewhat excited. No doubt Halifax was thinking of Hitler's assurance to him, less than four months previously, that there was no prospect whatever of German troops suddenly marching into Austria or Czechoslovakia. Chamberlain gave Ribbentrop his usual warning: the use of force against Austria would create a very serious situation for England. But the Germans were not using force, they were engaged in what they regarded as negotiations, which Lord Halifax had approved at Obersalzberg.

The *Anschluss*—the joining together—of Austria and Germany had been forbidden under the Versailles treaties, without the permission of the League of Nations; but Austria, shorn of her Central European empire and surrounded by hostile states, was always in danger of collapse. In 1931, the Austrian and German Governments had reached agreement on a customs union, which had been vetoed by France, Czechoslovakia and Italy. The great Viennese banking house, the Credit-Anstalt, failed, accelerating the economic landslide in Europe which among other things helped Hitler to power. The Fuehrer was Austrian by birth, and the *Anschluss* had for him an emotional as well as a strategic significance.

Hitler's opportunity to take Austria came out of the blue, and was certainly unplanned. It arose from a combination of Mussolini's increasing involvement in the Spanish Civil War, and a desperate decision by Schuschnigg, the Austrian Chancellor, to try to halt the ceaseless internal sapping by Austrian Nazis with an appeal to world opinion through a plebiscite. This move took the Germans by surprise. Only the most rudimentary military plans existed. In the late afternoon of March 10, less than forty-eight hours before his troops entered Austria, Guderian, commander of the German XVI Corps, was summoned to Berlin by

Beck, the Chief of Staff, told in the greatest secrecy that Hitler intended to incorporate Austria into the Reich, and warned to stand by for further orders. Late that night the orders came: Guderian was to alert his old 2nd Panzer Division and the S.S. Adolf Hitler Division, and assemble them in the neighborhood of Passau, on the Austrian frontier, over 400 miles away. These orders were so unexpected that the commander and staff of the 2nd Panzer Division were dispersed on a training exercise, and had to be hurriedly recalled. The division had no maps of Austria, but some Baedeker Guides were hastily assembled. It had no supply vehicles, except what could be commandeered from civilian firms. Guderian obtained petrol for his tanks by threatening to take it by force from German civilian petrol depots, and when he marched into Austria on the early morning of March 12, he got his supplies from Austrian filling stations.

British observers, convinced that Hitler's plans for Austria were part of an elaborate "grand design," were deceived by Guderian's supply difficulties into making exaggerated reports of a massive panzer breakdown, leading to the conclusion that the German Army was hopelessly unready for war. As Guderian had moved his tanks and troops over 400 miles in less than forty-eight hours by a series of the brilliant improvisations he was later to demonstrate in France, an exactly contrary conclusion might more prudently have been drawn.

If there had been a "grand design" to invade Austria, it seems unlikely that Goering, as commander-in-chief of the Luftwaffe, would have fixed the night of March 11 for a glittering reception to be given at Luftwaffe headquarters in Berlin. Shortly after ten o'clock, the first of Goering's thousand guests began uneasily to dance under the tinkling chandeliers. Their host, however, was conspicuous by his absence. He was with Hitler at the Chancellery, anxiously awaiting a telephone message from Rome which would decide the fate of Austria.

It came at twenty-five minutes past ten, and Hitler took it himself. The caller was Prince Philip of Hesse, who had been sent to Rome with a personal letter from Hitler to Mussolini, begging the Duce not to intervene if German troops crossed the Austrian frontier.

Hesse said, "I have just come back from the Palazzo Venezia. The Duce accepted the whole thing in a very friendly manner. He sends you his regards . . ."

Hitler broke in excitedly: "Then please tell Mussolini I will never forget him for this. Never, never, never, whatever happens . . . As soon as the Austrian affair is settled, I shall be ready to go with him, through thick and thin, no matter what happens . . . If he should ever need any help or be in any danger, he can be convinced that I shall stick to him, whatever may happen, even if the whole world were against him."

This was among the few promises Hitler ever kept, though he lived to regret having made it.

Mussolini's reply was not foreordained. He was not at all happy about having a German neighbour on the Brenner, and if he had encouraged the Austrians to resist, they might have done so. Hitler would then have been faced with a choice between backing down or entering Austria by force, which in turn would have faced Britain with a choice between backing down and going to war. It was not only Hitler who had reason to be grateful to Mussolini.

Greatly relieved at the knowledge of Mussolini's acquiescence, Goering went off to his reception, shook hands with a few guests, sat down at the central table, and gave the signal for the *pièce de résistance* of the evening, a performance by the ballet of the State Opera Company. Guderian's tanks had almost reached their assembly areas, and could be ready to advance at first light. Goering had one other source of worry. Keitel, Hitler's military adviser, had warned the Fuehrer that if Czechoslovakia mobilized, the whole Austrian operation would be endangered. The regular army of Czechoslovakia, French-trained, consisted of 14 infantry divisions, one mechanized division, and some miscellaneous troops. The German Army at this time had only 28 divisions, a proportion of which had to be held back in the west in case France gave trouble over Austria. It was common ground among the General Staffs of Europe that if Germany swallowed Austria, Czechoslovakia became indefensible.

There had been rumours in Berlin that day that the Czechoslovaks were mobilizing, but the rumours had been anxiously denied during the afternoon by Krofta, the Czechoslovak Foreign Minister, who volunteered, apparently without having been asked, that his Government was not contemplating any kind of measure.

Among the guests at Goering's reception was Dr. Vojtech Mastny, the Czechoslovak Minister in Berlin. Smallish, plump, with pretensions to being a bit of a dandy, Mastny is fated to make his few brief appearances on the stage of history at moments when he is being bullied by somebody. It is not clear whether Goering sought out Mastny, or Mastny sought out Goering, but they came together at the reception, and Mastny, according to Goering, was much worked up and was trembling. He begged for an assurance that the German measures against Austria were in no way directed against Czechoslovakia. Since it happened to be true, Goering gladly gave the assurance. The events in Austria, he said, were "a family affair"; Germany had nothing against Czechoslovakia and wished to continue the present relations with her.

Mastny hurried back to his Legation and telephoned this reassurance to his Government, who were in anxious session. He took back to Goering a message from the Czechoslovak Foreign Minister that "no one here contemplated intervening in the Austrian affair." Goering received this assurance as gratefully as Mastny had received the earlier one. He became genial and expansive: "I can give you the word of the Head of State and I can give you an entirely official declaration, because the Fuehrer has empowered me to conduct the highest affairs of State."

Goering afterwards maintained that this expansive undertaking had applied only to the specific circumstances of the *Anschluss,* and ten days later, when the crisis was safely over, Ribbentrop officially informed German representatives abroad that the pledge given to Mastny "did not apply to future circumstances." The Czechoslovaks naturally disputed this limited interpretation. One may perhaps assume that Goering would have said anything that night which served the German purpose of keeping the Czechoslovak Army quiet. It is also fair to suggest, however, that the Czechoslovak Government allowed itself to be somewhat easily reassured. German annexation of Austria turned the flank of the expensive Czechoslovak fortification system, which did not cover the southern frontier with Austria. In a bitter book written after the signing of the Munich Agreement, Colonel Emanuel Moravec of the Czechoslovak General Staff accused his masters not only of short-sightedness in basing their defensive plans on the assumption that Germany and Austria would never be united, but also of taking no serious steps to fortify the Austrian frontier even after the *Anschluss*. It was Moravec's complaint against the Czechoslovak politicians that they would neither make up their minds to defend Czechoslovakia nor agree in good time to reach the settlement with Germany that was the only practical alternative. They dared not do the latter, Moravec wrote, because for years the Czechoslovak people had been so worked on by propaganda that they hated the Germans, and would not contemplate coming to an agreement with them.

Certainly the Czechoslovak Government did nothing at the time of the *Anschluss* to convince the Germans that Czechoslovakia, with its 15 divisions and its frontier fortifications, would be a tough nut to crack. The fortifications, in fact, were not even manned.

In Prague, the editor of the Socialist newspaper *Pravo lidu* told an audience that the *Anschluss* did not concern Czechoslovakia at all. The Czechoslovaks were not like the Austrians, they would defend themselves. Besides, they had their pacts with France and Russia. The Germans would never dare touch them.

At nine o'clock on the morning of March 12, Guderian's first tanks crossed the Austrian frontier. They were not invading. They had been invited in by an Austrian Government headed by the Austrian Nazi Seyss-Inquart. Such are the blessings of negotiation, Nazi style. The Fuehrer crossed the frontier shortly after lunch, gave the house of his birth at Braunau a Nazi salute while standing in the back of his car watched by a small and unenthusiastic crowd, and drove on to Linz. Soon Jews in Vienna were being told to take off their clothes and walk on all fours, and elderly Jewish ladies were hoisted up into trees and instructed to chirp. They were not forced to do so, it was all a matter of negotiation.

The German people rejoiced. Their Fuehrer had done it again, and all without going to war. But not even the Germans received

the news of the *Anschluss* with greater rejoicing than a majority
of the Sudeten Germans of Czechoslovakia. They were more nearly
akin to the Austrians than to the Germans of the Reich, they
had never wanted to be detached from Austria after the First
World War, and the anticipation of reunion with their Austrian
cousins set in motion an avalanche of nationalist feeling.

Fifteen thousand, twenty thousand, twenty-five thousand demonstrators, many of them in the Henleinist uniform of shorts and
white stockings, marched through the streets of Sudetenland
towns, chanting, "One People, One Nation, One Leader." The
wildest rumors were put into circulation: the Fuehrer was coming
to liberate them, too. He was coming on April 10, the date set for
a plebiscite in Austria; or on April 20, his forty-ninth birthday.
Henlein issued a manifesto giving his fellow Sudeten Germans until May 31 to join him, with sinister implications of what would
happen to them if they did not jump on the Henleinist bandwagon. Posters appeared: "Be on the winning side! Join Henlein
Before It Is Too Late!" and "It Is Five Minutes to Twelve." Henleinist employers threatened to fire workers if they did not join,
and some who continued to resist were beaten up. Under this
sustained pressure, only about 400,000 Sudeten German Social
Democrats held out against joining Henlein, calling themselves
with pride as well as justification the last of the free Germans.

It is pleasant to be in the driving-seat of a bandwagon, but if
the vehicle only drives round and round in circles, there is the
danger that those who have so eagerly jumped on will become
equally eager to jump off. Unfortunately, the Fuehrer seemed to
be in no hurry to come to the help of the oppressed Sudeten
Germans, and there was always somebody claiming to be a better
driver than Henlein, who would really take the bandwagon somewhere.

Eisenlohr, the German Minister in Prague, was no Nazi, but
an astute career diplomat, assiduously pressing on with the German Foreign Ministry policy of helping the "chemical dissolution" of Czechoslovakia. He had secured from Hodza, the
Czechoslovak Prime Minister, a promise of concessions to the
Henleinists and a hint that they might be invited to join the
Government when the time was ripe. This fitted in well with

German policy, but not with that of the Henleinists. However gladly they might have joined the Government in the first excitement of their electoral success, to do so now, when the majority of their people were clamoring for immediate liberation, would be to risk losing their mass support.

At the time of the *Anschluss*, Frank, Henlein's deputy, was engaged in trying to push Eisenlohr into taking a more positive line. Eisenlohr was not going to have the hothead Frank upsetting his careful diplomacy, and snubbed him. Frank appealed to Berlin over Eisenlohr's head, and was snubbed again. The German Foreign Ministry, on Eisenlohr's advice, refused to see Frank, and so did the *Volksdeutsche Mittelstelle*, the organization set up by Hitler in 1937 under a major-general of the S.S., Werner Lorenz, to exploit the fifth column potentialities of German minorities abroad. Frank complained to friends in Berlin of the treatment he was receiving, and Eisenlohr was asked to explain himself. Meanwhile, Frank had returned from Berlin to Prague, and there he and Henlein decided on a bold step. They would write direct to Eisenlohr's new master at the German Foreign Ministry, Ribbentrop, congratulating him on "the happy turn of events in Austria," promising to render thanks to the Fuehrer "by redoubling our efforts in the service of the policy of Greater Germany," and asking if they might see him personally to discuss future plans.

This cast hooked a very big fish indeed: the Fuehrer in person. Henlein and Frank were invited to Berlin, and on March 28 spent three hours at the Chancellery in conference with Hitler, Ribbentrop, Hess and Lorenz of the *Volksdeutsche Mittelstelle*.

The meeting was of great significance, but not quite in the way that is usually given. It has been described as marking a decisive turn in the relationship between the Henleinist leaders and Hitler, the moment when Henlein agreed to follow the Fuehrer's policy of always making demands on the Czechoslovak Government which were not acceptable. But it was not quite like that. What must be remembered is that perhaps Henlein, and certainly Frank, had gone to Berlin to ask the German Government to intervene in the Sudetenland immediately and dramatically. Frank had come prepared with inflammatory information about Communist plots in Czechoslovakia, about plans for secret mobilization by the Czechoslovak General Staff and the possibility of a military *Putsch* against Benes and Hodza, with which he hoped to provoke Hitler into taking action. The Fuehrer no doubt listened with interest and tucked Frank's stories away for future use. He repeated the promise he had already made publicly, to settle the Sudeten problem in the not-too-distant future, and he added the assurance that he could no longer tolerate Germans being oppressed or fired on. But he did not offer to do anything about it. Instead, he turned all his considerable charm on the susceptible Henlein. He knew, he said, that Henlein was immensely popular, the rightful leader of the Sudeten Germans.

"I can only be a substitute for the Fuehrer," Henlein interjected hopefully; but the Fuehrer did not rise to the bait. "I will stand by you," he said grandiloquently. "From tomorrow you will be my Viceroy. I will not tolerate difficulties being made for you by any department whatsoever within the Reich." This instruction was rubbed into the intransigent Eisenlohr on the following day. But German policy remained what it had been: chemical dissolution. In a discussion of the tactics to be pursued by the Henleinists in the months ahead, Henlein agreed that, in spite of the favorable situation created by the *Anschluss*, he would not drive things to the limit, but would continue to put forward his previous demands. He summarized them accurately as "We must always demand so much that we can never be satisfied," and the Fuehrer agreed that this was correct. Henlein was also told that he would have to cooperate closely with the German authorities, although following his own tactical line.

The discussion ended with the Fuehrer applying some more lavish butter to his new Viceroy. He congratulated Henlein on his successful past visits to England, and asked him to go again as soon as possible to persuade the British to keep their noses out of Czechoslovak affairs. Henlein promised to do so, and in fact very usefully did.

But the most he could take back to his clamorous supporters was a promise from Ribbentrop that behind the Sudeten Germans stood a nation of 75 million people, who were no longer prepared to tolerate their suppression by the Czechoslovak Government. Meanwhile he was to negotiate—and make sure he kept his supporters under firm control while he did so.

At a second meeting at the German Foreign Ministry, the demands Henlein was to make on the Czechoslovak Government were hammered out. They included a stop to the building of Czech schools in the Sudeten German areas; the development of self-government, and the employment of Sudeten German officials; the holding of State and communal elections, which had been continually postponed, ostensibly because the Czechoslovak Government was afraid of disorder, but in reality, as the Henleinists suspected, because the Government knew Henlein would again sweep the Sudetenland; and the abolition of control in the frontier areas by the State police, a paramilitary force under control of the central Government, whose methods were not always above reproach. There was to be a further demand that Henlein's followers should be free to profess the Nazi ideology if they chose. This demand was not universally popular among the Henleinists themselves, and it was afterwards wrapped up in an assortment of euphemisms, and indeed at one point dropped altogether. But the demands discussed at this conference at the German Foreign Ministry are recognizably those that Henlein put forward to a massive Sudeten German rally at Karlsbad a month later, and which became known as the Eight Karlsbad Points. If they were accepted by the Czechoslovak Government, they were likely to lead inevitably to the secession of the Sudetenland. If they were not accepted—and nobody believed that they would be—then it would be publicly demonstrated that the Czechoslovak Government was unwilling to allow its Sudeten German minority even a reasonable measure of self-determination. What was to happen then remained to be determined.

It should be said in fairness to the "moderate" Sudeten German Party leaders that they did not know about these Berlin meetings with Hitler and Ribbentrop until the official German Foreign Ministry documents were published after the war. Some of them, however, have told me that they were already suspicious of Frank's activities and of his influence on Henlein, and it is perhaps surprising that their uneasiness did not cause them to resign, protest, or take any other of the steps open to politicians who find themselves in disagreement with the leadership. Their answer is that they believed they, not Frank, were in control of the machine. One may also guess that they, too, were swept away by the heady prospect of liberation from Czech domination, and were not inclined to inquire too closely how it was to be achieved. They were fools, like many nationalist leaders, but not, I think, anything worse—if, indeed, there is anything worse.

CHAPTER 5

Idiot's Delight

NEVILLE CHAMBERLAIN'S father, Joseph Chamberlain, had been among the most brilliant of late Victorian statesmen. Under his rule at the Colonial Office, vast tracts of Africa were annexed to the British Empire. He worked to achieve Anglo-German friendship and failed. In spite of his brilliant promise, he never became Prime Minister.

Neville's half-brother, Sir Austen Chamberlain, six years older, also had a remarkable political career, becoming a distinguished Foreign Secretary. Neville was generally considered the dullard of this talented political family. At the age of twenty-two, he was sent off to grow sisal in the Bahamas, a venture which failed and cost his father £50,000. By the time Neville Chamberlain was forty-six, the highest office he had achieved was that of Lord Mayor of Birmingham. He made an unfortunate incursion into Government administration during the First World War, at the invitation of Lloyd George, as Director-General of National Service. He withdrew to Birmingham after only a year in London, deeply hurt by his experiences and believing, not at all wrongly, that he had been badly let down by Lloyd George, whom he never forgave. After the war, he became M.P. for a Birmingham constituency, and in a Conservative Party deprived of a number of its leading lights by a split over the Lloyd George coalition, he rose by plodding steadiness from Postmaster-General to Paymaster-General, then to Minister of Health, Chancellor of the Exchequer, Minister of Health again, finally Chancellor of the Exchequer and heir-apparent in Baldwin's last administration. It was Neville the tortoise, not the brilliant hares Joseph or Austen, who became the Prime Minister of the Chamberlain family. When he succeeded Baldwin on May 28, 1937, he was already sixty-eight.

Chamberlain had a somber appearance, with bushy, grizzled eyebrows, a grizzled, untidy moustache beneath a prominent nose. His high, stiff collar and loosely knotted tie gave him a Victorian air. Priding himself on his own cold logic, he despised what he considered a lack of logic in others and took evident pleasure in exposing their inadequacies. He gave an impression of aloofness, arrogance, complete self-containment. "Cut that beggar in a million pieces, and there wouldn't be a drop of blood," said one of his political opponents. The appearance was deceptive. Chamberlain was shy, kindly, deeply sensitive. Those who worked most closely with him, and knew him best, still speak of him with a very real warmth.

He had in him the makings of a great peacetime Prime Minister. It was his misfortune that the virtues of such a role became vices in the part he had actually to play. As a practical businessman, and also as a former and efficient Minister of Health, he knew how desperately needed were better houses, more health facilities, all that is today commonly called Welfare. Left Wing opponents accused him of wasting money on armaments which should have been spent on eliminating poverty and disease. Nobody could have agreed with them more strongly than Chamberlain. He resented the money spent on arms. He was called a Fascist and accused of hobnobbing with Hitler and Mussolini of his own choice. He detested them both, but tried to operate the traditional British policy of maintaining a balance of power in Europe at a time when it seemed equally dangerous to support either Russia or Germany, and the only balancing-pole remaining was an uncertain Italy.

He is generally portrayed as a weak man unversed in foreign affairs who entered upon his contest with Hitler in the company of his equally ill-informed adviser, Sir Horace Wilson, "with the bright faithfulness of two curates entering a pub for the first time; they did not observe the difference between a social gathering and a roughhouse."

This does not stand up to very close examination. Chamberlain had never specialized in foreign affairs, but he was not a fool, he had been almost continuously in Government office since 1922, during which time he had seen official papers and given every evidence of having studied them. Throughout the Munich Crisis he worked with an Inner Cabinet consisting of the current Foreign Secretary, Halifax, and two of Halifax's predecessors, Hoare and Simon. The standard is perhaps not very high, but Chamberlain certainly did not suffer by the comparison.

His vanity led him to believe briefly, as others had done before him, that he might be able to tame Hitler, but in anticipation of his first meeting with the Fuehrer he wrote: "Is it not positively horrible to think that the fate of hundreds of millions depends on one man, and he is half mad?" This was a dangerous delusion—Hitler was not mad, he was a cool-headed and shrewdly calculating opportunist—but it does not sound much like the bright faithfulness of a curate entering a roughhouse.

Chamberlain's short-lived policy of appeasement sprang from the idea that Britain could not go on pretending, as it had done under Baldwin, that Hitler and Mussolini did not exist. They did exist, and something had to be done about them. But what? To Chamberlain, appeasement was rooted in a strong moral belief that wars are caused by international injustices, and that if these injustices were righted, Hitler and Mussolini would have no reason for going to war.

But mixed with the gold of this idealism were baser metals. Chamberlain had a considerable share of vanity, and it was his by no means unworthy ambition to go down in history as a peacemaker. On this issue he let his heart rule his head. A perceptive Conservative critic, Robert Boothby, studying Chamberlain in the House of Commons, noted that his "hatred of war burns him up. One felt that there were almost no limits to which he would not go in order to prevent the horrors of war which he so vividly described, and the thought of which, I am convinced, never for a moment leaves him . . . One would not, at first sight, suspect the Prime Minister of being an emotional man; but when the question of peace or war arises, his passion knows no bounds. This is at once impressive, formidable and dangerous."

Chamberlain was also a snob. He stemmed from that great English industrial middle class which had opened up, tamed and ruled the countries of the British Empire, and he had an inherited confidence in his own moral uprightness, his own fitness to decide the destinies of inferior people. Hitler, he considered after having met him, was the commonest-looking little dog that he had ever seen, without one sign of distinction about him. There is no doubt that he condescended to Hitler and that Hitler, with a woodyard of chips on his shoulder, detected and resented the condescension. One may surmise that the Fuehrer took a peculiar personal satisfaction in scoring over Chamberlain as a prominent representative of that European Establishment which had snubbed him, despised him, tried to use him—and run away at the first threatening flourish of the hippopotamus-hide riding whip he liked to carry in his early political career.

One of Chamberlain's first actions on becoming Prime Minister was to initiate what seemed at the time a massive program of rearmament, against which there was some agitation by pacifists and the Left Wing of the Labour Party. By the spring of 1938, it was still possible for a borough in London's East End to refuse representation on the county Territorial Association because "any kind of armed force was contrary to their principle, and secondly because the army was built on class distinction"; for the Bishop of Exeter to be bitterly assailed because he, a supposed Christian, had volunteered for the Air Raid Precautions Service.

It was the year of Robert Sherwood's *Idiot's Delight* in the London theater: "They're all talking about security. They're all jittery. So they get bigger cannons and sharper bayonets. And that makes them more jittery"; and "I'll tell you what else you can do in these tragic circumstances. You can refuse to fight. Have you ever thought of that possibility? You can refuse to use those weapons that they have sold you." Long queues waited outside a London cinema to see the French film *La Kermesse Héroïque*, in which the women of a prosperous Flemish town warded off the destruction of their homes, and enjoyed themselves greatly, by going to bed with the Spanish invaders; tactics the effectiveness of which the French themselves, though not the film's British admirers, were shortly to have an opportunity of testing.

And yet though much can, quite rightly, be made of the climate of pacifist opinion in 1938, this was not the root cause of British behaviour during that summer. The real cause was indifference

which, for lack of information—or a plenitude of misinformation
—later turned to sheer funk. One young man vividly remembers
his sense of outrage when, on the Friday evening before the German march into Austria, a companion remarked complacently,
"You won't see anything about that on the newspaper placards
tomorrow. There's football." That was in March. By the end of
August, an opinion poll conducted by the British organization,
Mass-Observation, was reporting that 40 percent of those questioned were taking less interest than before in the continuing
crisis: "I work in an office, but they don't talk now about it, they're
all sick with fright of it," and "When I see the paper I turn the
page over. I suppose it's because I'm windy."

This was the fruit of the long years of propaganda about the
knockout blow from the air, ranging from H.G. Wells's imagina-
tive novel and film, *The Shape of Things to Come*, which portrayed a world devastated by air attack, to the official A.R.P.
booklets which suggested, improbably though correctly, that the
horrors portrayed by Wells could be mitigated by sticking strips
of brown paper over the sitting-room windows.

This fear started with the politicians, since they were better
informed. In March, Malcolm MacDonald, a member of Chamberlain's Government, told Harold Nicolson, an influential Government backbencher, that war would mean a massacre of women
and children in the streets of London. "No Government could
possibly risk a war when our anti-aircraft defenses are in so farcical
a condition. Even if the Germans exploit our present weakness in
order to achieve an even stronger position against us, we must
take that risk." Chamberlain, flying in over London suburbs from
one of his meetings with Hitler, dwelt with horror on the impact
bombs would make on the close-packed houses beneath.

We now know that the fear was exaggerated, but in 1938 it
was real. Nor was Britain so far behind Germany in the vital field
of aircraft production as was supposed at the time. Goering and
Milch had made a practice of inviting influential foreigners to
inspect the Luftwaffe and German aircraft factories and giving
them a highly coloured picture both of the Luftwaffe's strength
and potential. Official British Intelligence assessments overesti-
mated the Luftwaffe's strength by 15 percent, and the output
of German aircraft by at least a quarter. The unofficial estimates

were even more wildly astray. Among Goering's visitors was the British aeronautical engineer, Roy Fedden, who visited Germany twice in 1937 and again in the autumn of 1938. Fedden's estimate, given to the Government in 1937, put German production for 1937 and 1938 at more than double the British figure and suggested that this gap would widen unless drastic measures were adopted. In an air defense debate in May, 1938, Lord Lothian and Sir Hugh Seeley, using figures which Fedden claims to have provided, estimated that by 1939 Germany would have 8,000 first-line aircraft of all types. In fact she had some 3,600 airplanes on the outbreak of war, as against 1,600 British and 1,100 French aircraft, and by the summer of 1939, thanks to the spurt in rearmament put on after the Austrian crisis, British monthly output had almost caught up with the German. A determined start even a year earlier might have transformed the situation, though it is an interesting speculation how a pacifically-minded electorate would have reacted to Fedden's prescription, "Without any doubt the British Nation's main energies have got to be given over completely to armament manufacture instead of their legitimate and normal business for the next five years . . . Such a program will entail considerable financial sacrifice: either several shillings on the income tax and perhaps even a capital levy, or the day of balanced budgets gone for some time to come." It cost them more than that in the long run, but perhaps Ribbentrop was not far wrong in his suggestion that the British people would only fight when they were convinced beyond any doubt that their vital interests were threatened. In 1938, that time was still two years away.

If a British Army had taken the field in 1938, it would have consisted of two divisions, about 60,000 men, without Bren guns, armoured carriers or anti-tank weapons, and with some battalions down to a strength of five officers and three hundred men. There were no light, cruiser or infantry tanks, and the only medium tanks available were obsolete.

The Royal Air Force had some 500 bombers, half of which, according to their commander, were not in operational condition. Of the 350 fighters, only 60 were modern Hurricanes. By September, 1938, there was radar cover only on part of the east coast, from the Wash to Dungeness, on the Strait of Dover.

At sea, Britain apparently still ruled the waves, but as Ribbentrop had pointed out to Hitler, if the British had to keep an eye on Italy and Japan as well as on Germany, the combined British and French fleets would be hard put to it to maintain supremacy.

This was a poor hand for any Prime Minister to be caught with, and Chamberlain was not a man to risk bluffing in a situation where his bluff might only too easily be called. His inclination to pacifism was fortified by the advice of his Chiefs of Staff after the *Anschluss* that nothing could now help Czechoslovakia, and that if Britain went to war with Germany, she might be beaten. At this point the head of Chamberlain, the coldly logical thinker, came together with the heart of Chamberlain, the man who hated war, and in the middle of March he committed to paper in a private letter his thoughts for the future. It was now evident, he wrote, that only force could stop German expansion, and that collective security was useless unless it could show what would now be described as a credible deterrent backed by determination to use it. The only thing to be done was to break off attempts to come to terms with Hitler, announce some increase or acceleration in rearmament, and continue to try to swing the balance of power by detaching Italy from Germany. "If we can avoid another violent coup on Czechoslovakia, which ought to be feasible, it may be possible for Europe to settle down again, and some day for us to start peace talks again with the Germans."

There is not much doubt that Chamberlain himself continued to hope, at least until the following spring, that Hitler could be persuaded to behave sensibly. But there was nothing in the Fuehrer's upbringing or experience which led him to believe that the human race was guided in essentials by what Chamberlain regarded as logic or common sense. Human affairs, on the contrary, were ruled by force, or by fear of force. Hitler greatly desired an agreement with Britain on the only terms that interested him, a free hand in Europe in return for a German guarantee of the British Empire. But this he never seemed likely to get. The British, like a lot of old-fashioned nannies, insisted on interfering in what did not concern them, and the bait of future talks which was constantly held out to Hitler by Chamberlain seemed to come down to nothing more substantial than Lord Halifax discoursing on disquiet in the Church of England. Ribbentrop can have had little difficulty in convincing Hitler that the British wanted agreement only on their own terms, and were simply stringing out negotiations for as long as possible in order to complete their rearmament program. It is perfectly true that many of them were.

There is a case for arguing that, if Chamberlain had contented himself with speeding up rearmament, which he did, and had meanwhile avoided any further commitments, his policy would have been perfectly sound.

No Prime Minister, however, operates in a vacuum. Although Chamberlain's Government commanded an apparently impregnable majority in the House of Commons of some 220 votes, there were divisions within his own party which limited his freedom of action. A substantial number of his supporters—perhaps a majority—would have been happy to see Germany encouraged to satisfy her ambitions at the expense of Russia, in the hope that Nazis and Communists would cut each others' throats, and without regard for the possibility that, if one or the other achieved complete victory, they would be in a position to dominate Europe. Churchill, who had an invincible faith in the might of the French Army and little understanding of contemporary warfare, favoured a preventive war against Germany. Anthony Eden, who had resigned as Foreign Secretary in February, 1938, was opposed not so much to Chamberlain's attempt to come to terms with Italy as to his making concessions before he received the *quid pro quo*. Both Churchill and Eden had sympathizers in the Cabinet. At least two ministers, Malcolm MacDonald and Oliver Stanley, had been close to resignation at the same time as Eden. Duff Cooper, the First Lord of the Admiralty, did resign after the Munich Crisis, and certainly three other ministers, Lord de la Warr, Walter Elliot and W.S. Morrison, together with a number of their juniors, were seriously shaken in their loyalty. None of these counted for a great deal unless they had been able to steel themselves to act in unison. Halifax, however, could certainly have brought the Government down by resigning, and he suffered qualms of conscience from time to time which needed only a little additional guidance from God, assisted no doubt by a sharp prod from Eden, Churchill and his Foreign Office officials, to have pushed him over the edge. The great British Conservative Party conceals its splits very well, but the splits were there, and the events of 1938 divided the party as deeply as anything in this century.

To these internal pressures on Chamberlain was added external pressure from the French and Czechoslovak Governments, each of which was pursuing its own ends. Under this combined assault, Chamberlain allowed himself to be pushed into an undertaking which could be made to mean anything or nothing. Britain's only continental commitment in the spring of 1938—apart from that to her oldest ally, Portugal—was a guarantee to France and Belgium, under the Treaty of Locarno, to go to the assistance of either in the event of an unprovoked attack. She was also a member of the League of Nations, which involved conveniently vague commitments to fellow members, including France and Czechoslovakia, but no automatic obligation to take military action. France, on the other hand, was bound by treaty to come to the help of Czechoslovakia, if the latter were attacked. She could effectively do this only by attacking Germany, and it was a matter of great concern to the French whether attacking Germany could be construed as the unprovoked attack on France which would bring Britain to her help under the Locarno Treaty.

On March 24, in a careful statement to the Commons, Chamberlain subtly widened the British commitment. In what was intended as a warning to Germany that a repetition of *Anschluss* tactics would not be tolerated, he emphasized that treaty obligations were not everything, and that if war did break out, the conflict would probably not be confined to those who had assumed such obligations. This was especially true in the case of two countries with such close ties as Britain and France. In other words, if Germany attacked Czechoslovakia, and France then attacked Germany, Britain might come to the help of France. On the other hand, she might not. Like Halifax's admission to Hitler at Obersalzberg, Chamberlain's Commons statement was an invitation to diplomatic blackmail, though in this case by France and Czechoslovakia. Naturally the statesmen of those countries availed themselves of every opportunity to push Chamberlain just a little farther in directions in which he had no wish to go.

CHAPTER 6

"Allons, Enfants de la Patrie . . ."

IF OPINION in Britain was confused, in France it was chaotic. Hitler was not entirely wide of the mark in his appreciation that the country was near to civil war, a consummation he devoutly strove to bring even nearer by a lavish distribution of subsidies.

The French Communist Party was the most powerful in Europe outside the U.S.S.R. It had taken part in a short-lived Popular Front Government under the Socialist Léon Blum. Afterwards, it went into opposition, and the French upper and middle classes feared that it was only waiting on the sidelines for an opportunity to seize power, by force if necessary, with the support of a Russian-dominated Republican Government in Spain.

The Communists' extremist opponents formed semi-fascist groups, the Croix de Feu and hooded Cagoulards, who waged guerilla war with Communist trade unionists. Demonstrations and riots were answered by strikes which brought armament production to a standstill. Like unskillful surfers, French politicians tried to ride these waves of violence, were capsized into the stormy seas, picked themselves up and, with remarkable resilience, mounted their surfboards again. The British Parliament, it has been said, is full of ex-future Prime Ministers; the French Parliament was full of past ones, each engaged with his band of followers in devious intrigues to save his country by his own return to office at the earliest opportunity.

The French people, watching this political carnival with cynical indifference, were not encouraged to rise above the level of their

59

politicians. Petty Government officials, of whom there were a great many, supplemented their low salaries with a system of rake-offs on Government contracts. After all, why not? It was only what financial scandals had taught them their political masters were doing on the grand scale. French workmen, having won a forty-hour week from the Popular Front Government, went on strike in protest against any infringement of it, and their supposed superiors coined a phrase, "Better Hitler than Blum," to express their feeling that at least Hitler knew how to deal with intransigent and disrespectful Communist workers. In Artois and Picardy, where the land had been reduced to undrained swamp twenty years before by the contending armies of the First World War, a farmer's plough struck against rusted steel helmet or dud shell, and the farmer spat and silently swore, "Never again."

The Prime Minister of this distracted and divided country was the fifty-three-year-old son of a Provençal baker, Edouard Daladier. Dark and thickset, Daladier looked to a patronizing British eye like an Iberian merchant visiting the Roman Senate. His chunkiness and ostentatious peasant bluntness had won him the nickname of the Bull of Vaucluse. If his behaviour sometimes more closely resembled that of another popular bull of the time, the pacifist Ferdinand who just wanted to smell the flowers, it must be remembered that Daladier, too, was working under the shadow of the knock-out blow; that his country had been devastated twenty years before by the most appalling war in history; and that he had nothing like the parliamentary security which Chamberlain on the whole enjoyed.

Daladier's Foreign Minister, Georges Bonnet, was an able and intelligent economist, a former French Ambassador to the United States who, according to Daladier, owed his appointment as Foreign Minister to the influence he was supposed to command in Washington. It is more probable that he owed it to his views on foreign policy. According to Paul-Boncour, Bonnet's predecessor, when Daladier became Prime Minister he considered retaining Paul-Boncour as Foreign Minister. Paul-Boncour was asked for his views on foreign policy and replied, according to his own account, that he would take a firm line towards Germany over Czechoslovakia. A few hours later Daladier telephoned him to say that this was a fine policy, thoroughly worthy of France—and Georges Bonnet would be Foreign Minister.

It ought to be said that French statesmen, when writing their memoirs, start with the incomparable advantage that a great many official French files were burned in 1940, and Paul-Boncour's memory may or may not be reliable.

Like the British Chancellor of the Exchequer, Sir John Simon, Bonnet was one of those human beings who feel the need to be loved; and like Simon, the more he sought popularity, the less he found it. His prominent nose and lank thin hair gave him, in some unfriendly British eyes, the unattractive look of a newly-hatched pigeon.

The French position when Daladier assumed office was not an easy one. In the days of a disarmed Germany and an independent Austria, the Czechoslovak alliance had seemed highly desirable to France as a potential menace to Germany in the east. Now Germany was armed and aggressive, Austria had been swallowed up, and the German jaws were closing upon the Czechoslovak tadpole's head. If German troops crossed the Czechoslovak frontier, France was committed to war with Germany. France's principal ally, Russia, was an uncertain—from a French bourgeois point of view, a hostile—quantity. The British, though they might declare that their frontier was the Rhine, seemed inclined to defend it to the last French soldier. The United States had washed her hands of Europe. The nightmare of French politicians since 1870, another war without allies against Germany, seemed on the point of coming true. Daladier and Bonnet played their shaky hand so well that, by the autumn, they had avoided war over Czechoslovakia, committed the isolationist British to involvement in any French war with Germany, and transferred to British shoulders a great deal of the public odium resulting from the treatment of Czechoslovakia.

The French, in fact, were trying to do almost the opposite of what they publicly said they were doing. In this respect they were no worse than the other principals in the crisis. Hitler was not greatly concerned about the rights and wrongs of the Sudeten Germans, only about Czechoslovakia as an anti-German base. Chamberlain used the crisis to demonstrate to Hitler the sincerity of his attempts to reach a settlement with Germany. Nor was poor little Czechoslovakia quite the innocent victim of Great Power politics that clever propaganda has made it seem. Benes was a skillful diplomat—perhaps too clever by half—who used all his considerable resources to play for time and demonstrate to the world how impossible it was to reach agreement with his Sudeten Germans. As for the Henleinists, who believed themselves to be at the center of affairs, manipulating events, they were used by everybody, outwitted by everybody, and, as generally happens, paid the heaviest penalty in the long run.

The first indication of the deviousness of French policy came at the end of April, when Daladier and Bonnet arrived in London to confer with the British Government about the situation arising from the mounting tension in the Sudetenland. Their visit was preceded by a chorus from sections of the French press on the theme, "Must three million Frenchmen die to keep three million Germans under Czech rule?" Some of this campaign was due to German subsidies placed at the disposal of certain French newspapers, but much of it came from the heart. Daladier and Bonnet undoubtedly had a great deal of popular support for their pacifism.

On the day after Daladier's arrival in London, the German Embassy received a report from one described in the published German Foreign Office Documents as a "confidential agent." This agent has been identified for me by Dr. Fritz Hesse, then the representative in London of the official German News Agency, as Maurice Gerothwohl, a former diplomatic correspondent of the London *Daily Telegraph.*

Gerothwohl reported that on the previous evening, Daladier had asked him to stay behind, after talking to him in the company of four or five other journalists. When they were alone, Daladier said abruptly, "Well, are you going to put pressure on Prague? Are you going to give the Czechs pressing counsels of wisdom?"

The British were only too willing to put pressure on Prague to make concessions to the Sudeten Germans. They had indeed suggested to Paul-Boncour, when he was Foreign Minister, that France and Britain should combine in exerting such pressure, but the suggestion had been received without enthusiasm.

Gerothwohl replied to Daladier that he thought the British had already exerted considerable pressure, but they did not want to go too far, since France, not Britain, was Czechoslovakia's ally.

"There you are wrong," Daladier answered, "for we are bound, bound in honor to Czechoslovakia by treaty. France has her hands tied. But you are free . . . The British Government must act in Berlin and in Prague; possibly in Prague even more than in Berlin . . . Mark my words, the peace of Europe probably depends at this moment on the Czechoslovak issue and on what your Government, and especially Mr. Chamberlain, will do in that direction."

Daladier, according to Gerothwohl's account, told him to "go and see our friend; I have told him to speak to you quite openly, as usual." "Our friend" was Count Fernand de Brinon, director of the Franco-German Committee, used as an intermediary by both Daladier and Bonnet. De Brinon became the Vichy Government's representative with the German occupation authorities in Paris during the war, and was shot for high treason in 1947.

De Brinon was considerably franker with Gerothwohl than Daladier had been. He explained to Gerothwohl that the French Prime Minister hoped Chamberlain and Halifax would themselves suggest that pressure should be put on Prague, when Daladier could acquiesce without seeming to have taken the initiative. Bonnet, said de Brinon, was even keener than Daladier on steering clear of France's obligation to fight for Czechoslovakia.

M. Daladier informs me that he has no recollection of any such conversation as that described by Gerothwohl. It is of course entirely possible that Gerothwohl, a man of great charm but without many scruples, invented it. Dr. Hesse has told me, however, that he also received information that this was Daladier's attitude from another fellow-journalist, Pierre Maillaud, a London correspondent of the French Havas Agency.

It is certainly true that in the official Anglo-French talks, which began on April 28, Daladier took an exactly opposite line to that ascribed to him by Gerothwohl. The first day's talks, which did not deal with Czechoslovakia, passed off amicably in spite of British inability to agree to a French request to hold joint naval staff talks. In the evening, Daladier and Bonnet went to Windsor

Castle, where they were taken for a tour of the royal pictures by the King and Queen and entertained by an orchestra playing traditional French tunes. Daladier, it seems, was particularly impressed by the graceful curtseys of Princess Elizabeth and Princess Margaret, and by the Queen's friendly remark, "How brave you are, Monsieur Daladier." The *entente* apparently could not have been more *cordiale*.

But from the French ministers' diplomatic advisers, left behind in London, arose a discordant note. Daladier and Bonnet, they declared, were profoundly upset by British reluctance to hold naval talks. In fact, by the following morning, Lord Halifax had been informed that the French were so devastated by this refusal that they were almost ready to make their own terms with Germany.

Thus suitably softened up, the British ministers began the second day of talks, which were largely concerned with the problem of Czechoslovakia. At impassioned length, Daladier resisted the British proposal to put pressure on Prague to make concessions to the Sudeten Germans. Chamberlain became alarmed: "Fortunately the papers have had no hint of how near we came to a break over Czechoslovakia," he noted in a letter. He also described Daladier as a simple and straightforward man. Quite suddenly, and to Chamberlain's relief, the simple and straightforward man gave way on the British proposals for Czechoslovakia. During luncheon, as a *quid pro quo*, he got his naval staff talks. Moreover, the pressure on Prague was to be accompanied by a British warning to the Germans that the British and French were doing their best to find a peaceful solution of the Sudetenland problem. And if in spite of the pressure on Prague no agreement could be reached, then it was up to Britain to tell Germany that, in the event of war, Britain might march with France.

Simplicity and straightforwardness are indeed major virtues in the field of diplomacy.

But this was not all. There had been signs from Prague itself that pressure was not unwelcome, as long as it was British. In the middle of March, immediately after the *Anschluss*, the Czechoslovak Minister in London, Jan Masaryk, had written a flowery letter to Sir Samuel Hoare, the Home Secretary and one of Chamberlain's close associates. Masaryk was the son of the Czechoslovak republic's great founder. He was immensely gregarious, though his sociability masked an inner unhappiness which was sometimes reflected in that sad, dark face, and it was his misfortune to mistake his great popularity for influence.

Masaryk's letter to Hoare was characteristic of the man. It began with a flourish nicely calculated to appeal to Hoare, who had a good conceit of himself: "You know how my father valued your friendship and how my sisters and I humbly follow in his footsteps in our devotion to Lady Maud and you." It carefully disavowed any ideas of guarantees or commitments from the British Government. What it sought was advice, "direct, blunt, concrete advice—not vague admonitions of the advisability of 'doing something.' My influence in Prague is not quite worn out and I would like to use it in the right direction."

Like most people, Hoare was only too delighted to give advice: "If I were in the position of Benes, I should ask the French and British Governments to give me their good offices in helping to make a really satisfactory arrangement for the Sudeten Germans." Halifax, when the exchange was reported to him, found the advice admirable. The use which was made of it, however, he found less admirable, for very soon it was being interpreted in Prague as an official British proposal that, if the Czechoslovak Government produced concessions to the Sudeten Germans which the British Government regarded as satisfactory, the British would underwrite them. Halifax drew back in alarm. And yet the logic of his own words to Hitler at Obersalzberg, allied with Chamberlain's commitment to France, forced the British inexorably on. They wanted to remain benevolent and impartial mediators, but now they were interested parties, at least half-committed to war unless they could extract from the Czechoslovak Government terms which Hitler was willing to accept.

CHAPTER 7

How to Make Your Own Crisis

ON MAY 2, 1938, four special trains rolled out of the Anhalter station in Berlin, carrying the Fuehrer on a state visit to Italy. With him went Ribbentrop and five hundred assorted diplomats, soldiers and party officials bound for Italian sunshine and Italian banquets.

It was the first meeting of the dictators since the *Anschluss*, and each was intent on impressing upon the world, and each other, that nothing existed between them save the strongest ties of brotherhood. The visit had been long planned. The Italians, indeed, had spent six months in preparing, and the military parades were to excel in brilliance and precision even those for which Nuremberg was famous. Mussolini, neglecting statecraft, had spent hours supervising the details. His Foreign Minister and son-in-law, Ciano, leaving the diplomatic telegrams to lesser men, had taken on his shoulders the burden of getting the streets suitably decorated for the Fuehrer. The shopkeepers of Rome, he reported testily, were showing a great deal of reluctance in putting up their distinguished visitor's picture.

Hitler on his side was equally determined to impress. The theatrical producer Brenno von Arent, assisted by Frau von Ribbentrop, had designed special dress uniforms for the German diplomats. By day they would wear a navy blue uniform with gold buttons and braid, silver shoulder-tassels and a sash with a dagger in it. For evening wear, the dagger was exchanged for a sword, and the lapels of the dark blue coat were embroidered with silver leaves. Paul Schmidt, the official German interpreter, commented sourly that the uniforms made them all look like level-crossing keepers. He also remarked upon the hardships of the itinerant diplomat's life: "Often, as we were going from one Italian town to another, we had to change our tailcoat for our day uniform, the knightly cloak for the admiral's greatcoat, the dagger for the sword, so that our compartment was far more like the wings of a studio during the shooting of a film than an ordinary sleeper."

Hitler, the artist, decided that Italy was wonderful beyond compare. No countryside could equal that of Tuscany and Umbria, no cities in the world were as lovely as Florence and Rome. A few years later, Hitler the strategist was prepared to destroy them all without compunction.

In Rome, he had to stay at the Quirinale with that snob, King Victor Emmanuel, and caused consternation when he went to bed by demanding a woman. It was later explained that the Fuehrer could not sleep until he had seen a woman remake his bed, but the King, who disliked the *parvenu* Hitler as much as Hitler disliked him, spread the scandalous story with relish, and added to it his belief that the Fuehrer injected himself with stimulants and narcotics.

These were but spots on the sun. Mussolini at his first meeting with Hitler four years before had described him as looking like a silly little clown. Now, with German troops on the Brenner, he could not help but be profoundly impressed by his fellow-dictator. They swore blood-brotherhood, and when they parted, Hitler's eyes were seen to be filled with tears.

Hitler, however, had intended to do some serious business during the visit. In between the parades, the opera, the speeches to cheering crowds, he hoped among other things that light would be thrown on the problem of what to do about Czechoslovakia, to which for the first time he had been giving his personal attention. The situation there was building up to a crisis. The Sudeten Germans, stimulated by German propaganda, were awaiting their liberator with increasing impatience. Prague was a hotbed of anti-Nazi activity, and there was always the chance of an explosive situation being created which could provide the excuse for a preventive war against Germany, unless Germany acted first. Nor did it seem likely that the Czechoslovak Government would or could make concessions without at any rate a show of force.

In preparation for his talks with Mussolini, Hitler had dictated to his adjutant, Schmundt, some rough notes which gave an indication of the way his mind was working. Mussolini had already swallowed Abyssinia and had become heavily involved in the Spanish Civil War. If that was enough for him, and he had no mind for further adventures which would keep France and Britain engaged in the Mediterranean, then the elimination of Czechoslovakia would have to wait—as Schmundt's notes put it, "return with bag empty." If, however, Mussolini felt inclined to try to extend his African empire, then Hitler would "return with Czechoslovakia in the bag."

In a talk with Keitel on April 21, Hitler had laid down the broad outlines of military operations against Czechoslovakia. He rejected the idea of an attack out of the blue: such measures were only justified for the elimination of the last enemy on the Continent.* There were two other possibilities. Germany could march in after a period of diplomatic discussion, building up gradually to a crisis and then to war; or the march-in might follow swiftly on an incident such as the murder of Eisenlohr, the German Minister in Prague, an incident which Frank would no doubt have been happy to arrange. Keitel was to go ahead with planning for both alternatives. The first four days of military action, the Fuehrer emphasized, would be decisive. Britain and France must be presented with a *fait accompli* as in the case of Austria, which would convince them of the hopelessness of military intervention. Hungary and Poland could be brought in: "wolf's nature; they want to share the loot." And before the incident, Czechoslovakia would have been so demoralized by propaganda that she would collapse from within.

The question was, when? On this vital point, the visit to Italy did not prove helpful. Mussolini had his hands quite full enough in Spain without adding new African adventures. He had just signed the Anglo-Italian Agreement, under which Britain recognized his Abyssinian empire in return for a promise to withdraw

*Such as Russia in June, 1941.

Italian troops from Spain, and for the time being he was quite happy to balance between Britain and Germany, until it became clear which of them was likely to offer the greater long-term advantages. It is just possible that he did agree in vague terms to launch an attack from Libya when Hitler was ready to act against Czechoslovakia, but when Ribbentrop produced a draft German-Italian treaty, both Mussolini and Ciano found a variety of reasons why the moment was not opportune to consider it. Hitler, in fact, left Italy with bag empty.

Back in Germany, he retired to Obersalzberg to recuperate from Italian hospitality and to do some more thinking about Czechoslovakia. He was visited there by Henlein, returning from the visit to London which the Fuehrer had asked him to undertake. Henlein was able to report that the visit had been remarkably fruitful.

The Sudeten German leader had passed through Berlin on his way to Britain, and had agreed with Ribbentrop on the points he was to make. He should put forward the Karlsbad demands as conditions which would satisfy the Sudeten Germans, but say that if the Czechoslovak Government procrastinated or showed signs of stubbornness, his people would no longer be satisfied with the Karlsbad demands, but would want self-determination. He was also to deny any suggestion that he was acting on instructions from Berlin. He did this very convincingly. In the course of a talk with Churchill, he went so far as to give Churchill his word of honour that he had never received orders or even recommendations from the German Government.

Henlein's bluff manner appealed to the British. Although Churchill afterwards claimed to have been suspicious of him, he found Henlein's demands reasonable enough to pass them on to Masaryk, who said that he would be happy to see a settlement along those lines.

Henlein was also entertained to tea by Harold Nicolson, vice-chairman of the influential Government backbenchers' Foreign Affairs Group. Nicolson himself was hostile to Chamberlain's foreign policy, and he had invited several critical Conservative M.P.'s to meet Henlein. Henlein told them that he was asking for local autonomy for the Sudeten Germans, but if they failed to get that by negotiation, they would be bound to ask for an international commission and a plebiscite. This seemed reasonable to the group, and Henlein was told that British public opinion would probably support his demands. He was warned, however, that if he and his followers went too far, opinion would turn against him.

Most important of all, Henlein renewed his acquaintance with Sir Robert Vansittart, now diplomatic adviser to the Government, and Henlein's original intermediary with Vansittart, Group Captain Christie. Vansittart, indeed, had actively encouraged Henlein's visit, and seems even to have hinted that Chamberlain himself should see him, though nothing came of this.

Henlein dined with Vansittart and Christie, and they talked for four hours. "I found Herr Henlein far more reasonable and amenable than I had dared to hope," Vansittart reported afterwards to Halifax, "and I am sure that he will desire to remain so unless he is too much interfered with by German pressure from across the border . . . He was evidently pleased by his visit, and I most certainly was, for if the situation created by it is handled promptly, and if the Germans will desist from blocking tactics, we may really have turned a crucial corner in European history."

This was a misreading of the situation, for it was Henlein—or at least Frank—who had been pressing the Germans for action. Hitler at this point was still holding back. But it is scarcely surprising, in the light of Vansittart's encouraging report, that Halifax hastened to impress upon Benes the importance of seizing this favourable opportunty for negotiations while Henlein was in such a reasonable mood.

From the German point of view, all this was very satisfactory. Influential British opinion was impressed with Henlein as a moderate man. The visit enhanced Henlein's prestige among his own people and so helped to discourage extremists. Meanwhile, if nothing better turned up, the process of "chemical dissolution" could continue. There can certainly have been nothing in Henlein's report to encourage Hitler to make a sudden snatch at Czechoslovakia. Nor was he contemplating doing so. He continued to work at Obersalzberg on elaboration of the long-term plans he had outlined to Schmundt and Keitel before his visit to Italy.

On May 16 and 17, there was an exchange of signals between Schmundt at Obersalzberg and Lieutenant-Colonel Kurt Zeitzler at Keitel's headquarters about the state of readiness of German divisions on the Czechoslovak border and the armament of the Czechoslovak fortifications. Schmundt asked questions, Zeitzler answered them. He advised Schmundt that twelve German infantry divisions could be ready to march within twelve hours of receiving a mobilization order. Zeitzler advised, however, that the Czechoslovak fortification system of interconnected pillboxes and machine-gun nests was formidable, and the artillery and ammunition necessary to deal with it would not be available until the autumn. Nor would the three armoured divisions and four motorized divisions be ready until the autumn, although these were not earmarked for any particular purpose in the intervening period.

On May 20, Keitel sent Hitler for approval a draft of an operation order for *Fall Gruen,* Operation Green, code name for operations against Czechoslovakia. This covered the period until October 1 and began with the words: "It is not my intention to smash Czechoslovakia by military action in the immediate future without provocation, unless an unavoidable development of political conditions *within* Czechoslovakia forces the issue, or political events in Europe create a particularly favourable opportunity, which may perhaps never recur."

While Hitler was engaged in these comparatively peaceful pursuits, he received the dramatic news that the Czechoslovaks were mobilizing.

In the late afternoon of Monday, May 2, as Hitler was preparing to leave Berlin for his Italian junketing, Jan Masaryk, the Czechoslovak Minister in London, called at the Foreign Office for a talk with Halifax. The ostensible purpose of his visit was to inquire what conclusions had been reached at the Anglo-French conference of the previous week, but Masaryk's sources of information were excellent, and he probably knew a great deal about them already.

The Foreign Secretary's room was vast and draughty, about as conducive to intimate conversation as a hotel foyer, with a desk and chairs perched uncomfortably in the middle of its echoing spaces. There Masaryk, the son of the founder of the Czechoslovak republic, with his haunted face, learnt officially the British verdict. Halifax, as always, was very polite, but the message was unmistakable. The Czechoslovak Government, he said, would have to go a very long way in concessions to the Sudeten Germans. The *Anschluss* had largely turned Czechoslovakia's defenses, Russia's support was uncertain, Poland none too friendly. However willing the French were to honour their treaty commitments, and even if Britain allowed herself to be drawn into war, it was physically impossible to prevent Germany overrunning Czechoslovakia. Even if a war against Germany were eventually won, Czechoslovakia would almost certainly not be recreated in its present form.

Masaryk knew all this as well as Halifax. The question was, what concessions was Czechoslovakia expected to make, and if she made them, would Britain guarantee the remaining state? If Masaryk still had any hope of a British guarantee, Halifax killed it. Even after concessions had been made to the Sudeten Germans, Halifax said, the British Government could not give a guarantee to Czechoslovakia, nor in its formal commitments go beyond the terms of Chamberlain's March 24 statement.

Masaryk, edgy but also polite, thanked Halifax for his frankness, which, he said, did not surprise or grieve him. He said Benes was prepared to go a very long way indeed in the matter of concessions. Perhaps it might be possible to work out some form of autonomy on the Swiss model. But, he emphasized, it would take time to educate the Czechoslovak Cabinet and public to accept this.

Masaryk may have been something of a political lightweight, but he was an experienced diplomat, and it must be assumed that his next remark was not made by chance.

"My father never wanted the Sudeten Germans in the Czechoslovak State," he said, "but they were forced on him by Lloyd George." He then took Halifax very much by surprise. In reply to a question, he said that if the Sudeten Germans got their autonomy, and if this led in time to their leaving Czechoslovakia and joining Germany, he did not think this would necessarily mean that the same process would be followed by the Polish and Hungarian minorities.

These remarks of Masaryk summarized the dilemma in which Benes found himself. The Czechoslovak President would have

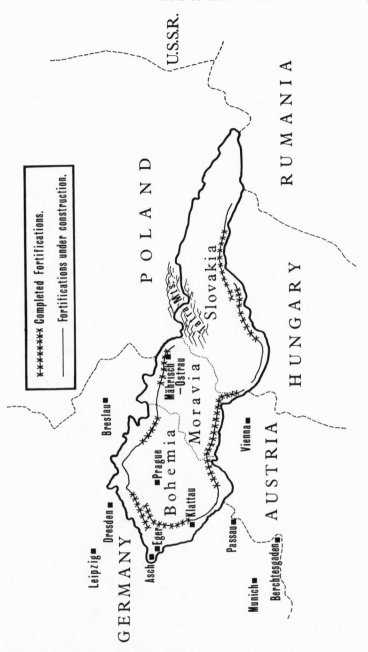

Czechoslovakia and her neighbours in 1938. The fortifications
varied in strength from continuous systems of underground concrete blockhouses to screens of wire and anti-tank ditches covered
by pillboxes.

been happy enough to get rid of his noisy and troublesome fringe of Sudeten Germans. The problem was how to do this without endangering his life's work, the Republic of Czechoslovakia. Benes was perfectly well aware that his other minorities would demand —or could be stirred up to demand—concessions similar to any granted to the Sudeten Germans. He was moreover to some extent the prisoner of the Czech patriotism which he himself had helped to build up. The Germans professed to believe that Benes, even if he wanted to, would be unable to make any really substantial concessions to the Sudeten Germans because he would be assassinated if he did so, and this belief, as will be seen, was not entirely without foundation. And there were the Czechoslovak fortifications which ran through the Sudeten German areas and which were guarded by the Czechoslovak Army. Both of these institutions were misleadingly publicized at the time. The fortifications were described as a Czechoslovak Maginot Line, but their strength in fact varied. In places they were strong, in other places little more than a screen of pillboxes, some unfinished. But they had cost 70 million dollars, and they were a symbol of national pride. The Czechoslovak Army, according to Benes, was one of the best in Europe. According to Churchill it had a mobilized strength of 40 divisions. Neither of these appreciations was accurate. The army's peacetime strength was 14 infantry divisions, one mechanized division, some fortress troops, mountain brigades, and frontier battalions. Fourteen days after mobilization, seven reserve divisions could be available, and there was a third series of seven reserve divisions, poorly equipped, giving a total mobilized strength of rather more than 30 divisions to defend some 1,300 miles of frontier. The army's equipment was probably the best in Europe, since it had started from scratch after the First World War, and its oldest gun dated from 1925. The quality of the officer corps, however, was doubtful. The senior officers like Syrovy, the Commander-in-Chief, and Krejci, the Chief of Staff, owed their rapid promotion to the fact that they had served with the Czech Legions which had deserted to the Allied side from the Austrian Army during the First World War. Their fighting qualities were distrusted by the younger officers, many of whom were Sudeten Germans denied promotion unless they had assumed

Czech names and nationalities. It is the opinion of Lieut.-Colonel F. O. Miksche, author of *Blitzkrieg* and at that time an artillery captain in the Czechoslovak Army, that if this army had had to fight the Germans, with or without the support of its allies, "the result would have been worse than Poland."

Czechoslovakia's allies, France and Russia, in fact, had only one value—as a deterrent. Once war began, neither of them could save Czechoslovakia from devastation. Benes's hope was that if they could be induced to make enough frightening noises, Hitler would be scared off going to war at all.

Thus early in the Sudetenland crisis one can begin faintly to see, through a haze of words and propaganda, the game of diplomatic chess which Benes set himself to play. He would concede some areas of the Sudetenland if he had to, but only under pressure which would convince Czech nationalists that he had no alternative. He would try to forestall trouble from his Hungarian and Polish neighbours. But he had no intention whatsoever of fighting if he could possibly help it.

Benes, however, like Chamberlain or Daladier, or indeed Hitler, was not operating in a vacuum. There was a group in Prague who were not only patriotically opposed to any concession to Germany, but believed that Hitler might even be brought down if his bluff was called. A German Foreign Ministry memorandum referred to them as "certain individuals in the Czechoslovak Government, as well as in the Czech Army and in the Prague Diplomatic Service, who take a pessimistic view of the future development of the Czech question . . . These persons are inclined to force the Czech-Sudeten German problem by an attitude of intransigence and to steer towards an international crisis." Henlein cannot be accepted as a wholly reliable witness, but in his talk with Churchill in London he claimed to have information from Osusky, the Czechoslovak Minister in Paris, that "there were certain circles among the Czechs who thought it would be a good thing to provoke an incident. They reckoned that Germany, knowing France and England were behind Prague, would not act, and this 'fainting-fit probe' could be exploited to destroy the Sudeten German Party."

Some of this group can be named. They included Moravec of the Czechoslovak General Staff; Jaromir Necas, the Social Democrat Minister of Welfare in Hodza's Government; and Franz Bleha of Hodza's secretariat.

Two days after the German Foreign Ministry memorandum was written there was an international crisis, and it began with the Czechoslovak General Staff.

On May 13, 1938, the men of a Czechoslovak customs post near Klattau, in the Sudetenland, close to the Bavarian border, began seeing things. Their report was conveniently vague: an unknown number of steel-helmeted German troops with machine guns was bivouacking in the forest.

Shortly after seven o'clock on the evening of Thursday, May 19, the British Foreign Office received a telephone message from the British Embassy in Berlin: "Acting Consul at Dresden reports that he has strong reason to believe that German troops are concentrating in Southern Silesia and Northern Austria. Leave suspended next Sunday." Sunday was in fact the day fixed for communal elections in the Sudetenland, and Sudeten German extremists had been confidently predicting that that was the day the Fuehrer would choose for a sudden coup.

This first message from Berlin was followed by another telegram received in the Foreign Office at nine-thirty next morning: "A British subject had come from Garmisch to Munich to report that a waitress had told him troops from the district were being moved to the Czechoslovak frontier in order to be ready for the elections."

On the face of it, none of these reports was strong enough to justify what followed, but the whole of Europe was in a state of jumpiness after the sudden German coup in Austria. The published messages from Berlin, moreover, were supplemented by information which has not been published, but was hinted at in a telegram from Krofta, the Czechoslovak Foreign Minister, to the Czechoslovak Ministers in London and Berlin: "We possess absolutely convincing proof that a few days before May 21 a concentration of several large [German] units in the Saxony region was accomplished. We inform only you confidentially that the English Intelligence Service checked this fact with their own means already before May 21, and fully confirmed our information."

Brigadier H.C.T. Stronge, the British military attaché in Prague at the time, has since put on record his conviction that this secret information, whatever it was, was manufactured by the Czecho-slovaks. Certainly no evidence has ever been published that there were significant German troop concentrations, and in view of Hitler's preoccupation at Obersalzberg with planning for the autumn, it seems improbable that there were.

At about midday on Friday, May 20, an agitated Krofta tele-phoned Eisenlohr, the German Minister in Prague, to tell him that information was coming in about German troop concentrations in Saxony. Eisenlohr told the Czechoslovak Foreign Minister that there was no such thing; then promptly telegraphed to Berlin to ask if there was.

Krofta also alerted Basil Newton, the British Minister, who in turn warned the British Foreign Office and Sir Nevile Henderson in Berlin. Henderson raced down to the German Foreign Ministry to make inquiries. At the time of the *Anschluss,* his inquiries about German troop concentrations had been met with indignant denials, and similar denials this time did not greatly impress him. On the following day, he sent his two military attachés on a tour of the areas near the Czechoslovak border, to make sure. Both reported that they could detect nothing suspicious.

But at half-past seven on that Friday evening, Ribbentrop began to take a hand in the game. He perhaps saw the chance opening up to further his own policy of pushing Hitler into action before Britain was ready, and he may have gone so far as to warn the German Legation in Prague that an ultimatum to the Czecho-slovak Government might be on the way. Certainly he did noth-ing to help the situation by sending for Mastny, the Czechoslovak Minister in Berlin, and bullying him about the reports of German troop concentrations which, he said, were being deliberately spread by the Czechoslovak Government to cover up Czech-provoked incidents in the Sudetenland. If Mastny's Government did not stop it, Ribbentrop said threateningly, there might be the most serious consequences. Mastny promised to do everything he could for peace, begged Ribbentrop to be patient, and hurried off to telephone a frightened message to his Government.

The Czechoslovak Cabinet, as it had amply demonstrated at the time of the *Anschluss,* was no body of fire-eaters. It was an

Sir Alexander Cadogan hurrying to the House of Commons with the last-minute invitation to the Munich Conference.

The devil and the curate. Hitler with Lord Halifax on his right at Ober-salzberg. The British Ambassador, Sir Nevile Henderson, is on the extreme right of the picture.

WHAT'S CZECHOSLOVAKIA TO ME, ANYWAY ?

ABOVE, *David Low in July pinpointed British indifference to the crisis. Two months later, the distribution of gas masks,* BELOW, *changed indifference to fear.*

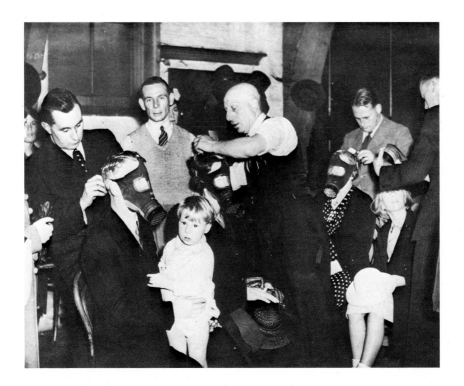

Jan Masaryk, Czechoslovak Minister in London.

Dr. Milan Hodza, the Czechoslovak Prime Minister.

President Benes of Czechoslovakia at army maneuvers with General Krejci, Czechoslovak Commander-in-Chief.

Prague, showing the Charles Bridge in the foreground and Hradcany Castle in the background.

Lord and Lady Runciman leave London for Prague at the start of the Runciman Mission.

Hitler with Karl Hermann Frank (LEFT) *and Konrad Henlein* (RIGHT) *after the German occupation of the Sudetenland.*

Germans against Hitler. Baron Ernst von Weizsaecker, ABOVE LEFT. General von Witzleben, ABOVE RIGHT. Dr. Theodor Kordt, "Herr X," greets Neville Chamberlain on his return to London after his first meeting with Hitler, BELOW.

ABOVE, *Neville Chamberlain and Sir Nevile Henderson pace the terrace of the Hotel Petersberg at Godesberg, awaiting a message from Hitler.*

BELOW, *Hitler under strain at Godesberg, with Chamberlain (RIGHT) and the official interpreter, Dr. Paul Schmidt (LEFT).*

ABOVE, *President Benes* (LEFT) *with General Syrovy after the Chechoslo-vak Government had accepted the Anglo-French terms.* BELOW (LEFT TO RIGHT), *Bonnet, Daladier and General Gamelin set off from the French Embassy for Gamelin's meeting with Chamberlain.*

ABOVE, *off to Munich. Chamberlain and his smiling Cabinet at Heston airport. Sir Kingsley Wood in black hat on left, Hore-Belisha between Chamberlain and Halifax (EXTREME RIGHT), Duff Cooper half hidden by Hore-Belisha.*

BELOW, *a smiling Hitler drives through the streets of Munich with Mussolini.*

The Munich Agreement is signed by Chamberlain ABOVE *and Hitler,* BELOW.

"*Peace for our Time.*" ABOVE, *Chamberlain greets the London crowd from the window of No. 10 Downing Street.* BELOW, *Londoners outside Buckingham Palace cheer the peacemaker.*

ABOVE, *Hitler's triumphant entry into the Sudetenland at Asch.* BELOW, *almost a million people welcomed Hitler's return to Berlin after signing the Munich Agreement.*

uneasy coalition, divided both politically and racially, many of whose members had learnt their politics in the day of the Austro-Hungarian Empire and could never quite convince themselves that that empire had ceased to exist. Asked to take decisions about 1938, they were apt to discuss at some length what had happened in 1918. Presented with a German ultimatum, they were likely to protest that it was not in accordance with the constitution of the Republic.

These men were now faced with information from their own Intelligence Service of German troop concentrations, and a demand from their own General Staff to call up five age-groups and to man fortifications which they had refused to man at the time of the *Anschluss*. In such a situation, it was their instinct to seek refuge in compromise, and they had no difficulty in agreeing with their Prime Minister that they should call up, not five age-groups, but one, together with about 100,000 technical and specialist reservists. This combined the maximum amount of provocation to their irascible neighbour with the barest minimum of defensive capacity. But to do more, Hodza, the Prime Minister, cautiously told them, "might lead the neutrals and the English to infer that the issue was not one of military measures and the German Government, but rather one of aggressive action on the part of the Czech Republic. This would cost us sympathy which is vital to our survival." They omitted, however, to tell either the French or the British what they were doing, which cost them even more sympathy.

Hodza was careful to emphasize that the President of the Republic approved this compromise, from which one may perhaps deduce that Benes was not disposed to take the Intelligence reports too seriously.

That night, as a result of their decision, tanks and troops, some of them trigger-happy, began to move into the Sudetenland, and on a road near Eger two Sudeten Germans in a motorcycle and sidecar were shot and killed when, it was alleged, they failed to stop in answer to a challenge.

By Saturday morning, the crisis was gathering its own momentum. One of the moderate Henleinist leaders, Neuwirth, read in his morning paper the incredible news that the Czechoslovaks were mobilizing, and hastened to telephone Dr. Walter Brand, the Henleinist representative in London.

Brand was appalled. He just had time to exclaim "Impossible!" when a voice said in Czech "I interrupt," and the line went dead. But Brand had heard enough to pass the news on to Christie, and either as a result of Brand's message or because of other information reaching the Foreign Office, Halifax decided to return to London from Oxford, where he had gone for the weekend.

Neuwirth, having alerted Brand, telephoned Hodza, with whom he was on friendly terms, about the shooting of the two motorcyclists near Eger. Hodza had not heard of the incident, and became very excited. Frank, who saw Hodza that afternoon, described the Prime Minister as in despair at the development of events. The Henleinists also saw the Minister of the Interior, Dr. Cerny, who was almost literally wringing his hands. When they asked him what was happening, Cerny answered, "I don't know what's going on. I can't answer you." His attitude confirmed their already strong suspicion that a military coup was taking place.

That afternoon, on Ribbentrop's instructions, Eisenlohr delivered a stiff protest to Krejci, the Chief of the Czechoslovak General Staff, against the mobilization measures. Krejci stormed at him that he had irrefutable proof of a concentration of between eight and ten German divisions in Saxony. Colonel Toussaint, the German military attaché, offered to let Krejci go wherever he wished, to see for himself, but the offer was swept aside. Eisenlohr reported to Berlin his opinion that the Czechoslovak generals had systematically tried to sabotage Henlein's negotiations with the Czechoslovak Government even before they had begun, and that the alleged concentration of German troops in Saxony was being used as a pretext for setting up military rule in the Sudetenland. At ten-fifty that night he telegraphed for authority to burn unnecessary papers—which included, no doubt, some very interesting ones.

News of these events, often garbled, came into the British Foreign Office all that Saturday in a series of telegrams. Halifax became very excited. He had been made a fool of over Austria, and was in no mood to be fooled again. Vansittart was also in a very excited state, and Brand was dispatched to Czechoslovakia with instructions to see Henlein and urge him to be patient, keep his head, and wait to see what the British Government could do for him. The routine Saturday morning Foreign Office press conference was postponed until 1:20 P.M., and then the head of the News Division, Rex Leeper, opened it in tones which hinted at least to one of his German hearers that he believed war was about to begin.

At three o'clock an alarming message reached the Foreign Office from Henderson in Berlin. He reported that he had seen Ribbentrop that morning, and found him in a highly excitable and pugnacious frame of mind. Ribbentrop confronted Henderson with the news that the Czechoslovaks were mobilizing, flourished at him telegrams about mounting casualties in the Sudetenland, and threatened that the German nation could not long tolerate such a situation continuing.

This looked only too much as if an Austrian-type coup were being manufactured, and at 3:45 P.M. Henderson was told to give Ribbentrop the emergency warning that had been agreed upon with the French: if Germany attacked Czechoslovakia, France would march, and "His Majesty's Government could not guarantee that they would not be forced by circumstances to become involved also."

It is significant that, during these rapidly-moving events, Chamberlain was out of London, and it seems possible that Halifax was not able to consult him by telephone until late that night, after the British warning had been delivered in Berlin. One wonders whether Chamberlain, if he had been in London, would have let the Foreign Office act quite so dramatically.

When Henderson arrived at the Foreign Ministry that afternoon with the British warning, he found Ribbentrop less excitable than in the morning. The reason for this changed mood may perhaps be found in an urgent demand to see the Foreign Minister made earlier by Brauchitsch, the Army Commander-in-Chief. Brauchitsch told Ribbentrop flatly that the German Army was not ready for operations against Czechoslovakia. Ribbentrop was completely taken aback. When Brauchitsch had gone, he said to the head of his secretariat, Erich Kordt: "Do you know our real military position? Brauchitsch has just told me that at present we aren't able to take on even Czechoslovakia. He says that in almost all arms we are absolutely inferior. If this is true, my policy is completely wrong."

In spite of this warning from Brauchitsch, Ribbentrop's language to Henderson was full of colorful aggression. The British were talking to the wrong address, he said angrily, it was Prague they should be bullying, not Berlin. The British had been talking about using their influence in Prague. Well, the only effect of that influence seemed to be to make the Czechoslovaks start shooting down Germans. And now Henderson was telling him that France and Britain meant to declare war on Germany, if she was not prepared to look on in silence while the blood of unarmed Germans on her frontiers was daily shed by people of an inferior race. The Czechs, he concluded ominously, were playing with fire if they relied on foreign help, because before it could reach them, there wouldn't be a soul left alive in Czechoslovakia.

Perhaps wisely, Henderson did not repeat most of this to London, contenting himself with reporting that Ribbentrop was in a state of considerable excitement, and adding his own opinion that unless pressure were put on Prague, "nothing I can say here will stop the German Government from intervening."

Europe awoke on Sunday morning to find itself close to the brink of war. Into one London newspaper office came a dramatic telephone call from its Paris correspondent: "The balloon's going up. The British Ambassador's laid on a special train to take the women and children out of Berlin." Henderson's explanation of this episode is that one member of his staff was going on normal leave with his family. Another staff member thought this a good opportunity to send his own children to England, but there was no room on the train. The railway authorities said, however, that they would add an extra coach if it could be filled, whereupon two other members of the staff decided to send their families.

Reports that the British Embassy was evacuating flew through an alarmed Berlin, and also reached the British Foreign Office, where Cadogan, the Permanent Under-Secretary, got Halifax's authority to stop what he called "this folly." But Halifax also sent for Dirksen, the German Ambassador, and gave him the same solemn warning that Henderson had given Ribbentrop the day before.

By this time, however, telegrams were coming in from Newton in Prague and Sir Eric Phipps, the British Ambassador in Paris, indicating that the British warning to Berlin had given a great deal of encouragement to Prague. Hints of a military take-over in Prague also reached the Foreign Office. London began to back-pedal. A telegram went off to Phipps, instructing him to make it quite clear that while Britain would honour her pledge to come to France's assistance if she were attacked by Germany, the French must not take it for granted that Britain would necessarily join in if France attacked Germany on behalf of Czechoslovakia. This was a message of which Bonnet was to make a great deal later on, but it must be seen in its proper context. The British, too, had heard the reports that there were people in Prague who would be not unwilling to provoke war with Germany, and the intention was to discourage any such development.

At five o'clock on Sunday evening, the British Cabinet met. They decided that there was nothing more to be done. The feeling on the whole seems to have been anti-Czech.

On this Sunday morning, Ribbentrop flew to Munich to consult the Fuehrer at Obersalzberg. He was seen off at Tempelhof aerodrome by Weizsaecker, the State Secretary, to whom he said, "We ought to provoke the Czechs."

One may assume that, in spite of the warning from Brauchitsch, Ribbentrop was still bent on war.

Weizsaecker, according to his own account, "roared at him, 'I must categorically contradict you.'" Sir Lewis Namier has unkindly remarked that if the devious and careful Weizsaecker roared at Ribbentrop, it must have been to make himself heard above the noise of aircraft engines. But Weizsaecker also wrote in his memoirs that Hitler found his attitude helpful in the May Crisis. There is no record of what passed between Hitler and Ribbentrop at Obersalzberg, but one may perhaps deduce that Ribbentrop's aggressive policy got a bloody nose. Hitler never paid too much attention to his military experts; but his intuition had not yet told him that the moment was ripe to take Czechoslovakia. The crisis, brief in its life as a mayfly, was over.

During these exciting events, the French Government was running some way behind the British. Gamelin, the French Commander-in-Chief, was recalled on Sunday from Brittany. He found Daladier and Bonnet in favour of going to Czechoslovakia's help if she were attacked. But they asked Gamelin, not for the first time, how he proposed to help the Czechoslovaks?

"I would attack," said Gamelin forthrightly, and then, as he always did, qualified this plain statement.

"But before me," he continued, "there would be fortifications and very soon most of the German Army, unless Poland intervenes, at least until Russia enters the war." There were at this period very few German fortifications, and Gamelin would have been naive indeed if he believed that Daladier and Bonnet wanted to hear about Russia. But the French General Staff had a fixed idea that their best chance of striking at Germany was to attack at the heart of German industry in the Ruhr by going through Belgium, and that if they made enough difficulties about any other direction of attack, the politicians might eventually give the Belgium plan their blessing, with or without Belgian consent. These ideas were well-known to the Belgian Government, and indeed the Belgian Foreign Minister sent for the French Ambassador during the May Crisis and told him pointedly, "We have just carried out maneuvers on the French border to demonstrate that, if you enter Belgium to support the Czechs, you will run into the Belgian Army."

With an attack through Belgium denied him, Gamelin always confessed himself bereft of ideas; and however belligerent Daladier and Bonnet might have felt, their belligerence was always cooled by this military douche of cold water.

Perhaps they did not feel so very belligerent. On this Sunday evening Daladier saw Welczeck, the German Ambassador, and told him that he had not made the alliance with Czechoslovakia, and was not happy about it. It did exist, however, and if Germany attacked Czechoslovakia, the French would have to fight. He then unwisely asked Welczeck for the German view on the Czechoslovak question. Welczeck reported with evident satisfaction, "I now had an opportunity of explaining to Daladier the whole maze of questions from a historical, geopolitical, economic, cultural and, finally, a moral point of view . . . Daladier thanked me for my clear and detailed exposé, from which he had learned much that was hitherto unknown to him."

On this same evening, Bonnet had a talk with Osusky, the Czechoslovak Minister in Paris. He warned Osusky that Czechoslovak mobilization without consulting France or Britain might have serious consequences. But the impression the French Foreign Minister seems to have managed to convey to Osusky, without actually saying so, was that the anxiety it was his painful duty to express originated from the British, not the French.

This was not wholly true. It was Bonnet who had first raised the matter with Phipps, saying he was going to give Osusky a warning. Phipps agreed, and suggested that the Czechoslovak Government should be told they had in effect broken their treaty with the French by their sudden mobilization. Bonnet was not yet ready to go quite as far as that, but he made sure Osusky was aware how much the French were being held back by the anxiety of their British friends.

Notwithstanding this, the British Government learned a few days later that the Czechoslovak Government felt Britain had been better than her word.

The Czechoslovak mobilization had been a great success. It had been anticipated that there would be desertions among the minority groups called to the colours, but there had been very few.

The communal elections in the Sudetenland passed off without serious incidents, though they resulted in a sweeping victory for Henlein.

And behind the guns of the Czechoslovak frontier forts now stood Czechoslovak soldiers: not only Czechs and Slovaks, but Sudeten Germans, Poles, Ukrainians. Ninety-eight percent of the officers and 85 percent of the N.C.O.'s were at any rate nominally Czechs, and there were complaints from the Sudetenland that some of them were behaving as if they were in enemy country. Watching the sullen crowds of white-stockinged demonstrators, they no doubt had their reasons.

CHAPTER 8

The Watchers in the Wings

TO ANYONE under forty who has grown up in a world dominated by Russia and America, it must seem curious that these two great powers played so little part in events which were to shape everyone's future. It is as if supporting players held the stage while the stars watched inconspicuously from the wings, preparing to make their own spotlit entrances.

But in 1938, only thirty years ago, the United States and the Union of Soviet Socialist Republics were no more than fledgling stars upon the world stage. Everyone recognized their immense potential. When the American economy sneezed, Europe caught pneumonia, and the domestic purges of the thirties in Russia affected the foreign policies of every European power. It must also be said, however, that these two giants were not exactly rushing to push themselves into the center of events.

America, having washed her hands of sinful Europe after the First World War and sought refuge in the normalcy of the unsinful President Harding, continued to be isolationist in her attitudes until at least 1940. Some of the most brilliant reporters of any age kept the American public fully informed of what was happening in Europe. Newspapers, radio, the cinema poured out information about the brutalities of the Nazi regime, which were indeed widely deplored. American public men were prolific of helpful advice as to what should be done about it. But whenever Roosevelt or Cordell Hull, his Secretary of State, proposed any action which could be construed as even remotely involving commitment outside the United States, they brought down upon their heads an avalanche of isolationist protest.

Chamberlain did not put himself out to encourage American involvement in European affairs. A proposal by Roosevelt in January, 1938, for an international con.erence to discuss disarmament and the sharing of raw materials was brusquely brushed aside, on the grounds that Chamberlain himself had just embarked upon his own attempt to reach some kind of settlement on those lines with Germany and Italy. Besides, as Chamberlain not unfairly remarked, "It is always best and safest to count on nothing from the Americans but words."

Chamberlain's rebuff to Roosevelt was the ostensible cause of Eden's resignation as Foreign Secretary, and it has been argued that if Roosevelt's offer had been accepted, it would have led to American involvement in the war at a much earlier stage than 1941. This is by no means certain. A new American Ambassador, Joseph Kennedy, arrived in London at the beginning of March and in a series of public and private pronouncements made the views of his fellow-countrymen painfully clear. "Right now," he told reporters before he left New York, "the average American isn't as interested in foreign affairs as he is in how he's going to eat and whether his insurance is good." He told a Pilgrims' dinner shortly after his arrival that "Americans were afraid of losing their jobs and getting into war. They would support every effort to preserve peace. . . . Others seem to imagine that the U.S. could never remain neutral in the event of a general war." Kennedy's forthright isolationism brought him into frequent conflict with the State Department, whose views he nominally expressed, but there is not much doubt that he did, as Richard Whalen, his biographer, says, express the feelings of the average American. According to public opinion polls, 95 percent of the American people were opposed to participating in another war, and two-thirds of them were unwilling to sell arms to the belligerents, even if the belligerents were fighting Hitler.

The position of Russia was very different. For one thing, she was not insulated from the scene of events by four thousand miles of the Atlantic. For another, Russian governments do not have to worry about opinion polls.

After the *Anschluss*, the Russian Government, like Roosevelt, proposed an international conference to consider steps against further aggression. This proposal also was turned down by the British. In private conversation, Chamberlain spoke of the Russians as "the Bolsheviks," and according to Maisky, the Russian Ambassador, he once absent-mindedly referred to Russia in Maisky's presence as "the enemy." He believed that the Russian proposal was simply a piece of mischief-making, and wrote of "the Russians stealthily and cunningly pulling all the strings behind the scenes to get us involved in war with Germany."

Behind much of Chamberlain's distrust lay the policy agreed at the 1935 Congress of the Communist International, that in the event of a "new imperialist war" breaking out, Communists everywhere should try to turn the war into one "against the bourgeoisie, for the overthrow of capitalism." The bourgeois governments of France and Czechoslovakia, as well as of Britain, showed a certain understandable reluctance to be maneuvered into a position where their throats could be slit under the cover of a patriotic People's War.

In addition, Chamberlain believed that Hitler was so bitterly opposed to the ideology of Communism that any Western involvement with Russia was likely to push him into war. The view was a simple one. Hitler was prepared to come to an agreement with the devil himself if it suited his purpose, and in 1939 did so, to the astonishment of the British.

In the light of postwar events, it can perhaps be argued that Chamberlain's attempt to keep Russia out of Europe was justified, if as misguided as that of the celebrated Dame Partington, who tried to expel the Atlantic Ocean with a mop. A more interesting question is whether Russia seriously wanted to become directly involved in the events of 1938.

The U.S.S.R. at that time was in the throes of the great purge which had followed the trial of the Old Bolshevik leaders, Zinoviev and Kamenev, on charges of conspiring against the state, and of which Tukhachevsky and a high proportion of military officers had become victims. The general opinion among foreign diplomats in Moscow was that the purges had drastically weakened Russia. The British military attaché gave his opinion that "from the military point of view there must be considerable doubt as to whether the Soviet Union is capable of fulfilling its obligations under the pact with Czechoslovakia and France by undertaking a war of offense. In defense of its territory, I still consider that the Red Army would be a formidable opponent."

In May, the Russian Foreign Minister, Litvinov, is said to have had a talk at Geneva with Benes's aide, Arnost Heidrich. According to Heidrich's postwar recollection, Litvinov said he considered war absolutely inevitable. The Soviets knew that the West wanted Stalin and Hitler to liquidate each other. Such a policy would not succeed because the Soviets had a very good memory about what the West did in the First World War. After the battle of the Marne, instead of launching an offensive action, the Western allies waited until the full strength of the German army could exhaust itself in the struggle against Russia. This piece of history would not be repeated, said Litvinov. This time the Soviets would wait to see how the Germans fought with the West, and they would intervene only at the end to secure a just peace. "If France goes to your aid," Litvinov told Heidrich, "then Russia will go too. But Benes is fundamentally wrong if he thinks that France will come to Czechoslovakia's help."

Either shortly before or shortly after this conversation, Litvinov also talked to Bonnet in Geneva. According to Bonnet, the French Foreign Minister asked Litvinov what Russia would do if Czechoslovakia were attacked. Litvinov answered that if France honoured her obligations, Russia would do the same, but only on condition that explicit consent was obtained from either Poland or Rumania for the passage of Russian troops and aircraft. Litvinov pointed out that France had treaties with Rumania and Poland, and should be able to get their consent. Bonnet records that he then saw the Rumanian Foreign Minister, who assured him that no Rumanian Government could agree to the passage of Russian troops across its territory. This would provoke the Germans, and Rumania would become a battlefield.

Rumania had taken advantage of Russian weakness after the revolution by annexing Bessarabia, and there was a well-founded fear that if Rumania allowed Russian troops into her territory, their first action would be to take Bessarabia back. The Poles had similar fears. The Polish Government was also violently anti-Communist, and had long-standing scores to settle with Czechoslovakia over the coal-producing area of Teschen, which the Czechs had annexed after the First World War.

It can be argued that Litvinov knew all this as well as Bonnet did, and that he was deliberately laying down conditions for Russian help which could not be fulfilled. The Russian account of Litvinov's Geneva interview with Bonnet, however, adds one significant fact. Litvinov reminded Bonnet that when the pacts with France and Czechoslovakia had been signed, it had been agreed to hold staff talks. This agreement had never been carried out, and he therefore proposed immediate talks between the Soviet, French and Czechoslovak General Staffs.

Bonnet "took note" of this proposal, and on his return to Paris sent for Coulondre, the French Ambassador in Moscow. Coulondre arrived on the eve of the May Crisis, and at that stage Bonnet proposed to him that military talks should be held between France and Russia. Coulondre pressed for the inclusion of Czechoslovakia, a suggestion which Bonnet countered with the extraordinary one that there should indeed be staff talks, but they should be separate ones between Czechoslovakia and France, Czechoslovakia and Russia, and Russia and France.

Coulondre returned to Moscow at the end of May with nothing firmly decided, but under the impression that staff talks would be held in some form. He heard nothing more until the beginning of July, when he learned in a roundabout way through the Czechoslovak Ministers in Paris and Moscow that the talks were off, "in order not to upset the British Conservatives." By that time, the French Government was reasonably sure the British had become so involved in the affairs of Czechoslovakia that France would not be left to face Germany alone. It perhaps marks the moment when the French felt it safe to forget their Russian alliance and concentrate on building up the English one.

Communist states, no less than capitalist ones, conduct their affairs on a basis of what they conceive to be self-interest, more or less enlightened, and it would not be surprising if internal weakness had combined with suspicion of French and British intentions to convince the Russian Government that the best policy in the circumstances was to wait and see which way the cat was going to jump.

No doubt there were Russian equivalents of those British Conservatives who would have liked to see their enemies destroy each other in an exhausting war. No doubt there was already in Russia, as in Germany, a section of influential opinion which favoured an alliance with Germany, and this section may even have included that hard-headed practitioner of *Realpolitik*, Stalin himself. Hitler bothered surprisingly little about Russia during the Sudetenland crisis, except as a potential source of supply for aircraft.

One may perhaps conclude that the Russian Government saw no advantages for itself in joining in a war over Czechoslovakia, although it would have been happy enough to see the fighting done by somebody else, as in Spain. And it was aware of the risk that, if it took any initiative without the agreement of the West, an opportunity might be found to turn the war into an anti-Communist crusade.

If we had Russian records and memoirs on the scale of those we have from Britain, France, Czechoslovakia and Germany, we might find that Russian politicians behaved as foolishly and indecisively under stress as those of other nations, wavering uncertainly between fear and sudden bursts of panic-stricken determination. That interesting but unreliable book, *Notes for a Journal*, ascribed to Maxim Litvinov though certainly not by him, hints that they did. But the Russians, perhaps wisely, allow their statesmen to present to the world only their public face. Stalin, Molotov, Voroshilov are always either heroes or villains. They are never by any chance simply human beings like Chamberlain, Daladier, Benes, who have to conduct negotiations when suffering from a heavy cold in the head or indigestion after a late night banquet.

CHAPTER 9

Facing the Consequences

CZECHOSLOVAKIA, wrote the British historian H.A.L. Fisher, was the child of propaganda; and of propaganda Benes was a master.

As the May Crisis died away, triumphant headlines flared in Prague, London, Paris, New York:

HITLER BACKS DOWN
DEMOCRACIES' FIRM STAND HALTS CZECH INVASION

When the British Parliament met on the afternoon of Monday, May 23, Harold Nicolson said to Clement Attlee, Leader of the Labour Party, "Well, are we seeing the turn of the tide?"

"I think so," Attlee answered complacently.

Chamberlain himself believed that Hitler had been halted in his tracks. "I cannot doubt in my own mind," he noted in a letter to his sister, "(1) that the German government made all preparations for a coup, (2) that in the end they decided, after getting our warning, that the risks were too great."

According to Sir Nevile Henderson's memoirs, the jubilation of the world's press over German discomfiture "gave Hitler the excuse for his third and worst brainstorm of the year, and pushed him definitely over the borderline from peaceful negotiation to the use of force. His fit of sulks and fury lasted from May 23 to May 28, and on the latter date he gave orders for a gradual mobilization of the army, which should be prepared for *all* eventualities in the autumn. He had made up his vindictive mind to avenge himself upon Benes and the Czechs."

Alas, very little of it was true. Henderson has been unkindly described as a "gent"—that is, someone aspiring to be a gentleman, but not quite achieving it—who was overcome by Goering's condescension in inviting him to shoot among the feudal splendours of Karinhall. Vansittart raged against him: Henderson was a complete Nazi, he could not be trusted to represent the Foreign Office point of view, he was stupid and vain, and had become almost hysterical in the Berlin atmosphere. Certainly Henderson lived very much on his nerves, was given to leaping ahead of his instructions, and was inclined to pour out his soul in long messages on a scale scarcely paralleled since General Gordon in beleaguered Khartoum flew to the electric telegraph as to the brandy bottle. But his assessments of German intentions, which were quite often correct, did less harm to the British cause than his propagation of the myth of Hitler the madman making policy in sudden, uncontrollable fits of fury.

Hitler had certainly been annoyed by the Czechoslovak mobilization and its consequences, which he described as "their rascally trick." Engaged in a vast confidence trick himself, he had to pay particular attention to his prestige, not only among his own people but in the world outside. He had had a sharp reminder, if he needed one, that the issues of peace and war did not lie entirely in his own hands. Most important of all, the unexpected British warning had reinforced his distrust of Chamberlain and Halifax. The British, he could reasonably have assumed, were working hand-in-glove with those Czechoslovak forces which were anxious to precipitate a preventive war before he was ready. There he had been, sitting peacefully at Obersalzberg, enjoying the view and doing nothing more offensive than planning a possible attack on Czechoslovakia in the autumn, when suddenly there was that hypocrite Halifax shouting and bullying almost as if he had been Hitler himself. One may perhaps surmise that the Fuehrer felt as shocked and outraged as if he had been abruptly knocked down by a curate of the Church of England.

Nevertheless, what followed was very little affected by the May Crisis. It resulted from the thinking aloud Hitler had been doing at Obersalzberg before his visit to Italy and after his return, and it would have been exactly the same if the May Crisis had never occurred.

On Saturday, May 28, the Fuehrer summoned to the Reich Chancellery his military adviser, Keitel, the Luftwaffe chiefs Goering and Milch, the Army Commander-in-Chief Brauchitsch, and his Chief of Staff, Beck, Raeder from the Navy, Ribbentrop and Weizsaecker from the Foreign Ministry, and the former Foreign Minister, Neurath.

Ribbentrop, still sulking from his rebuff at Obersalzberg, was given a lecture. Czechoslovakia, said the Fuehrer, could not be invaded immediately. The Army had not yet got the firepower to deal with the Czechoslovak fortifications, and progress on the West Wall, which would hold the French in check, was slow. There were indeed advantages in delay: more could be learned about Czechoslovak military plans, and the German people could be psychologically prepared to face a war.

Hitler made it quite clear, however, that sooner or later Czechoslovakia would have to be eliminated. He thought there would be no intervention from outside. The British would not be rearmed until 1941 or 1942. France and Russia were not prepared for offensive action.

But when was the elimination to take place? On this point Hitler's hearers seem to have been left in doubt. If the Fuehrer's personal aide Wiedemann is to be believed, the date was put as not before the end of September, perhaps not until March, 1939, whereupon Neurath, the former Foreign Minister, exclaimed, "Well, then, we have at least a year's time. Much can happen during that." The military formed a different impression. "The whole contrast becomes acute once more," Keitel's Chief of Staff, Jodl, noted in his diary, "the Fuehrer's intuition that we *must* do it this year, and the opinion of the Army that we cannot do it as yet, as most certainly the Western powers will interfere, and we are not as yet equal to them."

Two days after the conference, Keitel produced for Hitler a revised directive on Operation Green, which began with the words, "It is my unalterable decision to smash Czechoslovakia by military action in the near future. It is the business of the political leadership to await or bring about the suitable moment from a political and military point of view."

How near is the near future? It does not seem to have been very near, because another paragraph of the directive laid down that "An unavoidable development of events within Czechoslovakia, or other political events in Europe providing a suddenly favourable opportunity which may never recur, may cause me to take early action."

In other words, if Henlein's excitable followers got completely out of hand, if there were civil war in France, a Franco-British war with Italy, or some similar development, then Hitler might be forced to act quickly. Failing some such eventuality, the date was to be after the beginning of October and before the end of March, 1939. No earlier date was ever set, and as it turned out, it could not have been, without disrupting the building of the West Wall—or the Siegfried Line, as it was subsequently called. The point is of importance for an understanding of the events that followed. Hitler was never forcing the pace over Czechoslovakia. On the contrary, he was running as hard as he could to catch up, and running moreover with his feet slowed by the wet concrete of the Siegfried Line. For three dramatic days, from September 13 to 15, he had every reason to believe that, in Chamberlain's subsequently famous words, he had missed the bus.

In London, the Government continued to believe that its firmness during the May Crisis had secured a brief respite from war, and that every fleeting minute must be grasped if Europe were not to crash over the brink next time.

During the crisis, Brand, Henlein's representative in London, had been sent by Vansittart with a message to Henlein counselling patience. When he returned, he was met at the airport by Vansittart's intermediary, Christie, hurried straight through the customs and taken to Vansittart's private house in Park Street for a long talk.

Brand was surprised by the detailed nature of the discussion, which centered upon the meaning of the Henleinist demand for autonomy. Vansittart wanted to know how the Sudeten Germans planned to establish a civil service, build up local legislative and administrative bodies. At one point Brand was startled by a question from Vansittart: "How would it be if the Sudeten Germans had military units of their own?" This was a suggestion also made by Hitler in his March talk with Henlein, which even Henlein had begged to be excused from putting forward until later. At the end of his meeting with Vansittart, Brand said, "I don't believe the Czechs will give us autonomy to such an extent as we've been talking about. What will England do then?" Vansittart answered laconically, "Then we can't help them."

Newton, the British Minister in Prague, was constantly urged to keep up the pressure to get serious negotiations going between Henlein and the Czechoslovak Government, and was indeed moved to protest that the Czechoslovaks "will come to believe (as some already suspect) that we have no sincere interest in their welfare and are concerned solely for our own safety."

Henlein himself became anxious. The British were being really too obliging. What should he do, he asked his German advisers, if the Czechs acceded to all his demands, and in fact Hodza decided the time was ripe to invite the Henleinists into the Government? He himself proposed to accept the concessions, but immediately advance the demand that Czechoslovakia should break her agreements with Russia and France. This was at the beginning of June, and suggests that Henlein as yet had no inkling of the revised plan for Operation Green. He was still acting under his "chemical dissolution" orders of March. But even on the point of foreign policy the British were before him. The Foreign Office was already at work on a draft memorandum on the neutralization of Czechoslovakia.

In Paris, Bonnet followed his own devious paths. He had perhaps never greatly believed in the reality of the May threat, which he described as a balloon sent up by the Czechoslovaks to test British and French reaction, observing that "he could never quite forgive the Czechs their stunt of May 21." He nevertheless told the German Ambassador how he himself had often been on the telephone to Prague two or three times a day during the crisis, demanding that the Czechoslovak frontier officials responsible for the first misleading reports should be brought to book and punished. "If the Czechoslovak Government continued unyielding, the French Government would inform them that under these circumstances they would be obliged to submit their obligations under the alliance to revision."

The French Minister in Prague, however, seemed curiously unaware of his master's anxiety. While Newton was under almost daily bombardment from London to put pressure on Benes and Hodza to make concessions to Henlein, Lacroix, his French opposite number, had no instructions to do anything. The British became indignant, for it was after all Bonnet who had begged Halifax in the middle of May to "put as much pressure as possible on Dr. Benes to reach a settlement with the Sudeten Germans in order to save France from the cruel dilemma of dishonoring her agreements or becoming involved in war." By the end of June, Halifax was instructing Phipps to press Bonnet to give the Czechoslovaks the warning he was always saying he was going to give them, but never did: that if they continued to be unreasonable, France would wash her hands of the alliance.

Bonnet promised to instruct Lacroix to do so, but Newton reported more than a week later that although Lacroix had been to see Benes and Hodza, he had not spoken anything like as strongly as the British Government had been told that he would.

Bonnet then made the excuse that warnings sent through Lacroix did not convey any real weight or urgency; he would ask Osusky, the Czechoslovak Minister in Paris, to fly to Prague carrying a note which, Bonnet told Phipps, was couched in very strong terms. It was scarcely reassuring that the first intimation of Osusky's flight reached Phipps not from Bonnet, but from Count Fernand de Brinon of the Franco-German Committee. Halifax asked to see a copy of the note Osusky had been given. It took a fortnight for a copy to be produced, and then it so far failed to live up to Bonnet's description of it that Halifax protested again.

But perhaps the note was not everything. Bonnet has since written that he gave Osusky verbal instructions to see Benes and Hodza and "explain the situation clearly to them. Do not let them sleep under any dangerous illusions." It may be so. But in Prague, after Osusky's visit, Newton found Benes as fertile as ever in ingenious ideas for delay; and Lacroix had once more been left without instructions to continue the pressure.

The French, in fact, were content to leave the initiative to the British, who were becoming thoroughly ensnared. At the end of May, Halifax, anticipating the complete failure of negotiations in Prague, and noting "while we do not wish to be maneuvered into the position of arbitrator," began to take soundings about sending an international commission to Czechoslovakia. By mid-June, the international commission had shrunk to "an independent British expert . . . such as an ex-Governor of an Indian Province." Newton did not think the Indian ex-Governor was a good idea: "However foolishly, the connexion might be considered derogatory to both sides." The British thought again and came up with "some outstanding figure whose name would be known not only in England, but also abroad."

There seems to have been a shortage of outstanding figures who were burning to involve themselves in the insoluble problems of Czechoslovakia, for by July 16 the "outstanding figure" was revealed as that of the sixty-seven-year-old Viscount Runciman of Doxford, Elder Brother of Trinity House, Proprietor of the Isle of Eigg, former President of the Chamber of Shipping of the United Kingdom, former President of the Board of Trade. Coulondre has left a picture etched in acid of this estimable man: "Clean-shaven, impassive, buttoned up tight in a black morning coat, with his head perched on top of a prodigious stiff collar, he seemed to have dropped out of a page of Dickens and still to be feeling his fall." Mr. A.J.P. Taylor has also had his fun with Lord Runciman: "Once an Asquithian Liberal fervent for Free Trade, and later a National Liberal who welcomed Protection, he could be counted on to produce a 'soft' solution." Poor Runciman, in fact, has had a bad press, although he was a sick man, and it is certain that nobody, no international commission nor even an ex-Indian Governor, could have worked more conscientiously in impossible circumstances.

But the fact of his appointment served at once to precipitate events and to place the British Government in the very position they said they were trying so hard to avoid, that of arbitrators.

The German Government was embarrassed by the appointment. If they publicly approved of the Runciman Mission, would they not be bound to some extent to accept its findings? On the other hand, on what grounds could the Mission be directly opposed without alienating British public opinion? Fortunately, a premature "leak" in the London *News Chronicle*—which emanated, as so many of the best "leaks" seemed to do, from Bonnet's Paris—enabled Ribbentrop to mount his high horse: "The Reich Minister had been very much surprised that the matter had appeared in the press and had been confirmed by the British Government before we were informed. These were methods which we did not like. We declined to state our own attitude to the dispatch of Runciman and could only regard the Mission as a purely British affair."

Benes, when he heard about the Mission from Newton, "seemed greatly taken aback and much upset, flushing slightly and hardly recovering his full equanimity by the end of a conversation which lasted for over two hours." Benes saw that the game of playing for time was up. He would somehow have to force matters to a crisis before he was either committed to accepting Runciman's recommendations, or refusing them and losing all hope of British support.

Henlein and Frank were briefed by Hitler personally on the tactics they must adopt: "Hold out and wait." They did their best. They formed a Social Staff under the leadership of Prince Ulrich Kinsky, who had some excellent partridge shooting, and a Political Staff under Frank, who could be relied upon to cram Runciman with so much information—historical, geopolitical, economic, cultural and, no doubt, moral—that he would be permanently incapacitated from reaching any conclusions at all.

On August 4, the day after Runciman's arrival in what he was shortly calling "this accursed country," the Political Staff waited upon him at the Alcron Hotel in Prague and embarked upon an instructional session with his staff which lasted for over five hours. They were, Runciman reported to London, so anxious to leave nothing unsaid that they stayed in the hotel until half-past one the next morning. They kept him so hard at it during the next few weeks that he was forced to report he had been unable even to participate in Prince Ulrich Kinsky's partridge shooting.

CHAPTER 10

Plan Z

IN A FARAWAY country, white-stockinged young Henleinists provocatively jostled self-conscious young Czech militiamen who were letting their beards grow in an attempt to seem tougher than they felt. A Czech policeman forcibly tore the white stockings from a young German girl. Sudeten German students, going on strike at any imagined insult, shouted abuse at their Czech administrators. A mob of angry Czechs gathered outside a Sudeten German school, threatening to wreck it because the flag flown on Benes's birthday was an old one, a deliberate insult to their Czech president. From the Sudetenland spas of Karlsbad and Marienbad came a *cri de coeur*: would somebody please stop the crisis, it was ruining the tourist trade.

One has a picture of uncomprehending people frozen in their petty attitudes, like so many inhabitants of Pompeii in the moments before the lava flood.

In Berlin, Keitel's staff worked on the details of Hitler's plans for action. These, as formulated in a draft dated June 18, were governed by two important provisions. The first was that Hitler was "resolved, as from *October 1, 1938*,* to make full use of every favourable opportunity" for settling the Czechoslovak problem. The second was that "I shall, however, only decide to take action against Czechoslovakia if, as in the case of the occupation of the demilitarized zone and entry into Austria, I am firmly convinced that France will not march and therefore Britain will not intervene."

*Author's italics.

General Ludwig Beck, Chief of the Army Staff, "with his fine, intelligent and almost melancholic expression, weighed down, so it seemed, with responsibility,"* was a man of courage and integrity who continued to believe, in the face of a great deal of evidence to the contrary, that those qualities are more widespread than they are.

He refused to accept that France and Britain would not intervene. He believed that the French Army was the strongest in Europe; that on the first day of war, Britain would come out on the side of France; that Gamelin was a good general; and that infantry remained queen of the battlefield. Beck, wrote Guderian, had no understanding of modern technical matters and erected a barrier of reaction at the center of the army. Like his British and French contemporaries, he disapproved of all this damned newfangled nonsense about tanks. "I don't want to have anything to do with you people," he told Guderian. "You move too fast for me." An upright, honest, and dangerously unintelligent man.

By July, 1938, Beck had passed far beyond his first technical criticism of Hitler's military plans for dealing with Czechoslovakia, which he described as "a mad dream," and was trying to rally his fellow generals for more drastic action.

On July 19, he put his plans to his superior, Brauchitsch. He did not, he said, contemplate a military *Putsch*. Hitler would remain head of the State, but the evil geniuses—Ribbentrop and the Army's particular enemy Himmler, who was increasingly trespassing upon Army preserves—would be swept away. Brauchitsch behaved with his usual equivocation, but finally agreed to call a meeting in Berlin of the Army's senior generals to listen to Beck's views. They came, these distinguished men with their grey hair and upright figures, who had been officers in the First World War and now found themselves condemned to accept the strategic directions of Corporal Hitler. All but two agreed with Beck's thoughts on Czechoslovakia. Brauchitsch was requested to go and put them before Hitler. There was a stormy scene between the general and the former corporal. It was so painful that ever afterwards, when Brauchitsch heard his master's voice raised in anger, he came obediently to heel. Beck resigned in protest,

*Weizsaecker: *Memoirs.*

demanding that Brauchitsch should resign with him; but the Commander-in-Chief, in Hassell's graphic phrase, "hitches his collar a notch higher and says: 'I am a soldier; it is my duty to obey.'" The dissident generals, in the intoxication of their meeting, had agreed that none of them would take Beck's appointment if he did resign. General Franz Halder, however, felt the call of duty so strongly that he stepped into Beck's shoes, and continued to wear them for four years. So much for the solidarity of the generals' trade union.

A more important consequence of the generals' meeting was that Witzleben, commanding in Berlin, and Hoeppner, who held a command in Thuringia, astride the communications between Berlin and the south, began actively to prepare for a *Putsch* on the lines proposed by Beck. The plan, as it subsequently developed, was to begin with the seizure of the principal Government offices in Berlin and the arrest of the Army's enemies, Himmler and Heydrich. It must be emphasized that they were the primary targets of the plot. Hitler would be told that he must dismiss Himmler and Heydrich, and if he refused, he would be detained himself, and perhaps shot.

It is an interesting speculation how much Himmler and Heydrich knew about this plan. The Gestapo, like all bureaucracies, was fairly inefficient, but the generals' security was not particularly good. One of the plotters, Oster of the Wehrmacht Intelligence branch, had a habit of conspiring at the top of his voice in his Berlin club, to the dismay of his fellow conspirators. Goerdeler, the ex-Mayor of Leipzig, who was one of Beck's principal civilian collaborators, was so indiscreet that he could not be trusted with too many details. By September, news of the plot had reached the British journalist Vernon Bartlett, who tells me that he thinks he must have heard of it either from Goerdeler or Jan Masaryk. In the circumstances, it is difficult to believe that no whisper of it reached the ears of Himmler or Heydrich; and bearing in mind the alleged activities of Heydrich in the Tukhachevsky affair, one cannot entirely rule out the possibility that Himmler and Heydrich made use of the conspiracy for their own purposes.

In August, the conspirators sent at least two emissaries abroad with the object of seeking allies. One representative went to Switzerland, where a meeting had been arranged for him with Dr. Otto Strasser. Strasser and his brother Gregor had been early members of the Nazi Party, had broken with Hitler, and in 1938 Otto Strasser was conducting anti-Nazi activities with Prague as his headquarters. He does not—or is reluctant to—remember the name of the man he met in Switzerland, but says he described himself as "the general in charge of the invasion of Czechoslovakia."

Strasser was asked two questions: (1) Would Czechoslovakia fight if supported by her allies? (2) Would she fight alone if her allies deserted her? Strasser expressed his strong conviction that Czechoslovakia would be bound to fight in either event.

In that case, said the German, Hitler would be arrested as soon as the order to move against Czechoslovakia was given. He then told Strasser some details of the plan, including the information about Hoeppner's two divisions blocking the road between Munich and Berlin.

Strasser was understandably excited by this information, and on returning to Prague immediately told the Sudeten German Social Democrat leader Wenzel Jaksch. Jaksch too was excited, and arranged for the information to be relayed to Benes by the President's associate, the journalist Hubert Ripka. According to Strasser, whose account of this episode differs in some details from that given by Jaksch, Jaksch came back to him with an assurance from Benes that Czechoslovakia would fight even if her allies did not. The important point is that Benes apparently knew of the conspiracy, which placed him rather in the position of the goat tethered to attract the tiger, which will then be shot by ambushed hunters. The President may not have been greatly attracted by the role in which he was cast nor entirely confident of the hunters' marksmanship, but in a desperate situation goats cannot be choosers.

A second German emissary went to London. This was Ewald von Kleist-Schmezin, a Prussian landowner, whose visit to England was arranged through Ian Colvin, then a newspaper correspondent in Berlin. Kleist carried a dramatic message to the British Government from Beck: "Bring me certain proof that England will fight if Czechoslovakia is attacked, and I will make an end of this regime."

On August 18, Kleist had a long talk with Vansittart. He put his case in understandably alarmist terms, telling Vansittart that war was now a certainty unless Britain took a strong line.

"Do you mean an extreme danger?" Vansittart asked him.

"No," answered Kleist. "I mean a complete certainty."

Vansittart asked what was to be the date of operations.

Kleist laughed and answered, "Why, of course you know it."

Vansittart said that he did not.

"Well, anyhow your Prime Minister knows it," Kleist replied.

Vansittart said he did not think this was correct, and added that he was questioning Kleist about the date because it was obviously important to know how much time there was in which to act.

Kleist then gave a date: "After the 27th September it will be too late."

To men deeply suspicious of Hitler's intentions, who had been under mounting strain since at least March, this could only mean that on or after September 27, Hitler was firmly committed to marching into Czechoslovakia. In fact, there was no such clearcut intention. There was a requirement for the Wehrmacht to be ready by October 1 for all eventualities, which is by no means the same thing. But the British from now on were hypnotized by a date. Something had to be done before the end of September, or war was certain.

Halifax was sufficiently impressed by Vansittart's report to pass it on to Chamberlain. The Prime Minister was contemptuous of Kleist and his associates whom he regarded as weak and unreliable. But he had, as Kleist suggested, received similar information himself from the German generals through Lord Hutchison of Montrose. He was becoming increasingly distrustful of Benes and Bonnet, and he felt inclined to take some initiative. But what? He was not prepared to give any stronger commitment than that already given in March, since a stronger line seemed likely only to encourage Benes in his delaying tactics. Another warning to Hitler on the lines of that given during the May Crisis was considered, but Henderson was against it, and Wiedemann, Hitler's adjutant, who had visited London in July, had advised Halifax—on Hitler's instructions—that these public warnings only made the Fuehrer hard and uncompromising. Chamberlain therefore proposed that Sir John Simon should make a speech, and that Henderson should be publicly and pointedly recalled from Berlin for consultations.

Henderson came to London at the end of August, and Hoare has left a note of the impression he made, his sensitive nerves stretched almost to the breaking point by Ribbentrop's provocations.

In a long letter to Halifax written a few days previously, Henderson had left no doubt about his own considered views on the situation. "It is one of my duties to put myself under the German skin, if I can," he wrote, "and to report to you how they feel. Their whole experience of Benes is that he cannot be trusted and that whatever he may say, he always gets out of it. And they believe that the Czech military want war now, when they believe that they can drag France and ourselves in, rather than later, when the international position may be less favourable for them."

Henderson emphasized, correctly, that he did not believe Hitler had already decided on aggressive action. What Hitler wanted was autonomy for the Sudeten Germans, which would in time lead to secession. "Every German, however moderate, believes this to be inevitable in the long run, and since in politics geography always has the last word, it is more than likely. But for the moment a quiet life for the Sudeten would, I believe, satisfy Hitler; but if Benes won't give enough, then he may lose all."

"I would fight Germany tomorrow for a good cause," Henderson concluded, "but I refuse to contemplate our doing so for the Sudeten. If they were Hungarians or Poles or Rumanians or the citizens of any small nation, all England would be on their side. They are Germans, so we shut our eyes to realities and are influenced by other considerations, some honourable, some chivalrous, but many egotistical or inspired by fear."

There was a great deal of truth in this, particularly in that last sentence, but the man who came to London at the end of August with these ideas was not very likely to help on Beck's attempt to force a showdown.

Kleist's mission, in fact, had exactly the opposite effect to that intended. For on August 29 or 30, Chamberlain, Henderson, and Chamberlain's adviser, Sir Horace Wilson, conferring at 10 Downing Street, conceived an idea which the Prime Minister was to describe as "so unconventional and daring that it rather took Halifax's breath away. But since Henderson thought it might save the situation at the 11th hour, I haven't abandoned it, though I hope all the time that it won't be necessary to try it."

The idea was known as Plan Z. It was to be put into operation at any time between its conception at the end of August and what was regarded as the probable crisis date, September 17. It was to be a face-to-face confrontation between the British Prime Minister and the German Chancellor.

CHAPTER 11

". . . Le Jour de Gloire Est Arrivé"

IN THE MIDDLE of July, Welczeck, the German Ambassador in Paris, found Bonnet in optimistic mood: "I gained the impression that despite my very energetic remonstrance the Foreign Minister was not fully conscious of the gravity of the situation with regard to the Czechoslovak question." In fact, "the tones of the pipes of peace have . . . drowned the trumpet of war which we have sounded from time to time."

One may find a number of reasons for Bonnet's optimism. The British were becoming so thoroughly entangled with the problems of Czechoslovakia that, if the worst came to the worst, it was morally certain that France would not have to stand alone. The Czechoslovaks were digging their own grave by the slowness of their negotiations, since if matters came to a crisis, the French could tell them they had so wasted their opportunities that the terms of the Franco-Czechoslovak treaty had been broken. They could say, moreover, after an impassioned speech about French honour and the sanctity of alliances, that they took this regrettable action under British pressure. The only danger to this comparatively painless—except for the Czechoslovaks—process of disengagement was a crisis so sudden and violent that the French would find themselves dragged into war before they could help it.

Believers in the conspiracy theory of history will find a certain amount of evidence to suggest that, through De Brinon or some similar intermediary, a strong hint had already been passed to Hitler that the French were not going to fight. The representative of the German General Staff whom Otto Strasser saw in Switzerland told him that Hitler had given the German generals his "world of honour" that the French would not carry out their obligations. Hitler's word of honour was not perhaps a commodity to be valued very highly, but he seems to have been remarkably confident that he would have no trouble from France.

There is, however, even more evidence to support the views of those who continue to hold the old-fashioned belief that the human race conducts its affairs in a perpetual muddle of misinformation and misunderstanding.

During the first weeks of August, reports began to be published of what *The Times* called "a feverish and almost demonstrative erection of fortifications" on the German side of the French frontier. Most military commanders prefer to keep their operations secret, believing that surprise is often an essential element of military success. The German preparations were conducted in a literal blaze of publicity. Floodlights played night after night on the scene of two hundred thousand sweating men unloading, mixing and pouring concrete into the fortifications of the Siegfried Line. There were public announcements that a belt thirty-five miles wide had been declared a prohibited area, and rumours that the Germans intended to carry out a partial test mobilization in September. Bonnet did not seem greatly concerned. When the British Minister in Paris—Phipps was on leave—drew his attention to a newspaper report of the German mobilization, Bonnet said he did not know of the article, but would make inquiries and let the British Minister have any information the French Government had.

On August 16, General Vuillemin, the Commander-in-Chief of the French Air Force, visited Germany with a number of other air force officers. It was one of those invitations that Goering and Milch liked to give to influential foreigners. The French party spent several days inspecting German aircraft production, and their tour ended with a spectacular display of precision flying by the Luftwaffe, after which they were entertained by Goering at Karinhall.

There, Goering made an opportunity to take Vuillemin aside

and ask him if the French really meant to stand by the Czecho-slovaks. Vuillemin dutifully replied that they did.

Goering then began to shout abuse about the Czechoslovaks, who were, he said, intent on provoking Germany. He claimed to have in his possession a report by the Czechoslovak generals recom-mending war now, rather than in two years' time when the Ger-mans would be better prepared. If war began, Goering raged at Vuillemin, it would cause the massacre of millions of men for the Czechs, who weren't worth the trouble.

The combination of Luftwaffe maneuvers and Goering's vio-lence seems to have left Vuillemin in a highly nervous state. He told François-Poncet, as they drove away from Karinhall to-gether, "If there's a war at the end of September, as you say there will be, not a single French plane will be left after a fort-night."

By August 24, Vuillemin was back in Paris, reporting his im-pressions to Daladier, Bonnet and his political chief, Guy La Chambre, the French Under-Secretary for Air.

The French thought the Germans were probably bluffing; but just in case they were not, it perhaps seemed the moment to start preparing an alibi.

On the following day—at the request, M. Daladier tells me, of Guy La Chambre—Daladier asked William C. Bullitt, the American Ambassador in Paris, to invite Colonel Charles A. Lind-bergh to dine at the American Embassy to meet La Chambre.

"Lindy" had been the great American hero of the twenties, the clean-limbed, all-American boy who had flown the Atlantic solo in 1927 in the *Spirit of St. Louis*, and had managed to keep his dignity and modesty under the storm of ballyhoo which greeted his achievement, when 1,800 tons of ticker tape and torn-up tele-phone directories rained down on his triumphant progress through New York after his return. Then his only son had been kidnapped and, after a drawn-out agony of publicity, found dead.

Lindbergh's resulting views on democracy were no secret. As far back as 1936 he had told his British friend, Harold Nicolson, that if Great Britain supported the decadent French and the Red Russians against Germany, there would be an end of European civilization. Like Vuillemin, he had been a guest of Goering and

Milch, and his views on German air power were well-known. The German air force, he believed, was ten times superior to that of Russia, France and Great Britain combined. It is of course possible that the French Air Minister did not know what Lindbergh would say if asked about German air power; some politicians lead very sheltered lives. Perhaps he really did want an independent view of Vuillemin's account. On the other hand, perhaps not.

At Bullitt's dinner, La Chambre painted a gloomy picture of French air strength. French factories were turning out between forty-five and fifty planes a month, the British seventy, the Germans between five and eight hundred. What did Lindbergh think? Lindbergh was cautious about German production figures, but repeated his view that German air strength was greater than that of the rest of Europe. If Bonnet was looking for a well-known figure whose views could be used to confirm the report of the French air Commander-in-Chief, he now had it; and in transmission from Bonnet to Phipps, Lindbergh's dinner-table remarks gained a few dramatic if inaccurate additions, such as that Germany had 8,000 military aeroplanes and could turn out 1,500 more a month.

So far so good. But it is always better to over- than under-insure. On September 4, Bonnet accompanied Bullitt to the unveiling of a memorial to the American dead of the First World War. Bonnet—with the best of intentions, as he has made clear in his memoirs—had urged Bullitt to add a few words to his speech indicating that the United States might find herself drawn into a second European war. Bullitt, with the reluctant consent of the State Department, did voice the warning: "If war broke out in Europe no one could state or foretell whether or not the United States would be drawn into such a war." Bonnet in his own speech said that he was "touched, but not surprised, when your fellow-countrymen often tell me that if France were attacked once again, once again they would come to defend her."

As might perhaps have been anticipated by a former French Ambassador in Washington, a great many of Bullitt's isolationist fellow-countrymen were more angry than touched by these references, and Roosevelt was forced to calm the storm by publicly telling a press conference: "To include the United States in a Franco-British front against Hitler is a political columnists' inter-

pretation, and it is a hundred percent wrong." He also disavowed
Bullitt's speech, which did not "constitute a moral engagement on
the part of the United States towards the democracies."

Another brick was added to the alibi. There were to be several
more. A few days after the Lindbergh dinner, Bonnet had asked
Phipps if he could have in writing the warning that had been
given him verbally on May 22 about the limitation on British
commitments to France and Czechoslovakia. Phipps was told
from London that he might supply a copy, though in doing so he
was to make it clear that the British Government was not at this
moment repeating the limitations it contained.

To Lindbergh's views, Bonnet had added a little. From this
British message, Bonnet subtracted, circulating the May 22 document among "certain bellicose French ministers," but without the
attached proviso that what had applied in May did not necessarily apply in August or September.

In fact, at this particular moment, the British were prepared
to take a rather tougher line towards Germany than they were
willing to admit in Paris. For this reticence there were a number
of interconnected reasons. One of these was the warning given
by Wiedemann, Hitler's adjutant, that public threats would only
make Hitler hard and uncompromising, coupled with the unfortunate fact that things said in Paris had a habit of "leaking"
to the newspapers, especially those friendly to the French Foreign
Minister. But also there was the equivocal behaviour Bonnet had
shown throughout the summer towards pressure on Czechoslovakia. Chamberlain was prepared to take some notice of those of his
advisers who wanted another warning given in Berlin. He was
not, however, prepared to encourage the Czechoslovaks and
French to believe that, whatever they did, they would have
Britain behind them.

On Sunday, September 11, Chamberlain himself held an off-
the-record press conference. Although he cautioned his hearers
against regarding the situation as too serious, he also used the
words, "Undoubtedly, it is of the first importance that the German Government should be under no illusions in this matter and
that they should not, as it has been suggested that they might,
count upon it that a brief and successful campaign against

Czechoslovakia could be safely embarked upon without the danger of the subsequent intervention of France and later of this country."

This "guidance" emerged in much sharper form in a communiqué issued that Sunday evening by the Foreign Office: "In no event could Great Britain remain indifferent to a conflict in which the integrity of France might be threatened. It is of primary importance that the German Government should entertain no illusions upon this matter and that they should not suppose that a rapid and victorious campaign in Czechoslovakia could be begun without bringing about the possibility of intervention by France and subsequently by Great Britain."

On that Sunday, the Paris air was electric with rumour: François-Poncet, the French Ambassador in Berlin, had reported that the Germans were ready to march at the lifting of a finger. The date was to be September 24. The excuse for war would be a murderous attack on Runciman or Henlein.

The French Foreign Minister was in Geneva, where he saw Halifax's deputy, R.A. Butler. Bonnet told Butler, in a graphic phrase, that for France to envisage a war on three fronts, Spanish, Italian and German, "would be equivalent to jumping from the Eiffel Tower," which France had no intention of doing. He did not seem, Butler reported, to expect any further commitment from Britain. Bonnet also added usefully to his store of anti-war material. In Geneva he talked to Litvinov, his Russian opposite number, who had again been pressing for staff talks with the French. Asked by Bonnet whether Russia would honour her obligations if France did, Litvinov replied that she would. He had proposed, however, that the matter should be referred to the League of Nations, as a majority decision of the League Council would influence Rumania and perhaps Poland to allow the passage of Russian troops. It would also, of course, if one wants to be suspicious, give Russian troops an excuse for staying in Rumania and Poland if that seemed desirable. Bonnet added the information about reference to the League to his stock of useful material.

On the morning of September 12, Bonnet was back in Paris. The French press was splashing Sunday night's Foreign Office communiqué under such headlines as "England is with us!" and "The British Government do away with all uncertainty."

There was a meeting of the French Cabinet, after which, Alexander Werth reported, "Everybody looked very grim and determined. 'We have taken measures to meet every—*yes, every*—eventuality.' And when I asked one of the members of the Government what he thought of the British statement of the night before, he said: '*Je suis très, très, TRÈS, TRÈS satisfait.*'"

On September 12, however, Phipps in Paris received a reply from Halifax to a previous inquiry made by Bonnet. Bonnet had asked, "What answer would the British give to a question from the French in the event of a German attack on Czechoslovakia: 'We are going to march, will you march with us?'" In forwarding this question to London, Phipps had given his personal opinion that the question could not be answered in advance and without reference to the nature of the German aggression—in other words, the French and Czechoslovaks could not be given a blank cheque. He added to Halifax his own view that Bonnet was "desperately anxious for a possible way out of this 'impasse' without being *obliged* to fight."

Halifax's reply was most helpful: "The question itself, though plain in form, cannot be dissociated from the circumstances in which it might be posed, which are necessarily at this stage completely hypothetical . . . So far, therefore, as I am in a position to give any answer at this stage to M. Bonnet's question, it would have to be that while His Majesty's Government would never allow the security of France to be threatened, they are unable to make precise statements of their future action, or the time at which it could be taken, in circumstances that they cannot at present foresee."

Part of Halifax's reply, curiously enough, echoes the answer given by the American State Department to British inquiries about the American attitude in the event of war: "It would not be practicable to be more specific as to our reaction in hypothetical circumstances." The State Department's reply has escaped censure. Halifax's has been jumped on by everyone. Bonnet in his memoirs, as he is perfectly entitled to do, has made a great deal of it as an example of the lack of British support for French action, and indeed it was a foolish weapon to put into Bonnet's hands at such a moment. But it meant no more than that the British were not prepared to leave a decision on peace or war to the French.

By the evening of September 12, however, the French press, or some sections of it, were playing down the forthright Sunday communiqué of the British Foreign Office and playing up a new note of uncertainty which, it might be deduced, was being drawn from a confidential "leak" of Halifax's message.

On this same September 12, Léger, the permanent head of the French Foreign Ministry, saw Gamelin, asking him: "You have no other solution but to attack the German fortifications through Lorraine?" Gamelin had already said so on a number of occasions, and he said it again, adding that he could do nothing else, since he was not being allowed to go through Belgium.

Later in the day he was sent for by Daladier, who also called in Georges and Billotte, the French generals responsible for operations against Germany in the event of war. Daladier repeated the old question: what could the French Army do to help Czechoslovakia? Georges answered that it could not conquer the German Army before Czechoslovakia lost an important part of her territory. Czechoslovakia, he added, would be like Belgium, Serbia and Rumania in the First World War.

The earliest date the assembled generals could give for a French offensive was the seventh or eighth day after the declaration of war. Georges, indeed, put it as late as the tenth day. Gamelin uttered one of his Delphic assurances: whatever happened at the start of a war, "the democratic nations would dictate the peace."

The French alibi was now complete, a masterpiece of diplomatic art. The United States had disassociated herself from the crisis. The British would give no firm answer when asked if they intended to march with France. The Russians proposed to refer matters to the time-wasting League of Nations. Lindbergh supported Vuillemin's opinion that France was disastrously outnumbered in the air. The French Army could do nothing to save Czechoslovakia, and its only way of helping would be to hurl French soldiers against German fortifications. What an opportunity for the passionate and mellifluous evocation of 1917, a million French dead, mutinies, the Communists waiting their chance to take over. . . .

On the evening of September 12, the Fuehrer was to utter his own thoughts on peace or war at the Nazi Party rally at Nuremberg. Whatever he said, the French Government—or at any rate its Foreign Minister—felt armed at all points and calmly confident of outfacing the enemy.

CHAPTER 12

Czech-Mate

THE RUNCIMAN Mission arrived in Prague on August 3, in the middle of a heat wave. It immediately impressed the natives by appearing at a formal reception in all the glory of top hats, morning coats, and somewhat limp stiff collars.

The Mission had been hastily scrambled together in London, and consisted of Runciman himself, who was quickly dubbed The Lord; Frank Ashton-Gwatkin, a Foreign Office expert on economics; Geoffrey Peto, a company director and former Conservative M.P. who had been Runciman's parliamentary private secretary at the Board of Trade; and a banker, Robert J. Stopford. It was later joined by David Stephens, a bright young clerk in the Parliament Office of the House of Lords, who had made a study of Central European politics, and Ian Henderson, a member of the staff of the Prague Legation.

It is characteristic of the atmosphere of the time that Stopford was romantically, though incorrectly, believed by newspapermen to be a member of the British Intelligence Service sent to keep an eye on Ashton-Gwatkin, who in his turn was suspected of being engaged in secret negotiations with anti-Bolshevik White Russians in Prague.

The Mission was accompanied into Prague by a galaxy of those harbingers of disaster, the international journalists, who took up their posts in the Alcron Hotel, where the Mission was staying, or in the Hotel Ambassador. A number of the foreign correspondents came straight from the Spanish Civil War, and to the people of Prague this stark fact was often enough the first indication they had had that they themselves were now faced with an imminent crisis. One young Social Democrat student still remembers his sense of shock when he was introduced to a group of these distinguished veterans of Abyssinia, Spain, Austria, and was made to understand for the first time, "Good heavens, this means us next."

To a politically-conscious minority of Prague citizens, a visit to the lobby or bars of the Alcron and Ambassador now became an essential part of the daily round. It was here that the comings-and-goings of The Lord could be studied, together with those of other mysterious figures, French, German, British, who suddenly appeared. Among these were Professor René Brunet, sent by Bonnet to keep an eye on Runciman and perhaps to conduct some very private negotiations with the Henleinists; Dr. Kier, an Austrian Nazi now introduced, to the resentment of the Henleinist moderates, as adviser in constitutional law to Henlein and Frank; and the long-haired and cadaverous Lord Allen of Hurtwood, a pacifist Socialist British peer, who constituted himself an unofficial intermediary beween the Czechoslovak Government and Ribbentrop, and who probably did rather less mischief than he has taken credit for.

In the lobby of the Ambassador Hotel, the Henleinist press representative, a small man swelling with self-importance, held an informal daily press conference, and one British journalist at least was warned that, if he were so unwise as to take a hostile line towards the Henleinists in his reports, he might suffer unfortunate consequences on any subsequent visit to the Sudetenland. The Henleinist press representative assured the journalist that of course he himself would do his best to secure protection for him from the wrath of excitable Sudeten Germans, but still, accidents did happen, and it would be a pity if . . .

Both Czechs and Henleinists were past masters in the art of undercover work and of rumour-mongering. A favourite Henleinist story put about during the negotiations was that Benes was ill and not in full command of his faculties. Nor was security at that time as good as it has subsequently become, and the possibility cannot be entirely ruled out that both Czechs and Henleinists were able to obtain access to official British telegrams. Certainly at one tense moment an urgent official telephone message to a member of the Runciman Mission was put through by the Alcron switchboard to the special correspondent of the London *Daily Express,* who with almost inhuman self-denial caused it to be transferred to its proper recipient without learning the contents.

Against this slightly hysterical background, the Runciman Mission pursued its stately course. There is a legend that its members spent all of their time shooting Prince Ulrich Kinsky's partridges and hobnobbing with the Sudeten German aristocracy. This is not true. They all worked very hard indeed, and that, perhaps, was a fault.

The Mission's instructions from Vansittart and Halifax were to cultivate Henlein and try to influence him on the side of moderation. A second instruction was to play for time, since it was believed in London that if negotiations could be kept going until the end of September, war would be unlikely in 1938, and by 1939 there would be a considerable difference in the state of British rearmament.

The cultivation of Henlein presented the first difficulty, since for some time Henlein could not be found. The Henleinist tactics, as laid down by Frank, were so to cram The Lord and his staff with anti-Czech propaganda that they would return to London to report that the Sudeten German problem was incapable of solution, and that it was all Benes's fault. In pursuance of this game, Henlein was to remain incommunicado at Oberstdorf, in Bavaria, until he was required at the last moment to deliver the *coup de grâce.* But the Mission asked so insistently for Henlein that it became embarrassing to deny them a meeting with him.

It was promised that he would be present during a weekend Runciman was invited to spend at Kinsky's estate near the Saxony border. The opportunity was taken to give The Lord his first sight of conditions in the border areas: roads half-blocked with barricades of pine logs, Czechoslovak soldiers working on the frontier fortifications, a close security check on the Prince's guests. At the gates of Kinsky's park, a crowd of country people, mostly women and children, enticingly chanted, "Lord Runciman, we want to see you!" and when The Lord and his lady appeared, there was a chorus of that kind in which simple country people are so apt to express their spontaneous and innermost feelings: "We ask your help in our misery! Give us a fair solution!"

But there was no Henlein.

The Fuehrer's Viceroy appeared at last at the castle of another member of the Bohemian aristocracy, Prince Max of Hohenlohe-Langenburg, whom Vansittart, as well as the German Government, was to use as an intermediary during 1939 and 1940.

Once again Henlein was able to cast his spell over the British. He was at his most honest and appealing, all hearty simplicity, so different from those talkative Sudeten German lawyers who kept the Mission up until half-past one in the morning with their dissections of constitutional minutiae. So transparently honest was he that Ashton-Gwatkin conceived the idea of using him to help achieve the Mission's second object of playing for time. Henlein should be sent to see Hitler, to convince the Fuehrer of the sincerity of Runciman's attempt to reach a settlement, and persuade him that this was Germany's best way of gaining her ends.

Henlein was not without misgivings about the interpretation which would be placed by the Czechoslovak Government, and his own followers, on a public visit by him to Hitler. But he agreed to go, and Ashton-Gwatkin flew to London to discuss the proposal with the Foreign Office.

Neither Ashton-Gwatkin nor Runciman himself were at any time informed of Kleist's visit to London a few days previously and the threat under which the British Government now believed itself to be working, of a definite German attack on Czechoslovakia towards the end of September. There was, however, evident anxiety at the Foreign Office that some new approach to Hitler should be made, and Halifax, while accepting the idea of Henlein's visit, added to it a proposal that in addition Runciman himself should go to see Hitler. This proposal The Lord politely but resolutely declined. He had been impressed, however, by the growing tension in Czechoslovakia, the news of German Army maneuvers, and the prospect of a violent speech by Hitler at Nuremberg on September 12. He undertook to produce by September 15 a scheme of settlement if the Henleinists and the Czechoslovak Government had still failed to reach agreement by that date. The timing was designed to avoid appearing to rush

Hitler and encouraging him to keep the door open in his Nuremberg speech.

On September 1, Henlein, with a heavy cold, went off to Obersalzberg, carrying this offer from Runciman and a message from the British Government: if only the Sudeten German question could be got peacefully out of the way, it might be possible to negotiate an Anglo-German agreement over a wide, though carefully undefined field. This was a carrot Hitler had been offered before, and according to Henlein, he forbore to comment on it.

Henlein found the Fuehrer in a genial mood. Hitler took his Viceroy for a tour of his model farm, and went so far as to crack a joke, one of the few Hitler jokes on record. When they came to the cowsheds, Hitler said, "And here are the representatives of the National Socialist Cow Club." If it does not seem a very good joke, it must be remembered that at this moment the Fuehrer had a number of things on his mind. He was in serious trouble with his generals and his program. Beck had resigned as Chief of Staff; General Adam, the blunt old Bavarian who commanded on the Western front, was maintaining obstinately that he could not be expected to hold the French for longer than three weeks with the five regular divisions allotted to him; and the plans the Army High Command had produced for the conquest of Czechoslovakia seemed certain to lead to thirty-seven German divisions being bogged down for weeks in a slow and costly operation against the Czechoslovak fortifications. Hitler, who had been talking to Guderian, his tank expert, was pressing for the vital point in the whole operation, a quick victory to be achieved by an armoured thrust straight at Prague through the Egerland, at the western tip of Czechoslovakia. He did not get his way about this, however, until a conference at Nuremberg on September 9.

To Henlein, Hitler expressed doubt whether negotiations with Benes would ever produce any results, but instructed him to keep negotiating. The British Government, worrying about what Hitler was going to say at Nuremberg and about Kleist's warning of war on or after September 27, learned with some relief that Hitler had said nothing to Henlein about a date by which results must be achieved.

The British, however, now had another worry. Some time during

August, Brand, the Henleinist representative in London, had been asked by Christie, Vansittart's intermediary, to arrange another meeting between Christie and Henlein. Henlein was at Oberstdorf, and unapproachable except through Frank. Brand got to Oberstdorf and put to Henlein Christie's request for a meeting. Frank opposed the idea, and Henlein was won round with difficulty. The meeting took place at Zurich, Brand remaining in an outer room while Christie and Henlein talked. Brand does not know what was said between them, but has vivid recollection of Christie's concern afterwards. According to Brand, Christie told him that this was the first time he had heard Henlein threaten that Germany would go to war over the Sudetenland, adding the advice that since Germany was prepared to wage a war lasting ten years, Britain and France would be well-advised to keep out of it.

It seems probable that by the date of this meeting, Henlein and Frank, though not their subordinates, had been given some hint by Hitler of Operation Green, and that this hint was given at Breslau at the end of July, when Hitler watched a spectacular display by 30,000 Sudeten German gymnasts.

Afterwards, he had talked to some of the minor Henleinist leaders at their hotel. They were lined up in the foyer. The Fuehrer came down the staircase, accompanied by Henlein. He shook hands along the line, staring through and past them, then addressed them in staccato sentences: "Don't get impatient. Go back to your homes. Stand by your tasks. Stand together. Obey Henlein." It was the first indication most of them had had that the Fuehrer was interesting himself personally in their affairs. By the beginning of August, Frank, with his ostentatious inscrutability, was alarming his moderate colleagues by heavy hints: "It's all the same what's negotiated—everything will turn out differently," and suggesting that he had special information about the settlement of the Sudeten German problem by force.

But whatever Henlein and Frank had been told about Operation Green, they could not have been given a date for the start of operations, because none had been fixed. On August 19, Ribbentrop had told Weizsaecker, State Secretary at the German Foreign Ministry, that Hitler was determined to settle the Czechoslovak problem by force, and described the middle of October as the latest possible date because of technical reasons governing air operations. But Hitler himself was not nearly so definite. When Mussolini inquired anxiously about dates, he was told, at the beginning of September, "The Fuehrer is unable to state any definite time because he does not know this himself . . . For the rest, the Fuehrer will explain his attitude in detail when he makes his big speech at the Party Rally."

Meanwhile, in Prague, something momentous had happened: Benes himself had taken over negotiations with the Henleinists.

The information that he proposed to do so threw the Henleinist negotiators into a panic. They supposed, wrongly, that he was acting in combination with Runciman, and that they were about to be confronted by proposals which had Runciman's backing. Their principal negotiator, Kundt, was being kept from direct contact with Henlein by Frank, and sent an urgent request to Berlin for advice. This earned him a rebuke from Ribbentrop: "He did not like being approached so often by the Sudeten German Party for advice. Henlein had already received full instructions, and therefore it was not fitting that one gentleman or another kept appearing from Prague at short intervals to obtain decisions on individual questions. Henlein and his people must learn to stand on their own feet."

Ribbentrop did, however, go on to give some advice, warning the Henleinists of a danger they saw only too clearly for themselves. If they accepted the proposals Benes was now offering as a basis for negotiation, it would probably be "leaked" to the Czechoslovak and British press that they had accepted the President's magnanimous offer and were abandoning the Karlsbad points. The mass of Sudeten Germans, clamouring for liberation, might then get out of hand. If they refused the terms, Benes would have the valuable propaganda point that it was impossible to satisfy the Henleinists. Ribbentrop instructed Kundt that he must conduct negotiations in such a way that Benes was not stopped from implementing his proposals, though the Henleinists left themselves free to go on putting forward their Karlsbad demands.

There then began a curious contest in which both sides were less concerned with reaching agreement than with scoring a propaganda point. On the one hand was Benes, an incomparable negotiator; master of the small print in the contract, of every nuance of the conference table; skillful at manipulating strings which moved world opinion. He was fifty-four, at the height of his mental powers, but already showing some signs that the long period of strain was beginning to make him a tired man.

Opposed to him were two younger and less experienced men, the forty-year-old Ernst Kundt, who had studied law but had not finished the course, and a thirty-two-year-old doctor of law, Wilhelm Sebekovsky, one of the intellectuals of the Sudeten German Party, who had made himself an expert on the constitutional niceties of the Swiss cantonal system. Kundt, whose contacts were with Eisenlohr and the German Legation in Prague, was a "chemical dissolution" man, and to that extent in favour of moderation. Sebekovsky was a moderate, but he was by now doubtful whether popular opinion in the Sudetenland would tolerate anything less than secession.

Both burned with a fiery nationalist sense of Sudeten German righteousness and Czech hypocrisy. Neither trusted Benes. They regarded him rather as the Irish nationalists who came to London in 1929 to negotiate with the British Government regarded that other tricky operator, Lloyd George, and for whom Michael Collins spoke: "He [Lloyd George] is all comradely—all craft, and wiliness—all arm round the shoulder—all the old friend's act. Not long ago he would joyfully have had me at the rope's end."

The center of Prague, one of the most beautiful cities in Europe, is dominated by the thirteenth-century towers of the castle built on Hradcany Hill by Ottokar II, King of Bohemia. To the extent that Ottokar encouraged German immigration and was the unsuccessful rival of Rudolph of Hapsburg for the overlordship of Germany, King Ottokar had some responsibility for the Sudeten crisis of 1938. His castle had been destroyed by war, and replaced in course of time by a superb baroque palace, once the home of the Kings of Bohemia, then the Prague residence of the Hapsburg emperors, now in part the home and office of the President of the Republic of Czechoslovakia. There, in the President's big library, on August 24 and 25 Benes had two long meetings with Kundt and Sebekovsky which remained quite unknown to the international newsgatherers at the Alcron and Ambassador hotels, and to most of the people of Prague.

These two conversations, if one can forget for a moment that the lives of millions of people were to be affected by them, presented a scene of high comedy. Benes sought to project himself as the great father-figure of the Republic, the one man who had consistently advocated a settlement between Germans and Czechs, who was eager for good relations with Germany and regarded the Russian alliance as an unfortunate relic of an unhappy past. Kundt and Sebekovsky, who knew all about Benes's political methods, were under orders neither to accept nor reject the President's terms. They dourly asked for everything to be put in writing, and when they got it in writing, they ostentatiously took out a magnifying glass to read the small print.

Benes's offer was indeed a handsome one, and if it had been carried into effect a few years previously, it might well have kept Kundt, Sebekovsky and their party out of the presidential library altogether, and put Hitler to the inconvenience of finding another excuse for eliminating Czechoslovakia. The program proposed by Benes was in two stages. Immediately, the Sudeten Germans would be allowed to appoint their own fellow-countrymen as police and administrators; German would be recognized as an official language; and a loan would be raised to put Sudeten industry on its feet and help absorb the unemployed. In return for these concessions, Benes asked the Henleinists for a two-month truce in the propaganda war, which would allow the second stage of negotiations to begin. These negotiations would be concerned with the more fundamental question of self-government for the Sudetenland.

These proposals were handed over in writing on Tuesday, August 30, with a request for a clear "Yes" or "No" by Friday, September 2. Henlein took them with him on his visit to Obersalzberg and received Hitler's approval for continuing negotiations, though the Fuehrer professed himself skeptical about Benes's intention of implementing them.

The accepted version of what happened next rests almost entirely on an interview which Benes gave after the war to the British journalist, G.E.R. Gedye. The circumstances in which the interview was given are worthy of note. It appeared in the London *Daily Herald* of October 8, 1945, at a time when 2¼ million Sudeten Germans were being deported from Czechoslovakia under conditions which Gedye described on the following day as "an outrage to humanity." It is possible, therefore, that when Benes gave the interview, he felt the need to justify this postwar action of his Government by drawing as black a picture as possible of the Sudeten Germans' prewar conduct, though Mr. Gedye tells me that he does not believe this thought was in the President's mind.

In his interview with Gedye, Benes said: "It happened thus: I invited Doctors Kundt and Sebekovsky, two deputy leaders of the Sudeten Germans under Henlein, to visit me.

"Kundt . . . sat in the chair that you are sitting in now.

"I pushed a blank sheet of paper before him and said, 'Please write your party's full demands for the German minority. I promise you in advance to grant them immediately.'

"Kundt stared at me incredulously, 'Go on, write!' I said.

"Kundt was reluctant to write himself, so I wrote down at his dictation and I signed the document. The next day I informed Runciman of what I had done.

"Our unconditional acceptance of the most extreme demands created consternation in the German camp.

"Frank . . . rushed to see Hitler, who promptly called for a revolt by all Germans in Czechoslovakia. Henlein went to Germany, founded the Sudeten Legion to fight us."

Dr. Sebekovsky, the only survivor of the three participants in this dramatic scene, tells me that he has no recollection of anything of the kind taking place, and has given me a number of reasons to substantiate his statement. He is, of course, an interested party, and the most convincing reason in his support, it seems to me, is one he did not give—the question of dates. It was physically impossible for Hitler to invade Czechoslovakia before October 1, even if he had wanted to. All the instructions the Henleinists were receiving from Germany were to keep negotiations going. The man who did have an interest in forcing the Henleinists to break off negotiations was Benes, and what is interesting about the story is the reflection it may provide of Benes's own mind. One may surmise that this is what he would have liked to happen. But it did not.

At a meeting on September 2, Kundt and Sebekovsky, acting on the advice given by Ribbentrop, accepted some of the President's proposals, but put forward others of their own. Benes was now under very heavy pressure from both Runciman and Newton, who had told him that if the British people and Government had to choose between Henlein's Karlsbad points and war, there could be no doubt as to the decision. It was in these desperate circumstances that the so-called Fourth Plan was produced, and it owed more to the Sudeten German Social Democrats than to Benes's ready fountain pen. According to Wenzel Jaksch, the Sudeten German Social Democrat leader, "The various 'experts' in Benes's immediate office (as well as an entire division in the Foreign Ministry under Senior Governmental Counsellor Chmelar) had been concerned with the Sudeten problem only in a propagandist and negative sense. When the Sudeten German Social Democrats offered Benes's secretary, Prokop Drtina, a copy of their extensive memorandum to Lord Runciman, therefore, he seized it as a man overboard seizes a lifebuoy. An entire staff then worked all night to translate the Social Democrat proposals . . . together with certain concessions to the autonomist Karlsbad Demands, into a paper which the government could present as its own."

The Fourth Plan was officially handed over to the Henleinists on September 7, not by Benes, but significantly by Hodza. Benes himself gloomily told Runciman that the terms "amounted to capitulation and would in future years be regretted by Great Britain and France." The Henleinists naturally welcomed them. Kundt recommended them to his friends at the German Legation. If they were implemented, he pointed out, "chemical dissolution" would be well on the way. If on the other hand, as he believed, Benes had no intention of carrying them out, then the Henleinists would have won their propaganda point. It would be "proved to the world that Benes and his Government intend to continue in the main the post-1918 policy merely by means of new trickery." Even Frank described the terms as giving the Henleinists 90 per-

cent of what they wanted; and Henlein, nursing a high tempera-
ture in a hotel bed at Nuremberg, where he had gone for the Nazi
Party rally, gave his blessing to their acceptance, on the understanding that they were open to negotiation on points of detail.

At this triumphant point for the Henleinists occurred an "incident" in the largely Czech coal-mining town of Mährisch-Ostrau,
close to the Polish border, which needs to be examined with
some care.

A British report of the incident, made after what was described
as "careful investigation" by the British assistant military attaché
in Prague and the British consul at Reichenberg, laid the blame
for it wholly on the Henleinists. But this "careful investigation"
did not include hearing the stories of the three Henleinist leaders
concerned, and to that extent must be questioned.

According to the Henleinists—Dr. Franz Köllner, the party organizer, Dr. Neuwirth, a lawyer, and Franz May, a Henleinist parliamentary deputy—they were sent up to Mährisch-Ostrau by
Frank at the request of the local Henleinist organizer. A number
of Sudeten Germans, mostly small border farmers, were being
held in jail there on charges of gun-running and spying. These
charges were probably justified in some of the cases, but according to Neuwirth, Frank seemed to suspect that the Czechoslovak
State Police, whose methods were not always above reproach,
intended to beat up the men and extract from them confessions
that they were parties to a plan for an organized Sudeten German
rising. There may, of course, have been such a plan, or there
may not.

At Mährisch-Ostrau, Neuwirth found the imprisoned men had
indeed been beaten up, and May was struck and arrested by
Czechoslovak mounted police when he tried to stop them from
charging some Henleinist demonstrators.

Neuwirth, in a high state of self-righteous indignation, proceeded to make a row about this situation with the Czechoslovak
Government departments concerned. The Henleinist negotiators
in Prague, and their Austrian adviser, Kier, saw tactical advantages in it as a means of forcing further concessions out of Hodza,
and in particular making him remove the hated State Police from
the Sudetenland. They showed themselves affronted, and broke

off negotiations until they had had apologies and the guilty parties
had been punished.

It must be emphasized that, in the existing state of tension,
each side was deeply suspicious of the other. The Henleinists
believed that the incident had been deliberate provocation on the
part of the police. Hodza on the other hand demanded to know
from the Henleinists, "What orders have you got from Berlin?"
But the Czechoslovak Prime Minister was genuinely concerned
to reach an agreement, accepted the Henleinist denials, gave the
necessary apologies and promises about punishment, and it was
arranged between the two sides that negotiations should be resumed on September 13, the day after Hitler's speech at
Nuremberg.

Frank's attitude towards the resumption of negotiations was,
however, enigmatic. Ashton-Gwatkin and Stopford of the Runciman Mission saw him on the night of September 8, the night
following the incident, and had the greatest difficulty in persuad-
ing him to agree that negotiations should be continued. He did
finally agree, though according to Stopford, "Frank fought hard
and was nearly in a state of nervous collapse. When he left us at
2 A.M. he said to me: 'I am afraid to go home. I live in a lonely
suburb and I know the Czechs are waiting for me to kill me.' "

Frank was an excitable man, not very intelligent, with something like a conspiracy mania. He was almost certainly in possession of some guilty knowledge about Hitler's military plans, and
his fear that the Czechs might assassinate him seems to have
been genuine. It was in this state of mind that he journeyed to
join Henlein at Nuremberg for the Nazi Party Rally.

CHAPTER 13

Nuremberg-London

AT NUREMBERG in the second week of September the massed brass of the military bands crashed into Wagner's "March of the Nibelungs," the banks of floodlights played upon drilled ranks of thousands upon thousands of brown-shirted party faithfuls, the crowds in the immense open-air stadium roared their self-intoxicating *"Sieg Heil! Sieg Heil! Sieg Heil!"*

The annual Nazi Party rally at Nuremberg normally fulfilled two purposes. It was the great occasion of the year for thousands of local officials, representing three million party members throughout Germany, who came, swelling with pride and self-importance, to find themselves within touching distance of the great and to be rewarded for their loyalty by a smile, perhaps even a handshake, from the gods of the party hierarchy.

It was also the occasion upon which Hitler used the actor's controlled power to hypnotize both himself and his audience, and through the radio the German people, into a sense of mystic unity expressed in the person of a single man, himself. To this end no expense was spared, no device of theatrical art or military display neglected. The properties were thousands of perfectly drilled uniformed men, massed batteries of searchlights meeting thousands of feet up in the night sky, lines of light shining in a darkened arena from the shafts of red and gold standards borne forward through the silent ranks towards the rostrum. And finally the orgasm of the Fuehrer's oration, the white face, the increasingly frenzied gestures, the harsh, rasping voice rising to a scream, as he gave himself wholly, body and soul, to Germany, and Germany through the packed masses in the stadium gave herself to him.

Away from the intoxication of the rally itself there was intoxication of another kind, a great hearty Germanic swilling of beer and guzzling of *Wurst* and backslapping and jollity with the girls who came proudly in their peasant costumes to represent their town or village in the massed parade of German Youth.

Nuremberg was at once a religious ceremony, an American political convention, the Aldershot Military Tattoo, and a jumbo-sized spectacular in VistaVision and glorious Technicolor.

In 1938, it was something more. It was the place upon which the eyes of the world were concentrated, the city in which the world's future seemed likely to be decided.

Everyone was there; not only the leaders of the Nazi hierarchy, Hitler himself, Goering, Hess, Ribbentrop, Goebbels, but a multitude of generals and officials, foreign ambassadors, hundreds of journalists.

Everyone was looking for a sign. At a diplomatic reception, François-Poncet, the French Ambassador, tried to draw Hitler out: he hoped the Fuehrer would give him a favourable forecast.

"What about?" asked the Fuehrer with grim geniality. "The weather? The weather forecast is always wrong."

And so the world was left to its speculations. "Hitler to Speak on Monday," shouted the newspaper placards in a dozen languages. "Hitler: Will It Be Peace?" "Hitler: New Developments." How he must have loved it, the Vienna gutter-rat translated into this omniscient, omnipotent, barbarian god. But it was also very trying for his opponents' nerves.

The British Ambassador, sleek and suave, with his black hat and a red carnation in his buttonhole, reached Nuremberg on the early morning of Wednesday, September 7, and was conducted to a sleeping compartment in the train reserved for diplomats which stood in a siding at Nuremberg North Station. This tiny compartment was to be Henderson's home and Embassy for the next five days.

The Ambassador, already in poor health, was soon to feel much worse. He was taut and nervy by temperament, and the hysterical atmosphere of Nuremberg, piled on top of an international crisis and the claustrophobia of the cramped compartment, brought him almost to a state of breakdown.

He may have had some hope that the complete lack of secrecy in the crowded diplomatic train would at least give him a rest from the incessant bombardment of advice and questions from London. If he did hope so, he was to be disappointed. In London, Chamberlain's Inner Cabinet, Halifax, Hoare and Simon, together with a shifting population of advisers, Wilson, Cadogan, Vansittart, sat in an almost continuous huddle, worrying over the telegrams from Prague, Berlin, Paris, listening to the news reports on the radio, wondering what they could do to influence events, and changing their minds two or three times in the course of an afternoon.

On the day of Henderson's arrival in Nuremberg, they had been given a new date to worry about. This came by devious routes from Weizsaecker at the German Foreign Ministry, who was in touch with Beck and the other conspirators. Associated with Weizsaecker was another professional diplomat, Erich Kordt, head of Ribbentrop's personal secretariat. Erich's elder brother, Theodor, was Counsellor at the German Embassy in London, and a message from Weizsaecker was memorized by the Kordts' cousin, Susanne Simons, who conveyed it to Theodor Kordt in London. The older Kordt was enshrouded by the British even in their most secret communications in the mysterious identity of Herr X. Proclaiming that he put conscience before loyalty, Herr X conveyed Weizsaecker's message to Wilson, Chamberlain's adviser. The Prime Minister himself at that time was in Scotland, but Wilson took Kordt to Halifax, who thought the message so important that he asked Chamberlain to return to London.

Weizsaecker wanted the British Government to broadcast a message to the German people, telling them that war was inevitable if Germany attacked Czechoslovakia. This was thought to be as theatrical as Goerdeler's proposal in the following year that Chamberlain should broadcast to Germany from a battleship in the North Sea, and dismissed out of hand.

What did set the British gnawing their nails with anxiety was a statement from Weizsaecker through Kordt that Hitler had definitely taken the decision to march on September 19 or 20;

that is, in less than a fortnight's time. The information was untrue, and the evidence suggests that Weizsaecker must have known it was untrue. He no doubt wished to impress upon the British the urgency of the situation. What he succeeded in doing was to help bring about that "chemical dissolution" of Czechoslovakia for which he had been working so hard.

At the same time as Weizsaecker's message came the news that negotiations between the Henleinists and the Czechoslovak Government had been broken off as a result of the incident at Mährisch-Ostrau.

The combination of these two pieces of information led the Inner Cabinet to suppose on September 7 that German troops might already be on the move, and on that evening they began drafting a personal appeal from the Prime Minister to Hitler. Before the draft was finished, Wilson heard a news broadcast indicating that events in Czechoslovakia were not so serious after all, and this group of anxious and well-meaning men dispersed for the night to snatch what sleep they could.

On the following morning there was another huddle. All the old ground was gone over—would a new warning to Hitler do more harm than good? If not a warning, then what about Plan Z, Chamberlain's plan for flying to see Hitler, and if Plan Z was to be put into operation, what was the right time to do it—before Hitler spoke at Nuremberg on Monday, September 12, or afterwards? The huddle dispersed undecided, the Prime Minister to produce a draft of a message to Hitler saying he was coming, Cadogan to produce the draft of a warning.

The arrival of Chamberlain by aeroplane in Nuremberg, which seems to have been the original intention, would indeed have toppled that gathering over from hysteria into outright lunacy. But by late afternoon Chamberlain had decided to defer his flight until after the rally was over. There was still argument, however, about whether he should tell Hitler before September 12 that he was coming, in the hope that this would induce the Fuehrer to moderate his words, or whether if he did give Hitler this advance notice, the Fuehrer would rebuff him and so knock this last dramatic card out of his hand.

After more huddling, the Inner Cabinet decided to consult Henderson, and on the next morning a King's Messenger was sent flying off to Nuremberg with a request to the Ambassador for his advice. King's Messengers are retired officers of the British Army, more or less antique, and the original (and presumably hale and hearty) choice for the flight to Nuremberg could not be reached—he was out playing golf. The second string had had five teeth extracted shortly before and was in bed getting over the operation when the summons to duty came. His arrival in Nuremberg created a sensation. Was he the bearer of the British ultimatum which diplomats and journalists had been daily expecting? Of even greater moment, where was he to sleep? Henderson's official conducting-officer, a serious young lieutenant of the S.S., fought a long battle with the head of Protocol to secure accommodation for the King's Messenger in the diplomatic train. The head of Protocol was adamant; if he accommodated King's Messengers, he pointed out, he would immediately be confronted by extravagant demands from the Italian Ambassador, who was already plaguing the life out of him. The poor toothless warrior, nearly in a state of collapse, unfed since morning and able to masticate only scrambled egg, had to be tucked away in an overcrowded hotel.

Next morning, it was found that the King's Messenger could not get a civil flight beyond Cologne, and the British Government had to send a special plane to take him from Cologne to London. More sensational rumours. The advice from Henderson which he took back, however, was immoderately in favour of moderation. It was written for the most part on blank leaves torn from detective novels, because the Ambassador had omitted to bring any writing paper with him. Henderson did not think the Prime Minister should come to Nuremberg. Nor "for Heaven's sake" should there be another warning of the kind given on May 21. "The form of Hitler's genius is on the borderline of madness. He may already have stepped over the edge as some people believe . . . A second 21st May will push him over the edge. That I truly and honestly believe: if not of actual madness, of mad action." It was not Hitler, one may think, who was mad.

Henderson emphasized that he had talked to everybody at Nuremberg, except Hitler, telling them that if Germany marched against Czechoslovakia, Britain could not remain uninterested. He had found even Ribbentrop unusually reasonable. Goering, with whom he had paced for two hours up and down the terrace of a mountain hotel, had told him that the Czechoslovak question would have to be settled, but as yet there was no time limit.

The anxious men in London, studying these impassioned letters, decided to let Henderson have his way. No formal warning was to be given. Moreover, further movements of ships of the Royal Navy, about which there had been discussion, would be cancelled. This was a pity. A discreet announcement in *The Times* on the morning of Saturday, September 10, that the battleship *Royal Oak* and a destroyer flotilla had sailed from Rosyth, in Scotland, for Portsmouth on the English Channel, had brought the German naval attaché racing round to the Admiralty to ask for an explanation. The explanation he was given was not reassuring. He told the Director of Naval Intelligence that no one in Germany had believed Britain would go to war, and said twice that now he himself, for the first time, understood the possibility.

Deprived of that traditional British solace, the Royal Navy, the worried men in Downing Street gave themselves something to do by drafting and redrafting Plan Z.

In Nuremberg on that Saturday, Hitler stood in the pouring rain while thousands of uniformed Hitler Youth dedicated their services to him. Henderson noted that the Fuehrer was looking tense, unable to relax even among his young worshippers. The Fuehrer had reason for his tension. He had been up until half-past three that morning, hectoring his recalcitrant generals about Operation Green. They were still obstinately insisting on a Verdun-type siege of the Czechoslovak fortifications, instead of listening to the *Blitzkrieg* gospel of their Fuehrer.

"It is catastrophic for tanks to have to stop and wait for infantry," Hitler shouted at them. "This contradicts all laws of logic."

They went dutifully away to think again. But still no date was set for Operation Green.

Monday, September 12. The newspaper placards shouted: "Hitler Speaks Tonight." In London, the Inner Cabinet, having spent the day in a series of huddles, apprehensively turned on their radios.

In Nuremberg, the day began with one of those juggernaut displays of German military might which, as was part of the intention, sent shivers down the spine of poor Mastny, the Czechoslovak Minister. He said despondently to his military attaché, "We can never stand up to that."

"We have all that, too," the attaché retorted defiantly; but Mastny was not consoled.

In the Nuremberg stadium, at two minutes to seven, the searchlights hitting the sky proclaimed the Fuehrer's entrance. It took him twelve minutes to pass through the disciplined ranks to the rostrum, and to the world by its radios came a continuous savage bay, "*Sieg Heil! Sieg Heil! Sieg Heil!*"

At ten minutes past seven the Fuehrer's party deputy, Rudolf Hess, brown-shirted and beetle-browed, announced simply that the Fuehrer was about to speak.

And there he was under the spotlights, the man whose word meant peace or war, the failed artist who now had Europe for his canvas.

He began genially, warming up the audience with simple, ponderous jokes. Then the harsh voice began to rise as the orator seemed to lose control of himself but never quite did—the demagogue's clenched fist beat into the other open palm—a snarled "*Ich spreche von der Tschechoslowakei.*" Even Chamberlain, who spoke no German, could understand that Hitler had reached the subject of Czechoslovakia.

What followed sounded appalling, and in a sense it was. Such torrents of abuse of Benes and the Czechoslovaks were still at that time a shock to civilized sensibilities.

But what Hitler said left him carefully short of the brink. He made no new demands, not even the demand for a plebiscite in the Sudetenland which had been expected. He uttered no new threats, not even the hint of a date by which a settlement must be reached.

It was, Henderson assured his anxious masters, no more than a good debating speech, which left everybody back where they had been before the May Crisis.

But there were now two differences. In May, Henderson emphasized, there had been time for investigation or discussion. Now, only immediate implementation of genuine autonomy for the Sudetenland could stop Hitler from marching.

And since May, Henderson pointed out, Britain had so publicly committed herself to France that "if after all this, Germany deliberately and maliciously attacks Czechoslovakia and His Majesty's Government do no more than express their disapproval, we shall be regarded in Germany with universal contempt . . . We shall have irretrievably forfeited German respect and lost any chance of moderating vaulting ambition of extremists."

Henderson might have added that his Government would have irretrievably forfeited not only German respect, but that of the world. For this was what the good intentions of that decent, civilized, conscientious huddle of men had led them to.

CHAPTER 14

Eger-Prague

AT NUREMBERG, basking in an unusual and entirely welcome importance, were the Sudeten German leaders, Henlein and Frank, together with a number of their lesser colleagues.

A few days before Hitler's speech, Brand, the Henleinist representative in London, had been sent off with one of Vansittart's calming messages to Henlein. Would Henlein see the Fuehrer and impress upon him that nothing should be said at Nuremberg which would make war more likely? Brand set off for Berlin, where Bürger, the Henleinist representative there, put every possible difficulty in his way. It was not known where Henlein was, he could not be bothered with such a message, it was all impossible. Brand telephoned in turn to Prague, Henlein's home at Asch, finally Nuremberg. Henlein took a long time to come to the telephone, and when he did so, he was in a very bad temper, telling Brand he had no right to leave London at such a time.

When Brand gave him Vansittart's message, Henlein said crossly, "How can I speak directly to Hitler? I will see." This is a fair indication of the relationship between Hitler and himself. He was a man of no very great importance, and he knew it.

Henlein also, either in this telephone conversation or a later one, instructed Brand to meet him in Prague after the Nuremberg rally. This suggests that, although Henlein knew something was going to happen, it was not going to happen immediately after Nuremberg.

In Nuremberg, after the speech, the little group of Sudeten German leaders excitedly foregathered to discuss its implications. With them was Werner Lorenz, of the *Volksdeutsche Mittelstelle*. Neuwirth, bustling and self-important, left the group to telephone journalist friends in Prague, asking what the reaction to the speech had been. They told him it had caused a lot of excitement, but on the whole things were quiet, though nobody knew what Benes would do. Neuwirth made a note of these conversations, and took it to Henlein. Neither Henlein nor Frank showed any interest in the report, but Lorenz did, and insisted on carrying it straightaway to Ribbentrop. He returned a few minutes later with Ribbentrop's thanks and a reply: "You Sudeten Germans need not expose yourselves, it is not necessary."

Schnapps was poured out, and there followed an hour's genial conversation, during which there was no talk of war. In the course of it, Henlein told Neuwirth to telephone Sebekovsky in Prague and arrange for the remaining members of the party executive to meet him at party headquarters in Eger on the following day, September 13. If Hitler's speech was to be the signal for a rising planned by Henlein and Frank, as historians have suggested, then certainly they were in no hurry to place themselves at the head of it.

On the morning of September 13, the party left Nuremberg to drive to Eger. At the Bavarian frontier, they were warned by the German frontier guards that there was trouble in the Sudetenland. Henlein and Frank held a hurried conference in the road beside the cars. Henlein himself decided not to cross the frontier immediately, but to drive on to Selb, in Bavaria. Frank and the others continued to Eger, where, according to Neuwirth, there was much military and police activity, but no violence.

In the Sudetenland on the previous evening, towns and villages had seemed completely deserted. Everybody was at home or in the *Gasthaus*, listening to the broadcast of the Fuehrer's speech. Then they went out into the streets to discuss, argue, demonstrate, sometimes to fight.

Both Henleinists and their political opponents had some arms, and Sudeten German extremists certainly engaged in organized, if rather amateur, military exercises. Stopford of the Runciman

Mission found himself in the middle of one such exercise while driving by night from Prague into the Sudetenland.

On the night of Hitler's speech, shots began to fly in a dozen Sudetenland towns, and in some border areas Czech police and officials were besieged in their government buildings.

Every eye-witness with whom I have spoken, however—Sudeten German Social Democrat as well as Henleinist—is convinced that there was nothing amounting to an organized armed rising. Dr. Köllner, the Henleinist Party organizer, was one of the Henleinist leaders who returned with Henlein and Frank from Nuremberg. He is a forceful man, whose word in such matters carries conviction. He said, "I can assure you that if *we* had organized a rising, it would not have been like *that*." Herr Ernst Paul, a Sudeten German Social Democrat leader, was in Prague, in touch by telephone with his party branches throughout the Sudetenland. He tells me that in Eger itself, headquarters of the Henleinists, four revolvers fired by Social Democrats in an echoing archway started a wild rumour among the Henleinists that they were being attacked with machine guns. In another town, a couple of thunder flashes were enough to send hundreds of Henleinist demonstrators flying.

Not all the shots were fired by the Henleinists. Major Sutton-Pratt, the assistant British military attaché, reported from Eger that after Hitler's speech, thousands of Sudeten Germans marched out into the streets in frenzied, spontaneous joy. Some were carrying swastika banners, stones were thrown at the windows of Jewish shops, but most of the crowd were orderly. On the following morning in Eger, Czechoslovak police claimed that they had been fired on from a window, and shot back into the excited crowd, killing one man. The police sent for troops. Five tanks and two armoured cars drove into the town, indiscriminately firing blank cartridges, with some live ammunition. Sutton-Pratt tried to speak to the tank commander, who fired at him. When the British military attaché did manage to get near, the tank commander insisted that it was his duty to clear the streets, and continued through the town, still firing. "I consider the tank personnel quite lost their heads," Sutton-Pratt added.

Tachau was an almost wholly Sudeten German town some

eight miles from the Bavarian border. On the German side of the frontier a loudspeaker which could be heard two or three miles away blared out at regular intervals a march of patriotic significance to the Egerland, which had been adopted by the Henleinists, interspersed with the repeated message: "Wait! We Germans won't forget you!" On September 13, the people of Tachau gathered in the market square. They were excited, but there was no fighting. Shortly after one o'clock, Czechoslovak troops and armed police moved in. A company of soldiers took up station surrounding the municipal buildings. What provocation was offered is not known, but suddenly the troops opened fire. Among the eleven people killed was a doctor who had no politics and was married to a half-Jewish wife.

This was the situation in the Sudetenland which confronted the Henleinist leaders when they met at three o'clock on the afternoon of September 13 in their headquarters at Eger. Henlein was not with them, though he seems by that time to have crossed the frontier and to have gone straight to his own home at Asch, twenty miles from Eger. At one o'clock the Czechoslovak Government had proclaimed martial law throughout the Egerland. It can fairly be claimed that the situation justified them in doing so, but they certainly acted with unaccustomed decision. Frank, according to his colleagues, was in a very excited state, furious at the proclamation of martial law and at the resulting indiscriminate firing on Sudeten German civilians, of which highly coloured reports were reaching the Henleinist headquarters. In this mood, he telephoned Hodza in Prague, and roughly presented him with an ultimatum: the Government must immediately withdraw the State Police from the Sudetenland, repeal martial law, confine Czechoslovak troops to barracks, and transfer control of the police and security services to local Sudetenland authorities. He ended by giving Hodza half-an-hour to consider the terms and telephone back.

There is some confusion about where this ultimatum originated. One can say with fair confidence that it was not from Hitler. There is on record a brief snatch of telephone conversation between Henlein and Hitler on that day, which the Czechoslovak security services claimed to have tapped.

"You have presented an ultimatum to the Czech Government," said the Fuehrer, who, according to the transcript, sounded worried. "Was it well considered? What will you do if the ultimatum expires unanswered?"

"I shall immediately dissolve the negotiating delegation and break off the talks with the Czech Government," Henlein replied.

There was a short silence, then Hitler answered, "That's correct, Henlein, very well! Excellent! An excellent idea!"

Neuwirth, who was present at the meeting at Eger when the ultimatum was produced, believes that it was conceived by Frank himself, and was not subject to any discussion. Köllner, also present, thinks there was some discussion. Sebekovsky is not sure, but says that in any event he agreed with the ultimatum. When I asked Sebekovsky what it was intended to achieve, he said, "With hindsight, I suppose we thought we were appealing to France, Britain and Germany to help us against the Czechs. You may think us very naive, but we never believed that our affairs in the Sudetenland could possibly lead to war."

It was an anxious little group which waited in the Henleinist headquarters, expecting arrest at any moment, for the telephone call from Hodza. At the end of the stipulated half-an-hour Hodza did telephone, accepting the ultimatum on condition that a Henleinist representative went to Prague to negotiate a restoration of order.

Immediately after this conversation, according to Neuwirth, Frank turned to the group and said, "I am ordered by Henlein to dissolve the Sudeten German Party. No one has the right to negotiate with the Prague Government in the name of the Party." He then proclaimed melodramatically that he was going to Asch, "to the frontier," adding, "Who goes to the frontier shall follow me."

Some of those who followed him to the frontier were extremely half-hearted, and a few of the moderates, including Neuwirth, returned to Prague, where in spite of Frank's prohibition they tried to get negotiations going again. The German radio reported that they had been killed in Prague. In fact, they were not even put under very close arrest. On September 15, Neuwirth was sent for by the Minister of the Interior, who told him politely, "We can't guarantee your safety, so I will give you a secret agent of the State Police to look after you." With this escort, Neuwirth subsequently set out on a tour of the Sudetenland, including the fortified areas. It was a very civilized form of arrest.

Frank, however, remained on "the frontier," where he continued to behave like a Wagner hero. On the night of September 14, Brand, who had remained with Frank, claims to have overheard a telephone talk of great significance between Frank and Hitler. Frank implored Hitler to send tanks and troops to Eger and Asch. Hitler answered, according to Brand, "Frank, wait still some time. It is not the right time." On September 15, perhaps as a result of Frank's appeal, there was a discussion at Keitel's headquarters as to whether the preparations for Operation Green could be hurried forward. The decision was that they could not be, because of the rail commitments to the Siegfried Line.

It can be reasonably inferred from the behaviour of Henlein and Frank throughout this period that they had some knowledge of Operation Green, and that an "incident," perhaps even a rising, was to be provided in the Sudetenland to supply an excuse for the invasion of Czechoslovakia. But Operation Green could not begin until October 1 at the earliest. How, then, can one account for the events of September 12 and 13?

On the basis of the evidence I have outlined, I reject the answer usually given by historians, that Hitler's Nuremberg speech was the signal for a rising in the Sudetenland, which was to provide the excuse for a German invasion, and which misfired because of prompt action by the Czechoslovak Government. What is missing from such a story is any explanation of why Hitler, who was no fool, should deliberately create a situation in mid-September of which he was not prepared to take military advantage until nearly three weeks later. I think there was to have been an "incident" later, but the so-called "rising" on September 12 and 13 was not it.

There are, it seems to me, three possible answers. The first is that Sudeten Germans more extreme than Henlein and Frank were disappointed by the comparative mildness of Hitler's speech at Nuremberg and took matters into their own hands. This is quite possible, and would account for the patchy nature of the outbreaks of violence, and the inefficiency of their execution. But it would exonerate Henlein and Frank from a greater part of the blame history has laid on their shoulders.

A second possible answer is to be found in an examination of Frank's character. He was a hothead, described by Hitler as a damned fool, and he was in a highly romantic and excitable state. He had tried once, in March, to persuade Hitler to "liberate" the Sudetenland immediately, and had failed. He, too, may have been disappointed by the Nuremberg speech, and was trying to force Hitler's hand.

As an alternative to this answer, Frank may have acted too soon because he had not been told enough. It seems clear that he and Henlein knew something about Operation Green, but they may not have been given any indication of the delay before it could take place. Henlein and Frank were, after all, very small fry in the Nazi scheme of things. Frank was certainly indiscreet, and it is unlikely that they were told more than was strictly necessary. As against this line of argument, the whole tenor of what Henlein and Frank are known to have been told is summed up in the instructions they were given at Breslau: "Hold on and wait." The German loudspeakers were bellowing out to the Sudetenland the repeated message, "Wait." The telephone conversation between Hitler and Frank that Brand claims to have overheard repeated the same theme, "Frank, wait still some time." If Frank still had not got the message clear, then he was a bigger damned fool than Hitler believed.

I do not myself think, however, that the answer lies with Henlein, Frank, the Sudeten Germans or Hitler. I think it is to be sought in Prague, among those Czech nationalists who had been responsible for the May Crisis, and who were trying to repeat tactics which had proved so successful then.

It must be remembered that Benes was now a man under the most desperate pressure. He had been told both by Runciman and Newton that he must accept the Karlsbad terms, or lose any hope of British support. On the morning of September 7 a notorious leading article in the London *Times* had given a hint of worse possibilities. The Czechoslovak Government, warned *The Times*, might well consider allowing the Sudeten Germans to secede from Czechoslovakia. Although the British Foreign Office immediately denied that the article was officially inspired, it did in fact reflect views which Chamberlain himself had privately expressed. On September 8, Frank had presided in Prague over a joint meeting of Henleinists, Slovak, Hungarian and Polish separatists, who agreed to act together "on the urgent reconstruction of the Czechoslovak state"—a warning to Benes, if he needed one, that it would not be enough to satisfy only the Sudeten Germans.

The pressure on Benes for concessions increased the Czech nationalist pressure on him to take a firm stand. In explaining a few days later why the Government had been forced to proclaim martial law, Krofta, the Foreign Minister, said that part of the reason was "pressure of Czech circles dissatisfied with the Government's compliant attitude." On September 9, the Supreme Defense Council received a memorandum, nominally from Krejci, the Chief of Staff, but bearing some signs of the hand of that determined man, Colonel Emanuel Moravec. The memorandum urged the politicians to resist: "The army is under the impression that all the interminable negotiations and humiliations are the result of an overestimation of the strength of our northern neighbour and underestimation of our own potential strength . . . Even if we are unable to prevent a possible insurrection, we can make it more difficult and break it up right from the beginning."

It is evident from Moravec's book that he at least was constantly pressing for full-scale mobilization, and there were repeated rumours, as there had been in May, of a military coup if the Government would not agree. A supposed rising in the Sudetenland gave an excuse for mobilization, and there is no doubt that, from September 13 onwards, the Czechoslovak General Staff were quietly getting on with it.

It is not beyond the bounds of possibility that somebody knew his Frank, and counted on being able to stampede that erratic man into breaking off negotiations, at the very moment when they seemed on the point of presenting the Henleinists with a resounding triumph.

Historically, Henlein and Frank did break off negotiations over the Sudetenland, as Runciman duly reported. The question re-

mains, did they fall, or were they pushed; and if they were
pushed, by whom? It seems fairly certain that it was not by Hitler.
Benes, however, seems to have received the news of these events
with some satisfaction. When a Sudeten German Social Democrat
delegation went to see him at Hradcany Castle on September 13,
he greeted them with the words, "Gentlemen, diplomatically we
have won the war already."

There is no direct evidence to suggest that, if there was a plan
to stampede the Henleinists into precipitate action, Benes knew
of it or countenanced it. But one may briefly suggest certain
short-term advantages which such a plan might have been expected to produce. As a minimum, the breaking of negotiations
by the Henleinists presented Benes with a propaganda victory
which was invaluable in winning world opinion to the Czech
side. But there were gains which might be expected—a repetition,
for instance, of the British warning to Germany that had been
produced by the May Crisis. And if Benes knew of the German
generals' plans for action against Hitler when the order to march
on Czechoslovakia was given, he may have calculated that that
trap could be sprung if a crisis were manufactured in the
Sudetenland.

These are conjectures only, in that subterranean world of
political intrigue which threw up the Tukhachevsky affair, and of
which one can only say that everything is improbable, nothing
impossible. But if Benes, or anyone else in Prague, was thinking
in this way, their hopes were to be ironically disappointed. For the
events of May were not repeated. There was no firm British warning in Berlin. And far from having won the war diplomatically,
Benes had lost it. What remained to be seen was whether he was
prepared to fight it militarily.

CHAPTER 15

Tuesday the Thirteenth

IN THE EARLY DAYS of a golden September, as Londoners returned from their summer holidays to the realization that there was an international crisis, crowds began to gather in Whitehall, with its blocks of Government offices, and in Downing Street, that short, grey, undistinguished thoroughfare leading down from Whitehall to St. James's Park. Here, at Number 10 Downing Street, the Prime Minister's official residence, the anxious members of the Inner Cabinet sat in almost continuous conference.

The Times reported that on the evening of September 12, the night of Hitler's speech at Nuremberg, the crowds were curious, perhaps a little anxious, very quiet. "When there was conversation, someone recalled the first days of August, 1914, when exuberant processions marched round Trafalgar Square and the West End singing patriotic songs and waving Union Jacks and the French tricolor. 'You wouldn't get that now,' he said, and added an opinion that the present crisis would lead to no fighting."

An articulate young man expressed to a reporter a commonly held view: "I hate the Hitlerian philosophy. I believe it's a world menace. But our Government has made such a mess of everything that I would rather be shot than be led up the garden path."

By nine o'clock that evening, the crowd in and around Downing Street numbered about nine thousand people. Some were frankly sightseers. Any event in Whitehall, however insignificant, caused a stir of excitement. A red Post Office van pulled up in front of Number 10, and a woman called out dramatically, "They're bringing dispatches."

146

"Naw, lady, them's 'is love letters," came a shouted retort, capped by, "Who'd fall in love with Chamberlain's front teeth? Not me, I want something to look at."

But others were more serious. In Whitehall, it was noticed, men took particular care to raise their hats, or otherwise salute, when passing the Cenotaph, the memorial to the dead of the First World War.

The crisis, however, still did not command the popular attention which had been excited by the abdication of King Edward VIII two years before. A special edition of the London *Evening Standard*, published on the night of the King's abdication, sold nearly a quarter of a million copies. A special edition reporting Hitler's speech sold a hundred thousand copies fewer.

An opinion poll taken on September 13 showed that 55 percent of the people of Britain believed there would be no war. Another 30 percent said either that they did not know or did not care.

Throughout the morning and early afternoon of September 13, exaggerated reports of the rising in the Sudetenland flowed into Number 10 Downing Street. It seemed only too probable that this was the "incident" justifying the German march into Czechoslovakia of which Kleist and Kordt had given warning. The Inner Cabinet's huddles took on an even more feverish tone. Chamberlain was pressed to authorize mobilization, but he refused. He was, however, willing to allow some precautionary measures to be taken, but these amounted to little more than warning orders to territorial battalions to be prepared to mobilize.

In Paris, there was an important and acrimonious Cabinet meeting. The "hawks" of the French Government, Mandel and Reynaud, stiffened by Churchill, who was in Paris, were pressing for further mobilization measures. The doves deployed against them all the arguments so assiduously collected by Bonnet from Roosevelt, Halifax, Lindbergh, Gamelin, Litvinov. It seemed a cast-iron case, and yet it was not strong enough. Six members of the Cabinet remained in favour of mobilization, four were against it, and Daladier apparently sat on the fence. But Bonnet refused to admit defeat.

At half-past seven that evening, the first of a series of telegrams came into Downing Street from Paris. Phipps, the British Ambassador, reported that he had seen Bonnet after the French

Cabinet meeting. Bonnet was very upset and said that peace must be preserved at any price, as neither France nor Britain was ready for war. "M. Bonnet's collapse seems to me so sudden and extraordinary that I am asking for an interview with M. Daladier."

Phipps found a very different French Prime Minister from the firm, confident leader of a few days previously. Daladier told Phipps, "but with evident lack of enthusiasm," that if the Germans used force, France would be obliged to do so also. He added that of course he would have to be sure Czechoslovakia was in the right.

"I fear," Phipps added sadly, "the French have been bluffing, although I have continually pointed out to them that one cannot bluff Hitler."

Later, Daladier himself telephoned Downing Street, and there was a brief exchange over one of those faulty telephone lines which seem to symbolize Anglo-French relations between the wars. Chamberlain spoke little French and handed the call over to Cadogan, who told Daladier that it was hopeless to talk on the telephone and that the French Prime Minister must give a message to Phipps.

Phipps had gone to the Opéra-Comique, whence he was summoned by Daladier to the War Ministry. Daladier dictated to him a message which bears obvious marks of haste. Entry of German troops into Czechoslovakia must be prevented at all costs. If not, France would be forced to go to war. Daladier proposed that Runciman must either immediately publish his recommendations or somehow get the Henleinists and Czechoslovak Government together again. If neither of these things could be done, "I propose an immediate proposal to Hitler for a meeting of the Three Powers, viz: Germany for the Sudetens, France for the Czechs, and Great Britain for Lord Runciman, with a view of obtaining that pacific settlement advocated by Hitler in his speech last night."

When Phipps came down the steps of the War Ministry carrying this message, assembled journalists excitedly asked him if he had any comment. He answered cryptically, "This bickering will have to stop."

His report of this second Daladier conversation reached Downing Street at about eleven o'clock, and M. Daladier tells me that he received a telegram in reply stating that the British Prime Minister "had thought of something else similar and that he would inform me."

Daladier was hoping for a joint Anglo-French approach to Hitler. Chamberlain, however, had no intention of allowing the French to spoil his long-pondered attempt to meet the Fuehrer face to face. At last the moment had come. The weary, anxious hours spent during the last few days drafting and redrafting Plan Z had not been in vain. The message telephoned to Henderson shortly after eleven o'clock that night was Plan Z in its simplest form:

"You should ensure through Ribbentrop the delivery at the earliest possible moment of the following message to Herr Hitler as a personal message to him from Prime Minister:

" 'In view of increasingly critical situation I propose to come over at once to see you with a view to trying to find peaceful solution. I propose to come across by air and am ready to start tomorrow.

" 'Please indicate earliest time at which you can see me and suggest meeting. Should be grateful for very early reply. Neville Chamberlain.' "

CHAPTER 16

Priam and Achilles

AT ABOUT QUARTER PAST nine on the following evening, Wednesday, September 14, the crowds waiting patiently in Downing Street for something to happen were awakened to sudden life by the sight of forty or fifty men leaving the door of Number 10 and making at a sharp trot for the telephone kiosks round the corner in Whitehall and further afield.

People began to gather outside the kiosks, pushing and scrambling as they tried to read through the glass panels the message which the journalists inside were telephoning to their newspapers. The doors of the kiosks were soon jammed by dozens of milling people, and police had to be called to let the journalists out. But the message spread from mouth to mouth: the Prime Minister was flying to see Hitler. There was a cheer, and shouts of "Good old Chamberlain!"

In Berlin, a special edition of the *Deutsche Allgemeine Zeitung* was rushed on to the streets, with the news splashed across the front page like a declaration of peace. Crowds mobbed newspaper sellers in the Kurfurstendamm, grabbing the papers from their hands, and as people read the news, strained faces cleared, and there was talk and laughter.

One small group of Germans, however, was aghast. These were the Beck conspirators, who claim to have had their plans worked out in detail for a coup timed to take place in the interval between the issue of the order to attack Czechoslovakia and the beginning of troop movements. "As we waited with mounting anxiety in those tension-filled days of early September 1938," wrote Fabian von Schlabrendorff, one of the opposition group, "we received the news that Britain's Prime Minister was coming to Germany not to protest against Hitler's warlike tactics, but to talk peace with the German dictator." How they knew this is not quite clear, and Hitler himself seems to have believed the contrary; but for whatever reason, the wind was taken completely out of the conspirators' sails.

In Prague, too, the news was received with dismay. At first it was greeted with incredulity, as a wild piece of sensational reporting. When it was confirmed, there was consternation. Benes's close associate Hubert Ripka was at home with a group of politicians and diplomats when his paper telephoned the news to him. "We rang up the Government departments concerned to find out what they thought about it, and from all quarters came replies that it was 'very serious,' 'very bad,' 'extremely dangerous.'"

Mussolini, too, was shocked. "This is the liquidation of English prestige," he told Ciano. "In two years England has twice been floored." Goodbye to Chamberlain's hopes of detaching Italy from Germany.

But most of Britain did not see it as the liquidation of English prestige. In 1938, summit meetings between heads of Government were rarer than they have subsequently become, and what Léon Blum called the "noble audacity" of the sixty-nine-year-old Chamberlain caught the public imagination. The Prime Minister was so clearly an Edwardian, if not a Victorian, in dress and demeanour. Now he was making spectacular contact with contemporaneity by flying for the first time in an aeroplane. The gesture acquired almost the solemnity of a national sporting occasion: England playing Germany away, in the World Cup. "Good luck to the old boy, I didn't know 'e 'ad it in 'im," was a frequent remark, and "It took everybody by surprise, didn't it? I wish the Labour Party had thought of it. Now Chamberlain will go down in history for it. I used to think he was a twister, but this makes you think twice."

The popularity of the Prime Minister soared to dizzy heights. In March, according to an opinion poll, 28 percent of the population had been satisfied with the Government's policy, 32 percent were against it, 40 percent didn't know. Now 70 percent expressed themselves in favour of Chamberlain, 20 percent were not sure or didn't know, and only 10 percent were against him.

John Masefield, the Poet Laureate, whose duty it was to transmute the wine of his royal pension into the water which Englishmen regard as proper for official verse, voiced the feelings of many:

> As Priam to Achilles for his son,
> So you, into the night, divinely led,
> To ask that young men's bodies, not yet dead,
> Be given from the battle not begun.

The Prime Minister in fact left at half-past eight on the morning of September 15, in bright sunshine, but one must not debase poetry to the level of journalism by a pedantic insistence upon accuracy.

Another, though perhaps less widely held, view was that the British lion was about to utter a resounding roar. This was the opinion apparently held by Hitler himself, who later told Lipski, the Polish Ambassador in Berlin, that he thought Chamberlain was coming solemnly to inform him that Britain was ready to take armed action. Hitler's words are generally not to be accepted at their face value, but in this case he can probably be believed. The Wehrmacht could not be ready until October 1. Hitler's Viceroy in the Sudetenland had allowed himself to be completely outmaneuvered, and was now running round in ever-diminishing circles. The German generals had left the Fuehrer in no doubt about their opinion that Germany was not ready for war. Hitler had many reasons for thinking that he was about to be faced with a most unpleasant situation.

But Hitler's appreciation of Chamberlain's mind was as wrong as his later one that the old gentleman with the umbrella could be frightened out of any decisive action. It has been claimed on Chamberlain's behalf, and it can be demonstrated from his own contemporary words, that he was a shrewd statesman playing for time, following a realistic policy based on a cool calculation of British weakness, French instability, the impossibility of doing anything practical to save Czechoslovakia. These were the arguments which swayed Halifax and other members of the British Cabinet. They were considered by, but they did not sway, Chamberlain. His first consideration was, quite simply, the rightness of peace and the wrongness of war. It was right that the Sudeten Germans should be allowed to choose their own future. It was wrong that Czechoslovakia should be devastated and millions of people killed, wounded, rendered homeless and starving, to no useful purpose. This was the policy of appeasement in action. At the root of Chamberlain's belief was moral strength, not weakness. Whatever else he may have been, Chamberlain was no coward.

Churchill, asked later by Ian Colvin if he would have gone to meet Hitler, answered, "Yes, but I would have invited Herr Hitler to come and meet me, in the North Sea, on board a British battleship." The battleship's crew would undoubtedly have behaved as impeccably as those sad symbols of lost British naval supremacy, *Prince of Wales* and *Repulse*, sunk off the coast of Malaya in 1941 because they had no air cover. But certainly a more grandiose man than Chamberlain might have had ideas of flying to Germany in a bomber, with a fighter escort. Instead he went in a fast but small commercial plane, an eight-seater Lockheed-Electra of the nationalized British Airways. Churchill would no doubt have had a few imposing-looking generals and admirals among his staff. Chamberlain took with him two civilians, Sir Horace Wilson, his adviser, and the Foreign Office expert on Central Europe, William (now Lord) Strang. None of the three spoke fluent German. This small party was joined at Munich Airport by Henderson, jumpy, articulate, but still beautifully dressed. They were not perhaps men calculated to impress upon Hitler a sense of the awful might of the British Empire; but it was not Chamberlain's intention that they should.

The party took off from Heston Airport in brilliant September weather, but over the Continent the small twin-engined plane ran into thick cloud and had a bumpy passage through rainstorms. The Prime Minister, an elderly man, was nevertheless able to tell Ribbentrop, who met him at Munich Airport, that he had stood his first flight very well. Indeed, one of the remarkable things about Chamberlain was his wiry resilience. Within thirty-six hours, he was to spend fourteen hours in planes, trains and cars, hold an exhausting three-hour conference with Hitler, give an account of these proceedings to his Inner Cabinet, and at the end of it all find time and energy for an audience with King George VI, who had been complaining more in sorrow than in anger that he was not being told anything. The King was not alone. Most of the members of his Government had not been told very much, either.

At Munich railway station, a crowd of several hundreds cheered the British party and shouted *"Heil!"* and, according to a German observer, "it was a little, solemn moment when Chamberlain, at the side of Herr von Ribbentrop, walked with bared head past the bust of the Leader."

On the railway journey from Munich to Berchtesgaden, arrangements had been made for the Prime Minister's train to pass a troop train with hooded guns on trucks and rifles sticking out of the windows. According to Dr. Paul Schmidt, the official interpreter, a similar display mounted two years later for Molotov, the Russian Foreign Minister, drew from Molotov the dry comment: "Ah, now I see we can really begin to negotiate." Chamberlain, according to Schmidt, appeared not to notice the troop train, but continued talking to Ribbentrop.

Another drive by car through rain and cloud up into the mountains above Berchtesgaden to Obersalzberg, and there halfway down the steps of the Berghof stood a man, "bareheaded and dressed in a khaki-coloured coat of broadcloth, with a red armlet and a swastika on it, and the military cross on his breast. He wore black trousers, such as we wear in the evening, and black patent leather lace-up shoes. His hair is brown, not black, his eyes blue, his expression rather disagreeable, especially in repose, and altogether he looks entirely undistinguished. You would never notice him in a crowd, and would take him for the house painter he once was."

Thus Chamberlain's description of his first impression of Hitler. The Fuehrer has left no similar pen-portrait, but Dr. Schmidt tells me that Hitler took Chamberlain for the Minister of Finance and Lord Mayor of Birmingham he once was. They were both wrong.

Among Hitler's numerous entourage, Chamberlain noticed Keitel, "a youngish, pleasant-faced, smart-looking soldier," who was kept in attendance on these occasions as the recipient of ostentatious orders about mobilization and the deployment of troops. Keitel's services this time were as redundant as the troop train.

Tea was laid in the room with the big window overlooking an Austria now hidden by cloud. Behind the Prime Minister was a large Italian nude painting. The teatime chitchat has been described by Lord Strang as best left in oblivion, but Chamberlain thought one passage of it worth recording for posterity.

"I have often heard of this room," he said, "but it's much larger than I expected."

"It is you who have the big rooms in England," the Fuehrer answered politely.

"You must come and see them sometime," replied the Prime Minister.

"I should be received with demonstrations of disapproval," said the Fuehrer.

"Well, perhaps it would be wise to choose the moment," replied Chamberlain, at which Hitler permitted himself the shadow of a smile.

After a tea graced by such exchanges, Hitler asked abruptly what procedure Chamberlain proposed. Did he wish to talk alone or with his experts? Chamberlain answered that he would prefer to talk to the Fuehrer alone, with only an interpreter. According to Dr. Schmidt, this question and answer had been prearranged between Hitler and Chamberlain in order to exclude Ribbentrop. The German Foreign Minister was now regarded by the British as an evil influence on Hitler, in contradistinction to that well-known pacifist Goering. But Hitler also had recently been showing signs of impatience at Ribbentrop's insistent advice that now was the time to force war upon Czechoslovakia, even if this involved France and Britain. There is not much doubt that, up to the point of his first meeting with Chamberlain, Hitler had been following an anti-Ribbentrop line. The subsequent proceedings led him, temporarily at least, to change his mind.

The confrontation itself began with some flattering remarks by Chamberlain about his personal respect for Hitler and the work he had always done for Anglo-German understanding. Hitler had heard a great deal of this before from Halifax, and was almost

certainly expecting Chamberlain at some point to deliver a warning on the lines of that given to Ribbentrop in May. He came impatiently to the point: what was Chamberlain going to do about
the Sudeten Germans? Without giving the Prime Minister time
to reply, he launched into one of those torrents of historical dissertation which, according to Schmidt, he intensely disliked having
interrupted for translation purposes. They seem, in fact, to have
served the same role in Hitler's diplomacy as an artillery barrage,
to soften up the opposition before the real attack began.

If Hitler was indeed expecting an ultimatum, the Prime Minister's answer, when at last Chamberlain could get a word in, must
have forced the Fuehrer to reconsider his tactics.

Chamberlain wasted no time in argument. He simply asked
whether Hitler wanted only the return of three million Sudeten
Germans to the Reich, or was there something else? Would he
go on regarding what remained of Czechoslovakia as a spearhead
aimed at Germany's flank?

Chamberlain was no doubt trying to do two things. Cadogan at
the Foreign Office had been advocating for some time that an
attempt should be made to find out what Hitler really did want,
not only over Czechoslovakia, and to force him out into the open
instead of letting him shelter behind the smoke screen of his constant references to the injustices of Versailles. But although one
can discern this motive in Chamberlain's questions, it was less
important than his anxiety to establish in Hitler's mind the sincerity of his attempt to achieve a peaceful settlement in Europe—
in short, appeasement. A settlement of the Sudeten German problem was to be the pledge of Chamberlain's future intentions.

Hitler was clearly taken aback by Chamberlain's reply, and his
final answer, after some ducking and dodging, came straight out
of the "chemical dissolution" textbook: if the Sudeten Germans
came into the Reich, then the Hungarian minority would secede,
the Polish minority would secede, the Slovak minority would
secede, and what was left would be so small that he would not
bother his head about it.

Again Chamberlain did not argue. He said, "Well, you've stated
pretty clearly what your view is. I'll restate it to show that I've
got it right." He did so, Hitler confirmed it, and without further

discussion Chamberlain, "as a practical man," passed on to the next question. How much of the Sudeten German areas did Hitler want? Chamberlain suggested those with a population more than 80 percent German.

On or about September 15, the date of the Hitler-Chamberlain meeting, Henlein had written a memorandum for the Fuehrer, suggesting that he should demand the immediate cession of regions with more than 50 percent German population. He was to insist that this must be based on the 1918 population figures, before Czech settlers had begun to move into the Sudetenland. Henlein also recommended—a significant reflection of his belief that he and Frank had been tricked over the recent proclamation of martial law and would be tricked again if the Czechs got the chance—that the regions to be given up must be occupied within forty-eight hours by German troops. It is not absolutely certain that Hitler had received this brief in time for his meeting with Chamberlain, but even if he had, his fear may now have been of asking too little rather than too much. At the beginning of the talk, he had been expecting to be told that he would have to fight for the Sudetenland. He had in effect been asked if that was enough—wouldn't the whole of Czechoslovakia be better? And he had given the wrong answer.

He now began to shout that Sudeten Germans were being attacked by gas, "and from German territory could be heard the sound of artillery fire directed against defenseless German villages." At the same time, he said ominously, whole divisions were concentrated on the German side of the frontier and the Luftwaffe was standing ready.

Chamberlain, according to his subsequent accounts, certainly believed that Hitler was threatening an immediate invasion of Czechoslovakia. He had been conditioned to this belief by the warnings from the German generals and Weizsaecker. He afterwards emphasized to a joint Labour Party-Trades Union Congress delegation the Government's knowledge that Hitler contemplated action between September 20 and 28. He told the House of Commons of his conviction that "my visit alone prevented an invasion." He flattered himself. It was a combination of the inadequacy of the German railway system and Hitler's intuition. But intuition, and Chamberlain's calm acceptance of the German demands, was now beginning to tell the Fuehrer that Ribbentrop might be right after all. Chamberlain's reaction, however, was to harden his attitude. He became, as he characteristically put it, "indignant," and threatened to walk out. The Fuehrer, intensely sensitive to atmosphere, saw that he had gone too far, and began to subside in a series of growls. It might after all be possible "today or tomorrow" to explore whether a peaceful settlement could still be achieved. Everything depended on knowing whether the British were prepared to assent to the detachment of the Sudeten German districts on the basis of the right of national self-determination.

Chamberlain replied that he could not commit his Government, and he would have to consult the French Government and Lord Runciman—though not, apparently, the Czechoslovaks. He added that he personally favoured detaching the Sudeten areas, and was prepared to go home to find out whether his Government agreed with him. Then he and the Fuehrer could meet again. In the meantime, would Hitler give an assurance that he would not attack Czechoslovakia?

Then, Chamberlain said afterwards, Hitler's face changed, "and it was not a very nice change . . . Hitler said: 'I will try my best, and I will give you my word that unless something unexpected happens' (meaning unless Sudeten Germans killed or something), 'there will be no trouble on the part of Germany while the consultations are proceeding.'" That "or something" no doubt reflects German suspicion of the hawks in Prague.

Chamberlain added that "Hitler had given him the impression that he would be better than his word." One may note here what better than Hitler's word amounted to. Two days after the Obersalzberg meeting, he authorized the formation of a Sudeten German Freikorps, with the stated purpose of protecting the Sudeten Germans, but also "maintenance of disorders and clashes." A senior German officer with "far-reaching military powers" from the Fuehrer was attached to Henlein as adviser. On the following day, the concentration plan was issued for the five armies which were to attack Czechoslovakia, and Keitel's headquarters set to work on a summary of the military concessions to be exacted from the Czechoslovaks, which makes clear how little the operation had to do with the grievances of the Sudeten Germans. The terms included immediate abandonment of fortifications in the territory to be ceded and their occupation together with that of nearby rail junctions, towns and airfields; demobilization of the entire Czechoslovak armed forces in the rest of the country, and the discharge of all reserves; the discontinuation of the Czechoslovak armament industry until the end of all negotiations; and a ban on building any new fortifications to replace those taken over by the Germans.

The Fuehrer, who had a great talent for self-justification, would no doubt have argued that all these measures were forced upon him by the threat to peace which arose from the continuing existence of Czechoslovakia. They also reflect a hardening of his attitude that can be traced to the effects of his meeting with Chamberlain. The Prime Minister, on his return, told a number of people that he believed the impression he had made upon Hitler had been a good one. His belief rested on his conviction that he had stopped an immediate invasion, which was untrue, and on remarks made to Sir Horace Wilson by members of Hitler's entourage on the way back from Obersalzberg to Munich. Dirksen, the German Ambassador to Britain, said Hitler felt the Prime Minister understood him, and that Hitler appreciated the Prime Minister, "especially the directness with which he had talked and the rapidity with which he had grasped the essentials of the situation." Hewel, Ribbentrop's personal representative on Hitler's staff, revealed that "Hitler told me he was speaking to a *man*." Only Ribbentrop was too honest, or too sulky, to join in this lavish application of flattery.

Weizsaecker revealed what was probably the truth. He wrote in his memoirs of Hitler giving a "lively and joyful description of the conversation" between himself and Chamberlain. The Fuehrer clapped his hands as after a highly successful entertainment. "He felt that he had managed to maneuver the dry civilian into a corner." He had not. The dry civilian got into the corner of his own free will. God help him, he hoped to persuade the Fuehrer that honesty, straightforwardness and common sense could settle the problems of Europe and prevent war. The Fuehrer's opinion of this attempt seems to have been that Chamberlain was a *Schlappschwanz*, a word which cannot be adequately translated but which implies an unflattering appreciation of a man's virility. In that misjudgment lay one of the principal causes of the Second World War.

CHAPTER 17

Indian Summer of a Prime Minister

IN ST. JAMES'S PARK, the autumn crocuses were just coming up. There were as yet no unsightly gashes in the grass. The pretty secretaries and their escorts still made love, not war. The Prime Minister set to work to keep it that way.

Unlike Hitler, he was better than his word. He returned to Germany with the consent not only of his colleagues and of Benes's French allies to a voluntary dismemberment of Czechoslovakia, but with the consent of the Czechoslovak Government also. He achieved all this within the space of a week; and whether or not one agrees with the morality or expediency of it, it was certainly an astonishing *tour de force,* which should have ended before it began the legend of Chamberlain as a weak incompetent who did not know what he was doing.

This sixty-nine-year-old man reached Downing Street after his return flight from Germany at about twenty minutes past six on the evening of Friday, September 16. The Inner Cabinet was waiting for him, and within ten minutes of his arrival he was giving them an account of his first meeting with Hitler. He told them that he believed he had made a good impression on the Fuehrer, but left them with no doubt that this good impression would remain only as long as he delivered the goods. Nothing but self-determination for the Sudeten Germans would do, and the Inner Cabinet wasted no time in disputing his statement. Only the least likely member of the quartet, Sir John Simon, the Chancellor of the Exchequer, apparently considered that Hitler should be asked for some *quid pro quo*. But Simon was given to unexpected displays of belligerence at unlikely moments. They rarely lasted long, since his infinite capacity for seeing all sides of every question often caused him to argue cogently one day against the opinions he had expressed equally cogently the day before.

The full Cabinet, Chamberlain knew, was likely to be less obliging. Its members had been kept almost entirely in the dark about his intentions, they had been told of Plan Z only after the request for a meeting had been dispatched to Hitler, and some of them had reluctantly agreed to the meeting only on the understanding that Chamberlain was going to Obersalzberg to utter a firm warning.

The Cabinet met at eleven o'clock on the morning of September 17, and continued after a luncheon break until the early evening. One may assume that all was not sweetness and light.

Chamberlain does not seem to have thought it necessary to tell his colleagues that he had already given Hitler his personal opinion in favour of self-determination. He produced Lord Runciman to state the case for him, with a wealth of detail. This occupied most of the morning. Some members of the Cabinet, notably Duff Cooper, the First Lord of the Admiralty, resisted Runciman's views and reproached Chamberlain because he had not put to Hitler any of the less drastic propositions which the Cabinet believed he was going with. Chamberlain replied that the atmosphere would not allow it: only his direct intervention had prevented war. Duff Cooper tried to delay a decision by arguing that the Cabinet must have more time for discussion, and that in any event the French would have to be consulted.

Chamberlain coldly asked him if he favoured war. No, of course Duff Cooper did not—how could anyone say otherwise in the shadow of the knockout blow?—but he insisted that the least he was prepared to accept was a plebiscite under international control.

For reasons which will become apparent, this was the one thing Benes would not tolerate; but the proposal had a plausible, respectable ring about it, and although one or two ministers pressed their disagreement with Chamberlain to the point of resignation, they were not prepared to plunge over the brink. The only objection to a plebiscite came from Hore-Belisha, the Minister for War. If British troops were going to control the plebiscite, he pertinently asked, who would protect them if they were attackd by infuriated Czechoslovaks? To this awkward question the War Minister never seems to have got an answer. The agreed decision of the Cabinet was that they would accept an orderly transfer of Czechoslovak territory to Germany after a plebiscite.

Having settled his Cabinet, Chamberlain next turned to the Labour Opposition. That evening he saw the Labour leaders, Hugh Dalton and Herbert Morrison, and the general secretary of the Trades Union Congress, Sir Walter Citrine. The threat was held over the Labour leaders as over the Cabinet: "If Germany conquered Czechoslovakia, would Britain support going to war? Was it possible for the British people to resist the principle of self-determination?"

For the Labour Party, with its continuing pacifist tradition, this was a particularly difficult question and one which they knew they might well have to answer publicly at the polls in a General Election. There had already been hints that, if Chamberlain could secure an agreement with Germany over Czechoslovakia, he should capitalize on his popularity shown in the opinion polls by going to the country. The protagonist of this view in the Cabinet was Sir Kingsley Wood, the Air Minister, a professional politician to the last thinning curl of his cherubic head, whose attitude towards international affairs was summed up in a phrase he frequently used: "Our people"—Conservative workers in the constituencies—"won't like that." "Our people" in this case would very much like peace; and the Labour leaders, remembering the annihilation of their party in the General Election of 1931, had some reason to fear that their people might agree with "our people." The Labour leaders, while publicly making belligerent noises, in private walked with a statesmanlike circumspection. As Dalton put it, "My own view was that openly concerted action between our Party and other critics of the Government would be less useful at this stage than outwardly separate action. Alexander* was inclined to differ, but I warned him of the danger of upsetting a

*The Right Hon. A.V. Alexander, afterwards Viscount Alexander of Hillsborough, First Lord of the Admiralty in Churchill's wartime Government.

large number of people in our own Party, some of whom it had been hard work to bring up to scratch." Approaches to the Labour Party by Churchill for united action against Chamberlain were always rebuffed.

This caution on the part of the Labour leaders had important consequences. Jan Masaryk, the Czechoslovak Minister in London, with his tendency to mistake popularity for influence, was constantly sustained by the hope that Churchill, leading an alliance of Labour, Liberal and dissident Conservative M.P.'s, was strong enough to bring down, or at any rate stiffen, the Chamberlain Government. Churchill apparently did nothing to discourage such a hope. He was in almost daily touch with the Czechoslovak Legation as the crisis mounted towards its climax, and indeed on one occasion was being so abusive of Chamberlain over the telephone that the member of the Legation staff to whom he was talking thought it right to warn him that the telephone might be tapped.

"Egshactly sho, egshactly sho," answered that famous slurred voice, and carried on as before.

The story is characteristic of Churchill, at once funny, endearing, and demonstrating that wild indiscretion on account of which he was so widely distrusted by sound men of all British political parties, and which constantly frustrated Masaryk's hopes of an anti-Chamberlain coalition under Churchill's leadership.

Churchill was also in touch with Georges Mandel and Paul Reynaud, the "certain bellicose French ministers" for whose benefit Bonnet had asked the British Government to provide a copy of their cautionary words of May 22. Mandel and Reynaud were in a stronger position to bring down the French Government than was Churchill in relation to the British Government. But although Mandel and Reynaud may have been hawks, they were at best sparrowhawks. They were always on the point of causing a Government crisis in Paris by resigning, but never quite found the moment opportune to do so.

How far Benes believed Masaryk's sanguine assurances that the British and French Governments could be brought down is a matter for speculation. A practical politician himself, well aware of the ways of politicians, the Czechoslovak President probably did not pin very high hopes on them. But the possibility could be astutely exploited to put pressure on Chamberlain and Daladier, and so substitute for the major surrender which Benes knew Chamberlain had in mind the minor surrender for which he himself was prepared.

Benes prepared the way for this surrender with some care. On the eve of Chamberlain's visit to Obersalzberg, he told both the British and French Ministers in Prague that some areas of Czechoslovakia such as the Egerland could have been excluded from the republic at the postwar peace conference without endangering the existence of the state. He hastened to add that this could not be done now; "Parliament and public opinion would demand as a principle that the integrity of the frontier should be maintained." This was a slightly more concrete amplification of the hint dropped by Masaryk to Halifax in May. But Benes went further. At about this time, he sent Jaromir Necas, the Social Democrat Welfare Minister in the Hodza Government and one of the principal resisters, to Paris to see Léon Blum, the French Socialist leader. Necas carried a map showing what portions of the Sudetenland could be ceded without endangering the Czechoslovak fortifications. The notes of his instructions began with the words, "Never let it be proved that this plan sprang from the Czechoslovaks," and went on to warn that once the principle of cession had been admitted, there was a danger that the French and British Governments might give everything away. What Benes proposed was a limited cession of "so and so many thousand square kilometres of territory (I don't know exactly how many, but it will probably be four to six thousand; one should not commit oneself in this respect)" on condition that Germany also took over between 1½ and 2 million of the Sudeten German population who would otherwise be left in Czechoslovak territory.

The notes set out reasons for opposing a plebiscite which were nicely calculated to appeal to the Jewish Socialist Blum: a plebiscite would mean turning over several hundred thousand democrats, Socialists and Jews to Germany. But "show also, using the map, how our state would look after the holding of a plebiscite, in terms of its shape and the position of Germany." This of course was the real point. The Czechoslovak fortifications were in areas which, under a plebiscite, were certain to go to Germany, and without the fortifications, the Czechoslovaks could not put up even the pretense of resistance.

This brief was passed on to Daladier by Blum, and in spite of Benes's warning, the French Prime Minister seems to have been told where it came from. It was certainly in his hands by the time he and Bonnet left for London on September 18 to hear Chamberlain's report of what had happened at Obersalzberg. But as with so many other clever calculations during the crisis, the effect was the opposite of what had been intended.

The British Cabinet believed that they had firmly committed Chamberlain to a plebiscite. But when the British and French ministers met, Daladier, acting on Benes's brief, declared that it would be "almost impossible" for the French Government to agree to a plebiscite—the Czechoslovak Government would rather fight or cede territory than accept one.

Chamberlain certainly did not argue very strongly on behalf of his Cabinet's decision. He passed straight to the next point: on what scale was cession to take place? The Czechoslovaks would naturally wish to know how much territory they would be expected to give up. Hitler, Chamberlain said, wanted all those areas where more than half the population was Sudeten German. The French Government no doubt had maps which would show approximately what such a claim would mean. The French had indeed. They had the map supplied by Benes, which showed that cession on such a scale meant an end of the Czechoslovak fortifications, and so of Czechoslovakia as a useful ally of France.

Daladier and Bonnet put on a certain amount of shadow-boxing for the Benes line, but Daladier's most impassioned oratory was reserved for the question of a British guarantee of what would remain of Czechoslovakia. France, he said, must have some compensation for the sacrifice to be demanded of the Czechoslovaks. Small though Czechoslovakia was, the alliance was very important to France. From the map it could be seen that Berlin was nearer to the Czechoslovak frontier than Paris was to the German frontier.

"I will be quite frank," Daladier went on. "Measures have already been taken in the event of a German attack on Czechoslovakia to send French air squadrons immediately to that country. From there, they can menace Berlin from closer range than Paris can be menaced from Germany."

Even Chamberlain found this too much to take. In preparation for dealing with Daladier, he had asked for, and during the meeting received, a brief on the state of the French air force, according to which France had no more than twenty-one machines capable of standing up to the performance of German fighters and bombers, and about 700 hundred others, many of which were in North Africa. The British Prime Minister, possessing this knowledge, said coldly that he did not understand how a British guarantee of Czechoslovakia could increase French security. The answer was surely obvious. The French were in danger of a situation arising in which Germany would attack Czechoslovakia, and they would then be bound by a treaty to attack Germany without any firm British commitment to come to their assistance. The guarantee of Czechoslovakia, which Chamberlain had been refusing to give since March, was in effect a British commitment to France.

Chamberlain appeared to resist Daladier's demand, but when the conference adjourned for tea, he astonished his advisers by telling them that he had decided to give the French the guarantee he had been resisting so long and so obstinately. There was to be no consultation with the Cabinet, nor with the Dominions, about this new and, in its implications, far-reaching British commitment. But in return for the guarantee, Chamberlain got what he wanted: French agreement to the dismemberment of Czechoslovakia. Appeasement was to have its chance, and with French backing. During the adjournment, Chamberlain set the experts to work drafting a message to Benes, telling him he must surrender not only the territory outside the fortifications, but all the areas in which there was a Sudeten German majority.

By the time discussions were resumed at half-past seven, this draft message was ready. The French made some changes, which they considered might soften the tone. Chamberlain then pressed urgently for the amended message to be sent off to Prague that night. For once, Daladier dug in his heels. Perhaps he lacked Chamberlain's confidence in the amenability of Cabinets. The most he would concede was that he would let the British have a firm "Yes" or "No" by noon on the following day. Meanwhile, the agreed draft was to be sent to the British and French Ministers in Prague, with instructions to deliver it on receipt of a telephone message.

On the morning of September 19, Chamberlain imperturbably told his astonished Cabinet that there would be no plebiscite in the Sudetenland, that a telegram had been sent to Prague setting out the British and French terms, and that Britain was offering to guarantee the integrity of Czechoslovakia without its fortifications, although the British Government had been firmly saying for six months that it could not guarantee a fortified Czechoslovakia.

"Most of us disliked the idea," recorded Hore-Belisha, the War Minister, "but in the end there didn't seem to be any alternative because of the time factor, and we and the French have to be in agreement."

No member of the British Cabinet resigned, and even Churchill seems to have been temporarily tamed. That evening Halifax revealed to him enough about the French attitude to send him hastening over to Paris for a second time, to try to put some backbone into the French strong men, Mandel and Reynaud. Those two stout fellows, however, had proved to be no more belligerent than their British colleagues. When the French Council of Ministers met at the Elysée Palace at ten o'clock on the morning of September 19 to hear the terms with which Czechoslovakia was to be confronted, Daladier was able to present the London conference as a diplomatic victory for France. So indeed it was. Chamberlain had abandoned, on French insistence, the plebiscite which his Cabinet had demanded, and had conceded the guarantee of Czechoslovakia which he had previously refused. France, Daladier was able to point out, no longer stood alone.

According to Bonnet, there was some talk at this meeting of telling Benes that if he would not accept the Franco-British terms, the French Government would consider themselves freed from their treaty obligations, "but certain ministers felt that this was unnecessary at the present stage, so the idea was dropped." Anatole de Monzie, *plus Bonnet que Bonnet*, recorded in his diary that "the Franco-British plan was unanimously adopted in its wording and in its spirit. I asked that mention should be made of this unanimity in the communiqué, and this was agreed to. If it were unanimous, the communiqué would be of such a nature that it would bring the country and Mr. Chamberlain the comfort of our real and apparent understanding."

Mr. Chamberlain was not conscious of needing French comfort and understanding. Before he had the formal French approval, before the Anglo-French terms had been presented to Benes, he had instructed Henderson to tell the Fuehrer that their talk could be resumed on Wednesday, September 21. A later message to Henderson told him: "You may say from the Prime Minister that he learns that Czech reply will be available early this afternoon. He has arranged to consider it immediately with his principal colleagues and expects to be able to suggest later in the afternoon a time for his meeting with the German Chancellor."

He had had very little trouble with his own Cabinet, the British Labour Party, or the French Government. He had already been given reason to suppose that there would be no trouble with the Czechoslovak Government, either.

CHAPTER 18

Peace Breaks Out

A MAN LOOKING from the windows of Hradcany Castle, if he were not too mentally weary to take in what he saw, might reflect upon the multifarious business of the people, each intent upon his own affairs, crowding into the narrow streets of the old city. His eye might perhaps follow the progress of a car across the river towards the suburbs, where more than a million men, women and children had their work, their homes and their schools.

He might remember that twice in its history, Prague, that beautiful and civilized city, had been devastated by war; and there might recur to him some words of General Bodenschatz, Goering's aide, which had been reported to the Czechoslovak Government at the time of the Austrian crisis: "The flying personnel of all bomber aircraft already know exactly which targets [in Czechoslovakia] are to be attacked during the first minutes of enemy action and which later. The target plans are not lying in the drawers of command posts, but are already in the hands of those bomber squadrons whose task it will be to destroy the targets. These plans and documents are not merely deposited with the squadron or wing commanders, but the bomber crews know them in detail, have them distinctly illustrated on relief tables on which they rehearse, assuming all combat and meteorological conditions which could be encountered, should these plans have to be realized."

He might, as Benes later did, recall two major weaknesses in Czechoslovakia's defenses. The first was the unfinished state of the fortifications on part of the southern frontier with Austria. The second was that there was almost no defense for the civilian population against air attack.

At two o'clock on the afternoon of Monday, September 19, Newton, the British Minister to Czechoslovakia, and Lacroix, his French colleague, presented themselves at Hradcany Castle. Bonnet made a belated attempt to stop them from acting together, but this time Chamberlain had been too quick for him. There was to be no more shifting of French responsibility on to British shoulders.

Neither Newton nor Lacroix liked what he was doing. The terms, as Daladier had said, were "certainly very distressing," and though their presentation might have been softened on French insistence, they were not, in the notorious phrase of *The Times*, likely to make any prima facie appeal to the Czechoslovak Government. Chamberlain by this time did not disguise his dislike of Benes. He had quoted Runciman to the French: "Any sacrifice of Czechoslovak interests could only be laid at Dr. Benes's door. He had throughout been dilatory and had delayed putting forward the necessary proposals until the time when they might be accepted had long passed."

The terms now put to Benes involved the transfer to Germany of those Sudeten areas where more than half the population was German, "but we should hope to arrange by negotiations provisions for adjustment of frontiers, where circumstances render it necessary, by some international body including a Czech representative. We are satisfied that the transfer of smaller areas based on a higher percentage would not meet the case."

In return, the British Government was prepared to join in an international guarantee of the new boundaries of Czechoslovakia against "unprovoked aggression." Newton had queried the meaning of this last paragraph: did it mean a guarantee against claims on Czechoslovak territory by Hungary or Poland? No, Halifax replied hastily, it did not—unless the claims were enforced by "unprovoked aggression." And what is "unprovoked aggression"? Did not Czechoslovakia provoke it by, like Mount Everest, being there? In view of the British reservations, Newton asked for, and was given, permission to withhold for the time being any explanations about the guarantee.

Benes was requested to accept or reject the Anglo-French terms by "tonight or tomorrow."

The President, reported Newton in the dry language of diplomatic documents, "was greatly moved and agitated . . . Speaking with self-control but with bitterness he showed that he felt that, after all the efforts which he and his Government had made, they were being abandoned. I pointed out to him that at least he was being given a new and important guarantee by His Majesty's Government . . . Dr. Benes listened with attention but showed that he felt guarantees which he already possessed had proved valueless."

In the final paragraph of his dispatch, Newton gave a hint of things to come: "My impression . . . is that President Benes is more likely to accept than to refuse and is very receptive to any reason which will help him to justify acceptance to his people."

This was an opinion which, in various forms, Newton was to repeat a number of times in the next twenty-four hours, culminating in the warning to Halifax on the following night: "If I can deliver a kind of ultimatum to President Benes, Wednesday, he and his Government will feel able to bow to force majeure. It might be to the effect that in the view of His Majesty's Government the Czechoslovak Government must accept the proposals without reserve and without further delay, failing which His Majesty's Government will take no further interest in the fate of the country."

The British and French Governments have been condemned for their brutal ultimatum delivered to Benes at two o'clock on the morning of September 21. Their conduct was certainly not very heroic, but the ultimatum had been asked for by both the British and French Ministers in Prague, and the necessity for it had been foreshadowed in Newton's report of his interview with Benes on September 19.

All this bears out the contention of Colonel Emanuel Moravec that the Czechoslovak politicians dared not come to terms with Germany because they were afraid of their own people. There is an episode in Bohemian history known as the Defenestration of Prague, when two unpopular ministers were hurled from the windows of Hradcany Castle into the ditch. Some Czechoslovak ministers were almost as much afraid of another Defenestration of Prague as they were of Hitler. A scapegoat had to be found. It was readily available. Even before the Anglo-French terms had been officially delivered, a member of the Czechoslovak General Staff showed himself acquainted with their contents, telling the British military attaché that Czechoslovakia would not fight. "In view of the fact that Czechoslovakia was being betrayed by France and abandoned by Britain, it would be suicidal to fight Germany single-handed." At that stage, the French and British had neither betrayed nor abandoned anybody, though it was no doubt apparent that they would gladly do so if requested.

The Czechoslovak Government was a coalition. The most powerful element in it was the Agrarian Party. The Agrarians had always looked with favour upon an agreement with Germany and distrusted Russia. The Czechoslovak Prime Minister, Dr. Milan Hodza, was an Agrarian. Although he cultivated the air and manners of a Hungarian aristocrat, he was a lawyer and a Slovak, who had learned the art of political tight-rope walking in the days of the Austro-Hungarian Empire. His attitude towards Czechization had always been ambivalent, and he had made a number of attempts to reach agreement with the Sudeten Germans. He was on good terms with several of the more moderate Sudeten German leaders, and also worked amicably with Eisenlohr, the German Minister in Prague. On one occasion during the long drawn-out negotiations of the summer, he had asked Newton—"though it may be regarded as treasonable"—to invite the British Government to put pressure on Hodza's own recalcitrant colleagues to make concessions to the Henleinists. Hodza was intelligent, well-intentioned, and certainly not the man to lead a forlorn hope.

The minority of the Czechoslovak Cabinet which was opposed to the Hodza faction consisted mainly of the Czech nationalists of Benes's own National Socialist Party, the Social Democrats, and, the most intransigent of all, Monsignor Sramek of the Catholic People's Party. But these were uneasy bedfellows, and they were hopelessly divided in their attitude to Russia as an ally. Most of them were prepared to accept Russian help if France was also standing by their side, but only a tiny Left Wing minority would contemplate the thought of Russian help alone.

On the evening of Monday, September 19, after the Anglo-French terms had been delivered, the tall first-floor windows of Hradcany Castle blazed with light as these talkative but not particularly resolute or able men contemplated their appalling predicament. Their first reaction to the Anglo-French terms seems to have been that they could not possibly accept them. Their second was to ask the French Government point-blank whether they would or would not hold to their engagements if Germany attacked Czechoslovakia. It would perhaps not be unfair to suggest that some members of the Government—possibly a majority —hoped the answer would be that France would not. But Bonnet still would not make the unequivocal statement he had been telling the British and German Ambassadors all summer that he was going to make.

During the evening, Benes sent for Alexandrovsky, the Russian Ambassador, and asked for an urgent reply to two questions: would Russia send immediate help to Czechoslovakia if France also sent help? Would Russia support Czechoslovakia if she appealed to the League of Nations? The first question was surely unnecessary—the Russian Government had publicly stated on a number of occasions that they would honour their obligations if the French Government honoured theirs.

Benes told Alexandrovsky that he assumed a German attack would begin on September 22 if Chamberlain either did not go for his second meeting with Hitler, or went without a satisfactory reply. "Even under these conditions," Alexandrovsky reported, "Benes regarded the proposal of England and France as unacceptable and war as unavoidable, *because the people would not allow anything of this kind.*"*

A subsequent visitor found the President rather less positive. This was Klement Gottwald, secretary-general of the Czechoslovak Communist Party, which, the Czechoslovak Government feared, would seize any chance of popular unrest to stage a coup.

*Author's italics.

When Gottwald asked whether the Czechoslovak Government had decided to reject the Anglo-French terms, Benes gave an evasive answer. He repeated several times, however, that the Government would defend Czechoslovakia against direct attack.

The Russian Government's reply to the Czechoslovak questions was telephoned through to Benes by Alexandrovsky at about seven o'clock on the evening of September 20. In the state of communications between Prague and Moscow, a delay of some twenty-four hours from question to answer cannot be considered unduly long. Anti-Communists inside and outside the Czechoslovak Government, however, were able to make capital out of the delay, and the Agrarian Party newspaper appeared on September 21 with an accusation that Czechoslovakia had been betrayed by "a country of the Slav race." Czechoslovak politicians were at least adept at providing scapegoats for people of all political points of view.

The Russian answer to both questions was "Yes." The answers may or may not have been designed as propaganda, but in any event they arrived too late to influence the Czechoslovak Cabinet, which by the time it adjourned at one o'clock on the morning of September 20 was swinging strongly towards surrender. Newton heard from what he described as "a reliable source" that the Czechoslovak Government had decided to make a formal protest to the British and French Governments. "My informant believes that the very fact of protest if in fact made will indicate that the Czechoslovak Government is resigned to the necessity for compliance." Newton's informant asked for an additional British and French push "in order to help Czechoslovak Government take the plunge," and this was duly given.

The Czechoslovak Cabinet met again at eleven o'clock on the morning of September 20, under Benes's chairmanship. Some members were tearful, the Catholic Sramek argumentative, but the discussion mainly centered upon finding a form of words which would suggest patriotic withdrawal rather than surrender.

During the afternoon, Newton's valuable but unknown informant gave him another hint of what was being prepared. It would be a proposal for arbitration as a concession to die-hard elements, "but my informant believes Czechoslovak Government will then give way unreservedly if forthwith pressed sufficiently hard by the French and British Governments . . . I am therefore sending this warning so that you may be ready."

At five o'clock the Cabinet met again, and between half-past seven and a quarter-to-eight their official reply was handed over, first to Lacroix, then to Newton. As both had forecast, it was not an outright rejection, but a proposal for arbitration coupled with an appeal to Britain and France to think again.

Very shortly after Newton received this official reply, he telephoned London, "I have very good reason from an even better source to believe that formal reply handed to me by Minister of Foreign Affairs should not be regarded as final. A solution must however be imposed upon Government as without such pressure many of its members are too committed to be able to accept what they believe to be necessary." Newton went on to suggest an ultimatum to Benes, adding, "I understand that my French colleague is telegraphing to Paris in a similar sense."

There cannot be much doubt that Newton's source on this occasion was Hodza. It was certainly Hodza who urgently sent for Lacroix while the French Minister was drafting his message to Paris containing the Czechoslovak reply just received.

It was a dramatic interview, during which Lacroix, though not apparently Hodza, burst into tears. According to Lacroix's postwar evidence to a French parliamentary commission, Hodza's first question was, "Are you sure that France will back out if it comes to fighting?"

In view of all Bonnet's assurances to the British about how tough he had been with Prague, Lacroix's reply is surely startling.

He said, "I cannot tell. Would you like me to ask Paris at once by telegram, calling for a firm answer?"

Hodza impatiently swept this offer aside. "No, it will take too long," he said. "I assume that France will not march. If you can obtain a telegram from your Government confirming this tonight, President Benes will yield. It is the only way of saving the peace."

Lacroix asked if Hodza was acting with Benes's agreement. Hodza replied that he was, and with that of the General Staff, which advised that war against Germany without the support of France would be the equivalent of suicide.

Benes afterwards denied that Hodza was acting with his knowledge or authority, a denial which would carry more conviction if he had not also denied that he had offered to make territorial concessions when he had sent Necas to Paris with just such an offer. While Hodza and Osusky, the former Czechoslovak Minister in Paris, were in exile in London during the war, Hodza confirmed to Osusky that he had been acting with Benes's knowledge, and there are certain minor circumstantial details to confirm Hodza's story. The Czechoslovak Prime Minister had asked Lacroix for a reply to his request by midnight if possible. Benes waited up until after midnight, and only then went to bed. Hodza and the Inner Cabinet remained at Hradcany Castle, and were immediately available to consider the British and French ultimatums when they came.

But if Benes did know, one may perhaps advance a reason for his actions. Churchill, he knew, was in Paris, putting pressure on Mandel and Reynaud, whose resignations—or threat of them— might still force the French Government to support the smaller territorial concessions which Benes was prepared to make. Surely an ultimatum of the kind requested, if discreetly published, would provide Churchill, Mandel and Reynaud with valuable ammunition.

It was two o'clock on the morning of September 21 when Newton and Lacroix again presented themselves at the Castle and asked to see the President. Benes, according to his subsequent accounts, was roused from an exhausted sleep. According to Lacroix's postwar testimony, at his first words Benes collapsed "as if I had hit him with a club," and burst into tears. Newton's contemporary dispatch tells a less dramatic but perhaps more truthful story. While the British and French notes were being read, Benes carefully took them down in writing. He then produced a map, drew attention to the dangers likely to result from the narrow waist left to Czechoslovakia under the proposed new frontiers, and questioned the two Ministers about the meaning of the guarantee Britain and France were offering to the truncated state.

"M. Benes," reported Newton, "said that he took our demarche to be a kind of ultimatum, and indeed only such an ultimatum could justify him and his Government in accepting Anglo-French proposals without obtaining beforehand sanction of Parliament as was constitutionally required. We therefore told him our demarche had character of an ultimatum in the sense that it represented final advice of our Governments and, in their view, the last possible moment for acceptance of their advice, if his country was to be saved."

Benes's words and actions as reported by Newton do not seem to be those of a man utterly exhausted and suddenly awakened from sleep to cope with an entirely unexpected situation. The President clearly still had his wits about him. He made a note of what was said and used it to good propaganda effect in London and Paris in the days to come. He carefully pointed out that only an ultimatum would justify him in accepting the terms without recalling Parliament, the members of which would certainly have provoked Hitler by making long and patriotic speeches, if nothing else.

Either while the British and French Ministers were still with the President, or shortly after they had left, the resisters in the Government seem to have made a last attempt to rally some support. The Social Democrat Minister Necas and Ripka, Benes's journalist associate, telephoned Oreste Rosenfeld, editor of Léon Blum's paper *Le Populaire*, in Paris. They told Rosenfeld that the Czechoslovak Cabinet was in session but had postponed their discussions because Benes wanted to consult Rosenfeld before taking a final decision. What were the chances of a change in French public opinion, and in the attitude of the French Government, if the Anglo-French terms were rejected, Germany then attacked Czechoslovakia, and the Czechoslovak forces could hold on for a fortnight? This assessment of Czechoslovak resistance was certainly realistic rather than encouraging, but it is charitable to assume that Necas and Ripka wanted a brave answer. If so, they did not get one. Rosenfeld was told that Benes begged him to consult Blum and Edouard Herriot, the French elder statesman, and his callers said they would telephone again in two hours for a reply. Rosenfeld did consult Blum, and by five o'clock Necas and Ripka had Blum's answer: Czechoslovakia could not count on any such rapid change of French opinion.

An hour and a half later, Hodza's private secretary telephoned the British Legation to say that the Government would accept the Anglo-French terms, and that an official reply would be sent as soon as possible.

The information was premature. The Czechoslovak Inner Cabinet had indeed accepted the terms, and so did the full Cabinet, meeting at half-past six to ratify their decision, though the Catholic Monsignor Sramek still held out for the recall of Parliament. But by nine o'clock Hodza was in trouble with the leaders of the political parties, and while he was wrestling with them came a message from Osusky in Paris, urging delay.

This was Churchill's work, but if Benes heard it as the first faint trumpet-call of the rescuing cavalry that he was waiting for, the cavalry themselves never arrived—Mandel and Reynaud did not resign, there was no Government crisis in Paris, and it is not the least irony of this story that the man who dissuaded the French ministers from the resignation to which they had almost steeled themselves was Churchill. He did so, he wrote after the war, because their sacrifice could not alter the course of events, and would only leave the French Government weakened by the loss of its two most capable and resolute men. With this explanation Churchill coupled the opinion that "Benes was wrong to yield. He should have defended his fortress line. Once fighting had begun, in my opinion at that time, France would have moved to his aid in a surge of national passion and Britain would have rallied to France almost immediately." This is the Churchillian way of saying that the French Army would have made a half-hearted foray against the Siegfried Line, and that Britain would have sent two unequipped divisions to France. Meanwhile, Prague would have been bombed and Bohemia overrun. From this fate Benes was determined to save his country and his people.

At five o'clock on the evening of September 21, Krofta, the Czechoslovak Foreign Minister, formally handed over to Lacroix and Newton his Government's acceptance of the Anglo-French terms.

Shortly before this, at about half-past four, Benes was in consultation at Hradcany Castle with Krejci and other members of the General Staff when he received an unexpected visitor.

This was General Lev Prchala, commander of the Czechoslovak

Fourth Army, which was on the Austrian frontier. Prchala was a man who perhaps deserves the not dishonourable epithet, a simple soldier. Most of the Czechoslovak generals were French-trained and Maginot-minded. The fortifications on the Austrian border were weak, and Prchala had therefore evolved a plan for defending his sector of the front by attacking. After mobilization, he would have had fourteen divisions, four of which were mechanized, including an armoured brigade in each, and his intention, after he had halted the first German assault, was to head straight for Vienna with his mechanized divisions. One may have reservations about the effectiveness of such a plan, but at least it would have had the merit of causing high blood pressure among the older German generals and delighting Guderian, who would have recognized a kindred spirit.

Prchala's view of politics, and his opinion of politicians, may be judged from the purpose of his visit to Benes. He came to deliver an ultimatum: the President must dissolve the political parties, arrest the members of the Government, set himself at the head of a military dictatorship, and wage war against Germany in alliance with Russia. In case Benes refused this ultimatum, Prchala came with his pistol loaded and intended to shoot the President.

Prchala found Benes completely shaken. He urged his proposals upon the President.

"In that case," Benes replied, "the whole of Europe would turn against us and also against the Bolsheviks. There is no other alternative but to accept the German terms."

"Which Europe?" Prchala contemptuously asked. "Those cowards who have betrayed us? And Germany will turn against us anyway. Russia will send an ultimatum to Poland and Hungary, and will drive the Rumanians against the Hungarians, and there will be peace."

Benes turned to a map behind him to controvert this perhaps over-simple view of European politics. If he had shouted at that moment, Prchala afterwards claimed, he would have been shot, but he spoke gently, and the general saw before him not the omniscient, omnipotent founding father of the Republic, but a tired man. He kept his pistol in its holster. He may, of course, also have reflected, even in his high romantic mood, that if he shot the President, he himself would have been unlikely to leave the Castle alive.

The map behind Benes was already marked with indications of the territory to be handed over to Germany. Benes explained, "After all, this does not mean anything. Even if we hand it over, we shall remain an independent free nation. We shall be among ourselves. We shall arrange our lives according to our own wishes."

Prchala protested, "How do you make a foreign policy when you have handed over the fortifications? Foreign policy depends on bayonets. After six months even your domestic policy will be made by Hitler. He will say: out with the Jews, out with the Marxists, out with the Freemasons, and so on."

"There will be a revolution in Europe," Benes answered, "and we shall again get out of all this, without fighting."

"After another three hundred years," retorted Prchala scornfully.

That evening, Prchala tried to whip up some support among Krejci and other members of the General Staff. But, as he wrote in his diary, "the soldiers speak about Poland, Hungary and the doubtful help of the Soviet Union. Nobody, it seems, wants to die honourably."

Apparently, however, somebody did.

During Prchala's talk with Benes, the President left him to speak to a minister in another room. At that moment, through the open windows, a swelling volume of sound was heard, and when the President returned, Prchala remarked ominously, "Do you hear, Mr. President? The people are marching on the Castle."

"Yes," answered Benes, "they are calling for the Army."

Since the early morning of September 21, rumours of the Czechoslovak Government's surrender had been spreading, at first among supporters of the Social Democrat and National Socialist Cabinet members, then among the assembled foreign correspondents, finally among the people of Prague themselves.

Wenzel Jaksch, the Sudeten German Social Democrat leader, heard them and stamped into his party headquarters with a woebegone face, announcing glumly, "Peace has broken out."

Nobody could believe it. The propaganda for the Czechoslovak Maginot Line, the Czechoslovak Army, had been only too convincing. Although Benes had known at least since May what the British attitude was, although he himself had proposed concessions, little had been done to prepare public opinion for any surrender at all.

By the time the Czechoslovak Government's acceptance had been handed over to the British and French Ministers, there were ten thousand people in Wenceslas Square, and about the bronze equestrian statue of St. Wenceslas, the national hero, dense knots of men and women slowly spread and thickened until the square was packed.

At seven o'clock in the evening Hugo Vavrecka, the Minister of Propaganda, officially announced the surrender in an emotional broadcast: "God knows that at certain times one needs greater strength to live than to commit suicide. Dear brethren, sisters, fathers, mothers, children, we shall not today reproach those who left us alone and unsupported. History will pronounce its judgment on the events of these days. It is our duty to look ahead, and to build up and unite the nation which lives today and which will live tomorrow. We shall now be quite alone, we shall be strong, and it will depend on you whether out of the darkness which enshrouds us for a time the rays of a new dawn will shine upon us."

Crowds in the squares and cafés, hearing these official outpourings with tears of rage and shame, failed to agree with the Minister of Propaganda. It is noteworthy that, although armed guards were ostentatiously mounted on the British and French Legations, nobody went near them. The Prague crowds had no doubt who were the architects of surrender. They marched on Hradcany Castle.

Soon there were something like a quarter of a million people moving through the narrow streets of old Prague, over the Charles Bridge with its double row of baroque saints on either parapet, up Hradcany hill and into the square in front of the castle. They sang a fifteenth-century Hussite hymn, "Fear Not Your Enemies," and shouted a slogan, "We won't give the Republic to the German house painter." There were calls for the resignation of the "Surrender Government" and for the appointment as Prime Minister of General Jan Syrovy, Inspector-General of the Armed Forces and virtual Commander-in-Chief.

There is no doubt that in its early stages at least this movement on the Castle was entirely spontaneous. "It was the nearest thing to a revolution I have ever seen," an eye-witness has told me. "It seemed the way I had always imagined a revolution would be."

Whether this genuine outburst of patriotic fervour would have survived German bombs is a question which cannot be answered. It was not called upon to do so. Syrovy, for whom the crowds clamoured, had been built up as a Czechoslovak legend. He had commanded the Czechoslovak Legion on its march through Siberia at the end of the First World War. Like Jan Zizka, the Czech general of the Hussite wars, he had lost an eye and wore a swashbuckling black eye-patch. Syrovy, however, was no Zizka, but a fat and frightened middle-aged man.

At ten o'clock that night, after agitated conferences behind the scenes, Syrovy was brought out to face the crowds. He told them, "I am conscious of my responsibilities. Have confidence in me. Military dictatorship would be of no help to us. You do not know the causes which forced the Government to make its decisions. We cannot lead the nation to suicide."

The crowds went on shouting, "Better death than surrender!" "We want to fight!" "We will not surrender our frontiers!" The only comfort they got from Syrovy was an assurance that they were helping Hitler.

At first light on the morning of September 22, the crowds began to assemble again, and by this time the politicians had had a chance to catch up with popular feeling. The second day's demonstrations were to some extent organized, notably by the Social Democrats who brought in supporters from outside Prague in commandeered lorries and buses. All the party leaders, from Communists to the extreme Right Wing, hastened to scramble aboard the patriotic bandwagon. They had to. "If anybody had talked of surrender on that day, he would have been torn in pieces," one of the demonstrators has told me.

The crowds now numbered some hundreds of thousands. They marched on the Castle with posters demanding the resignation of the Government and the distribution of arms. They were terrifying in their orderliness, flowing irresistibly on in ranks of twenty and thirty abreast. Neither police nor troops could have stopped them, even if the Government had dared to give the order.

The Government, however, had no such rash intention. They met for the last time as a Government at eight o'clock on the evening of September 22. They were resigning, Hodza carefully emphasized, only for constitutional reasons—nothing whatsoever to do with the crowds outside. He went on to say that as it was not certain whether they would be at war, General Syrovy had been suggested as Prime Minister. He had indeed been very forcibly suggested, by half a million voices. So a new Government was appointed under Syrovy's premiership, including some politicians and "first-class civil servants such as the President of the High Court of Justice." Benes himself made the real decisions, after consultations with Hodza's Inner Cabinet, which continued to meet.

In this way the people of Prague were assured that they had got their Zizka, and dispersed peacefully, without defenestrating anybody.

CHAPTER 19

"Courage to Be a Coward"

AS THE ANGLO-FRENCH terms to Czechoslovakia became known in Britain and there were discreet "leaks" of the early-morning ultimatum to Benes, British public opinion began once more to swing.

Seventy percent of the British people had been in favour of Chamberlain's first flight to see Hitler. On September 21, 36 percent of a Mass-Observation poll expressed themselves as indignant with the terms offered to the Czechoslovaks. By September 22, the day of Chamberlain's second flight, this figure had risen to 44 percent. Remarks like "I used to be proud to be British, but now I'm ashamed of my own race" were commonly recorded. And one which, as a criticism of Chamberlain's policy, has not often been bettered: "Why didn't he say straight out six months ago that he wasn't going to do anything about anybody except our own coasts?"

Mrs. Edgar Dugdale, niece and biographer of the former Conservative Prime Minister, A.J. Balfour, told Harold Nicolson that she had been physically sick twice in the night of September 19 over "England's shame," and when she read on the morning of September 20 *The Times*'s reference to terms which had "no prima facie" appeal to the Czechoslovak Government, she went out to the lavatory and was sick again. It was the beginning of a sense of outraged national helplessness, of nostalgia for an omnipotent imperial past, which was to reach its climax at Suez eighteen years later.

In the face of mounting political demonstrations—hundreds, where in Prague there were hundreds of thousands—and a press almost unanimous in its verdict that Czechoslovakia had been betrayed, Cadogan recorded in his diary: "How much courage is needed to be a coward!"

Chamberlain did not lack courage, but even he seems to have felt that he had gone as far as he could go. He told the Inner Cabinet so on the morning of September 21, after the first premature report of the Czechoslovak surrender had been received, and that afternoon he came under heavy pressure from the full Cabinet. Churchill was told later that those unhappy men were at last taking a firm stand, and that Chamberlain had gone to Godesberg to demand early German demobilization, an agreement that transfer of the Sudeten German territories would be undertaken gradually by an international commission, "no nonsense about Polish or Hungarian claims," and a guarantee for what remained of Czechoslovakia.

Against this stiffening of opinion among the civilians must be set the growing pacifism of the military. General Sir Edmund Ironside, soon to be sent out to command British forces in the Middle East, recorded with characteristic emotion in his diary for September 22: "Chamberlain is, of course, right. We have not the means of defending ourselves and he knows it. He is a realist, and any plan he could devise would be better than war . . . At no time could we stand up against German air bombing. Chamberlain knows this. He dare not say so to the people. What a mess we are in."

The French said the same. Colonel Gauché, head of the Deuxième Bureau, told the British military attaché in Paris, "Of course there'll be no European war, since we're not going to fight." He added that France could not face the German air threat. Asked about this opinion two days later, General Dentz of the French General Staff made no comment, but "merely pointed out that French cities would be laid in ruins and that they had no means of defense. They were now paying the price of years of neglect of their Air Force."

There are not many things one can say with absolute confidence about the Munich crisis, but one of them certainly is that the generals—German, Czechoslovak, French and British—would with few exceptions have made admirable members of the Peace Pledge Union.

Godesberg is a fashionable spa on the Rhine, some thirty miles from Cologne. There Chamberlain flew in his British Airways plane on the morning of September 22, taking with him the same advisers as at Obersalzberg: Wilson and Strang. Henderson joined the party at Cologne, as did Ivone Kirkpatrick from the Berlin Embassy, who was to act as interpreter and note-taker for Chamberlain. According to Dr. Paul Schmidt, the official German interpreter, who may in this matter harbour the natural feelings of a professional at the intrusion of an amateur, Kirkpatrick did not do a great deal of interpretation: "We had a discussion as to who would interpret what. Finally I interpreted, with Kirkpatrick putting in an occasional phrase to show his master that he was following the proceedings." Kirkpatrick's presence did, however, ensure that there could be no repetition of the German tactics after the Obersalzberg conference, when Chamberlain had been denied access to Schmidt's official note of the proceedings.

On this second visit, lavish preparations had been made to impress the British Prime Minister. A guard of honour from the Fuehrer's own bodyguard was drawn up at Cologne Airport, and the road between Cologne and Godesberg was decorated with alternate swastikas and Union Jacks. There were crowds along the route, most of whose cheers were spontaneous.

The British delegation were accommodated in the Hotel Petersberg, on one side of the Rhine, that traditional frontier between civilization and the barbarian. The barbarian chieftain held his court in the Hotel Dreesen, on the other side of the river, from where he had issued some four years before to give orders for the bloody Roehm purge. The Hotel Petersberg was owned by the manufacturer of the original and celebrated *Koelnisch Wasser*, who had provided for his British guests no fewer than fifteen samples of his products, ranging from hair lotion to bath salts. Kirkpatrick has engagingly revealed that, even with war and peace hanging in the balance, he could not resist taking some of these scents and lotions back to Berlin for his wife.

At four o'clock in the afternoon, after a hurried buffet lunch, the British party crossed the wide river by ferry, with two police launches as escort, under the eyes of thousands of onlookers who lined the banks "in a manner reminiscent of the Varsity boat-race day," as Henderson put it with his sure British eye for a sporting simile.

The Fuehrer met the Prime Minister at the door of the Hotel Dreesen, and led him upstairs, followed by Kirkpatrick and Schmidt. The rest of the British delegation waited in the foyer downstairs, enduring hours of tedium. Lord Strang has described the scene: "The hall was thronged with members of the Fuehrer's entourage, prominent members of the National Socialist Party, senior military officers and officials of the German Ministry for Foreign Affairs, laughing and talking. . . . When the Fuehrer came out from the conference room he advanced towards the company, halted, and fixed them with his eye. They rose to their feet and froze to immobility and silence. The Fuehrer then turned on his heel without a sign and moved away."

The conference room upstairs, normally used for board meetings of prosperous Rhineland industrialists, was provided with a long baize-covered table, surrounded by twenty chairs. Hitler took one at the head. Chamberlain sat on his right, Schmidt and Kirkpatrick on Hitler's left. When they were seated there was a brief silence, then Hitler gestured to Chamberlain as if to say, "Your move."

Chamberlain began with a recapitulation of his agreement at Obersalzberg to secure the views of his Cabinet on the principle of self-determination for the Sudeten Germans. He announced with justifiable pride that he had come back with the agreement, not only of his own Cabinet, but also of the French and Czechoslovak Governments, to very wide territorial concessions. He went on to give a characteristically lucid and practical summary of the British proposals for the next stages of negotiation. There were detailed references to adequate safeguards for minorities, compensation for Czechoslovak buildings and banks taken over, the question of German willingness to shoulder responsibility for a proportion of the Czechoslovak national debt.

When he had finished, Hitler said in a dry, rasping voice, "*Es tut mir leid, aber das geht nicht mehr"*—"I'm very sorry, but this is no good any more." He pushed his chair back from the table, crossed his legs, folded his arms, and turned to scowl at Chamberlain. Schmidt translated the remark, and there followed a long pause of pained silence.

At Obersalzberg, expecting a British ultimatum, Hitler had asked rather tentatively for the Sudetenland. The calm acceptance of that demand by Chamberlain seems genuinely to have convinced him that Ribbentrop was right and that now was the time to eliminate not only Czechoslovakia, but France as well, while British rearmament was still incomplete. Before the Godesberg meeting, Hitler had told the Hungarian Prime Minister that he was going to present the German demands to Chamberlain with brutal frankness, and his principal fear was that the Czechoslovaks would frustrate a military solution by submitting to them. A message to the same effect reached Ciano, the Italian Foreign Minister, a few days later. This bellicose talk could be dismissed as an attempt to impress reluctant allies, if there were not the additional evidence that Wehrmacht headquarters had been warned to stand by on September 22 for a firm date for starting Operation Green. That would have meant an attack not only on the Sudetenland, but on the whole of Czechoslovakia, which would have left the French no option but to declare war on Germany. Despite the advice of his generals, Hitler seems to have been prepared to risk it, believing—as he rightly did in 1940, again against the advice of his generals—that the French Army could be knocked out, with or without British support.

It is, of course, entirely possible that Hitler was bluffing, that he had no intention at any time of marching into Czechoslovakia, and that at Godesberg he was merely intent on increasing the pressure he had begun to exert at Obersalzberg. But Hitler afterwards complained to Guderian of Chamberlain's "improper behaviour" at Godesberg, which he claimed had annoyed him. No doubt it had. Instead of allowing himself to be shouted at and bullied, as the Fuehrer expected, the *Schlappschwanz* became indignant, meeting the Fuehrer's onslaught with that icy cross-examination on points of detail which so infuriated his political opponents in the House of Commons, and which generally revealed that they had not done their homework. "What exactly did Herr Hitler mean by . . . How did Herr Hitler propose to . . ." Herr Hitler, indeed, had not done his homework, beyond warning the Wehrmacht to stand by for orders.

The unhappy meeting broke up at seven o'clock that evening, and almost immediately afterwards the Wehrmacht was told that there would be no orders that day. In Czechoslovakia also, things were not going according to plan. Henlein's Freikorps, with a stiffening of German S.S. and S.A. detachments, had virtually taken over Eger, which the Hodza Government had seemed inclined to abandon. Now Czechoslovak tanks and troops were moving into the Sudeten border areas, and that night Hitler ordered the Freikorps to withdraw.

But the strain on the Fuehrer was beginning to tell. William S. Shirer, reporting the Godesberg conference for C.B.S., noted the ugly black patches under Hitler's eyes, the nervous tic with which he walked, cocking his right shoulder nervously every few steps, his left leg snapping up as he did so. Shirer also wrote of Chamberlain "looking the image of an owl, smiling and apparently pleased in his vain way with some manufactured applause by a company of S.S. guards before the door." Poor Chamberlain, he gets no credit even for self-control. When the crisis was over, he walked up through the green and gold splendour of the autumn woods at Chequers, which he loved, and there "I came nearer to a nervous breakdown than I have ever been in my life." But of that, nothing was allowed to show in public.

That night there were anxious conferences on both banks of the Rhine. Hitler was under pressure from Ribbentrop to precipitate war—from his military advisers and Foreign Ministry officials not to push things too far. There has been disagreement among historians on the point at which Hitler finally made up his mind not to invade Czechoslovakia. Paul Schmidt, who was frequently with the Fuehrer during those days and whose opinion must obviously command respect, puts it as late as noon on September 28. It seems probable to me that Hitler, while keeping as many of his options open as possible, took the crucial decision on the night of September 22 at Godesberg. On the morning of that day he was prepared to follow Ribbentrop's advice and force a showdown with France and, if necessary, Britain. After he had encountered Chamberlain in an obstinate mood, he concentrated on making sure of getting the Sudetenland with its fortifications. Once he had those, he could take his time about the rest. But he could not yet be sure of the Sudetenland. The new Government in Prague was an unknown quantity. There had been a Czechoslovak broadcast during the day, indicating that Syrovy would not abide by his predecessor's acceptance of the Anglo-French terms. This was probably done to quiet the crowds in Prague, but Hitler was not to know that. He had, therefore, to maintain the pressure and guard against the possibility of any more such "incidents" as those of May 21 and September 13. Hence the insistence on a short time-limit for transfer of the ceded territory. But in fixing this time-limit, Hitler presented himself with another complication which further restricted his options. There is a difference, slight but decisive, between the logistics of an occupation, with its need for a host of policing infantry, and an invasion, with its armoured spearheads and close-support aircraft. Hitler had to convince the Czechoslovaks, French and British that he was still preparing for an invasion, when in fact he was preparing for occupation. But the more credible this threat was made, the stronger the likely reaction from the Czechoslovaks, who were prepared to surrender the Sudetenland, but whom not even Benes could have dissuaded from fighting if Hitler had seemed to be threatening the Czech heartland of Bohemia.

On the British side of the Rhine, Chamberlain maintained his determination not to give way on Hitler's demand for immediate occupation of the ceded areas—an ultimatum, as he later described it, rather than a negotiation. As for the rest of the Fuehrer's angry tirades, it was almost impossible to tell what he was asking for. It was, as Horace Wilson reported to London that night, "all words."

At half-past ten, Chamberlain telephoned Halifax in London to say that he proposed writing Hitler a letter, making it clear that British and French opinion would not go beyond the proposals already accepted by the Czechoslovak Government. If that led to a break, he would return to London on the following day. Chamberlain's letter was drafted with anxious care during that

night and the small hours of Friday morning. It sought to avoid
provoking a break, while at the same time maintaining firmness.
Its key phrase was: "In the event of German troops moving into
areas as you propose there is no doubt that the Czechoslovak
Government would have no option but to order their forces to
resist, and this would mean destruction of the basis upon which
you and I a week ago agreed to work together, namely an orderly
settlement of this question rather than a settlement by the use
of force."

It can be argued that this warning should have been more
forcibly expressed, but there is not much doubt that Hitler understood what it meant. Receipt of the letter at the Hotel Dreesen,
according to Schmidt, was followed by a long and feverish discussion between the Fuehrer, Ribbentrop and their advisers.

Through the long, tense morning the British delegation strolled
on the terrace of the Hotel Petersberg, keeping an eye on the
Hotel Dreesen through field glasses for any sign of Hitler's reply.
It had been promised before lunch, but by lunch time it still had
not come. The British sat down to a funereal meal which was
scarcely enlivened by reminiscences from Chamberlain of his
early days in Birmingham. It is noteworthy that, in spite of the
strain he was under, he was the only man with sufficient spirits
to talk at all.

At about three o'clock, Paul Schmidt emerged from the Hotel
Dreesen with a large brown envelope under his arm. He was immediately set upon by a milling crowd of journalists with shouts
of: "Do you bring peace or war?" Scarcely daring even to shrug
his shoulders, Schmidt marched through them, crossed the river
on the ferry, and was taken to Chamberlain. The Prime Minister
gave no sign of excitement, but greeted him like a casually encountered acquaintance. In a room of the Hotel Petersberg fitted
up as an office, Schmidt translated Hitler's letter to Chamberlain,
Wilson, Henderson and Kirkpatrick. It began with the customary
historical dissertation: "For nearly two decades the Germans, as
well as the various other nationalities in Czechoslovakia, have
been maltreated in the most unworthy manner, tortured, economi-
cally destroyed, and, above all, prevented from realizing themselves also the right of nations to self-determination." President

Wilson's Fourteen Points, unhappy victims of Czech tyranny, the German Reich's determination to end this state of affairs, jostled each other across the excited pages. There were no concessions.

Before facing the assembled journalists on his return to the Hotel Dreesen, Schmidt felt it necessary to brace himself with several drinks. Hitler was almost as excited as the journalists. "What did he say? How did he take my letter?" he eagerly demanded of Schmidt. Schmidt described Chamberlain's calm demeanour, and the Fuehrer seemed reassured that he had not gone too far.

In fact, Chamberlain's first reaction to the letter seems to have been to return to London. No doubt he should have done so, but as Henderson put it, "The Prime Minister's patience was not yet finally exhausted. He was unwilling to refuse discussion of proposals which he had not actually seen in writing."

At five o'clock, two more emissaries made the long passage of the river under thousands of curious eyes. These were Henderson and Wilson, sent to ask Ribbentrop for a written memorandum of Hitler's exact proposals.

Then the British party settled down again to their anxious waiting.

Communications between Godesberg and London were appalling. Telephone messages were partly inaudible, telegrams garbled and indecipherable. Halifax, Simon, and Hoare, sitting in one long, tense huddle, knew only that things were going badly, that Chamberlain was talking of returning home, and that they were being bombarded by requests from the Service ministers for at least some preparatory measures of mobilization. Throughout September 22, there were reports from Prague of the Freikorps activities at Eger, which seemed to be a preliminary to the expected German invasion, and the Czechoslovak Government were pressing for permission to mobilize.

There is no doubt that the Czechoslovak General Staff had been quietly taking at least preliminary mobilization measures since September 13, and that the Czechoslovak Government's request had a dual purpose: to frighten off a German invasion, certainly, but also to keep the Prague crowds quiet. The Syrovy Government, controlled by Benes, never had any intention of going back on acceptance of the Anglo-French terms, but in the existing situation in Prague it was scarcely politic to say so publicly.

At four o'clock on the afternoon of September 23, after a confusion of orders and counter-orders, Halifax authorized Newton to tell the Czechoslovak Government that the British Government could no longer continue their previous advice not to mobilize. This had been cleared with the British delegation at Godesberg, though the Godesberg authorization stipulated that the Czechoslovaks should not make a public announcement. Half an hour later, Halifax telegraphed Chamberlain for permission to take preliminary mobilization measures in Britain.

In Paris, a firm statement by Daladier was issued to the press: "France has gone to the extreme limit of concession. She cannot cede more. M. Daladier authorizes me to say that if Germany carries out a coup de force against Czechoslovakia, France would fulfil her commitments." That night, the French Government authorized the mobilization of sufficient reserves to bring the Maginot Line defenses up to full strength, and to dispatch seven fresh divisions to the German frontier, bringing the total strength there to fourteen.

At five minutes to ten, the British Foreign Office received a message from Henderson in Godesberg: "We propose to leave early tomorrow morning. Decision as to further step (preliminary mobilization measures) might await arrival."

Half an hour later, Chamberlain again crossed the Rhine to receive Hitler's promised memorandum.

Set against the background of a continent moving inexorably towards war, the mobilization notices being distributed in France, the battle fleet at Rosyth awaiting orders to sail, the rattle of machine guns along the Sudetenland border, this second meeting at Godesberg demonstrates the eternal failure of politicians to live up to the grandeur of events which they purport to control. It was purest farce.

Hitler, having tried bullying the day before, now set out to exert his utmost charm. Never had there been a statesman so sorely tried, so inexhaustibly patient, so grievously misunderstood. Chamberlain, smarting from his treatment on the previous day, was stiff and prickly. Hitler's memorandum was produced: it represented, said the Fuehrer, essentially the ideas he had expressed at the previous meeting. In that case, said Chamberlain, glancing at it, public opinion would not be satisfied. Besides, the whole thing was in terms of dictation, not negotiation.

At this point there was an interruption which Paul Schmidt has compared to the bang of a big drum during a symphony. It may perhaps be more aptly compared with the noise of a man slipping on a banana skin. Ribbentrop entered the room and announced portentously that the Czechoslovak Government had ordered general mobilization.

Chamberlain, according to Schmidt, went white at the translation of Ribbentrop's announcement. Hitler said in an unusually gentle tone, "In that event, things are settled."

With some knowledge of the background to Ribbentrop's announcement, one may perhaps try to read the minds of the British Prime Minister and the German Chancellor at this solemn moment. Throughout Chamberlain's previous meetings with Hitler, a series of messages had been brought into the room at apparently fortuitous times: thirty Sudeten German hostages had been shot, helpless civilians were being fired at, and so on. At first, to the apparent surprise of Hitler and Ribbentrop, the British had checked on this information, found it baseless, and confronted Ribbentrop with the evidence. Then there were so many messages, so wildly exaggerated, that they gave up the attempt.

Henderson afterwards claimed to Ribbentrop that Chamberlain did not know of the British authorization to the Czechoslovaks to mobilize. Perhaps he did not. The Halifax telegram may have been answered by Wilson or Henderson without consulting Chamberlain, or after a brief consultation which in the press of other anxieties he had forgotten. In that case, Ribbentrop's entry into the room must have seemed prearranged, the production of another phoney message which would be the signal for Hitler to announce that his troops were already on the march.

It seems more likely, however, that Chamberlain did know, but was not expecting a public announcement. In that case, he might reasonably anticipate that the Fuehrer, in his intransigent mood of the day before, would immediately send for Keitel and give the order to march.

But the Fuehrer was not in his mood of the day before. He was being altogether more cautious. And with his memories of May 21, he may have seen the mobilization announcement as a British-Czech trick, the signal for Chamberlain to tell him that he was going home, and that war would follow. It was September 23, and the Wehrmacht could not move for another week.

One point seems clear from Schmidt's account of the meeting. After the mobilization announcement, both the pacific Chamberlain and the militant Hitler were considerably more subdued. They had both been given a glimpse of the brink. Neither liked what he saw.

There followed an unedifying wrangle about who had mobilized first.

"The Czechs," maintained Hitler, with his memories of May 21.

On the contrary, retorted Chamberlain, Germany had mobilized first; she had called up reserves and moved troops to the frontier.

The Fuehrer said ominously that when Germany did mobilize, Mr. Chamberlain would see the difference between the peace and war strength of the German Army. And things had gone on long enough—Germany had been trying to get a peaceful solution in the Sudetenland for eighteen years. There was a German proverb: "An end, even with terror, is better than terror without end." He must take the appropriate measures to meet the Czech mobilization.

In that case, said Chamberlain, there was no point in negotiating further. He would go home with a heavy heart, since he saw the final wreck of all his hopes for the peace of Europe.

"But my conscience is clear," he continued. "I have done everything for peace. Unfortunately, I have not found an echo in Herr Hitler."

Ribbentrop thought this moment suitable to remind the British that they had not read the memorandum which they had so insistently asked for, which they had been awaiting all evening, and which they had crossed the river to discuss.

Wilson picked up the memorandum which Henderson had been translating, glanced through it, and exclaimed in dismayed tones that it laid down a timetable for the Czechoslovak evacuation of the Sudeten districts, with dates and even hours. Evacuation was to begin on September 26 and be completed by September 28.

Chamberlain picked up the paper, looked at it, and threw it on the table in disgust.

"It's an ultimatum, not a memorandum," he said.

"*Ein Diktat*," put in Henderson, to remind Hitler of his repeated fulminations against the *Diktat* of Versailles.

Hitler looked pained.

"It's headed 'Memorandum,' not 'Ultimatum,'" he pointed out, quite truthfully.

"I'm more impressed by the contents than by the title," Chamberlain retorted frostily.

There was more wrangling, then Hitler took out a pair of spectacles, picked up a pencil, and went through the memorandum, altering the word "demands" to "proposals," crossing out the September date and substituting October 1.

In a hoarse voice, and with a penetrating stare at Chamberlain, he said, "You are the first man to whom I have ever made a concession."

Chamberlain seemed unmoved by this display of generosity. He said merely that he would undertake to transmit the memorandum to the Czechoslovak Government, without any recommendation as to whether they should accept or reject it.

As he told the assembled journalists afterwards, "It's up to the Czechs now."

The memorandum required the withdrawal from defined areas of all Czechoslovak armed forces, police, and customs officials, and the handing over of these areas to Germany by October 1. In some additional areas, a plebiscite was to be held before November 25 under the control of an international commission. Everyone residing in those areas on October 28, 1918, or born there before that date, would be eligible to vote, which excluded the subsequent Czech settlers, and a simple majority would decide their future. An appendix to the memorandum laid down that all military, commercial, and rail installations must be handed over intact, and that no foodstuffs, goods, cattle or raw materials were to be removed.

It was a very far cry indeed from the terms Chamberlain had told his Cabinet he was going to Godesberg to insist on.

When Henderson had seen off the Prime Minister's party at Cologne Airport on the morning of September 24, he went into Cologne Cathedral, knelt down in the nave, and prayed for peace.

CHAPTER 20

Entente Incordiale

AT FOURTEEN MINUTES past one on Saturday, September 24, Chamberlain's British Airways plane touched down at Heston. As the Prime Minister appeared at the top of the gangway he was smiling, and the small waiting crowd of politicians and diplomats cheered him enthusiastically.

The newsreel cameras were ready, and Chamberlain made one of those airport statements which had become a ritual: "My first duty now that I have come back is to report to the British and French Governments the result of my mission, and until I have done that it would be difficult for me to say anything about it. I will only say this. I trust all concerned will continue their efforts to solve the Czechoslovakian problem peacefully, because on that turns the peace of Europe in our time."

There were cheers for this statement, and more cheers as the official cars drove away towards London. Whitehall was crowded with people when the Prime Minister reached it just before two o'clock. As his car swept into Downing Street, the cheering of the crowds was taken up by civil servants and journalists waiting in Downing Street itself, and there was enthusiastic clapping from people at windows high up in the upper stories of Government offices. Chamberlain seemed moved by his welcome. He stood on the steps of Number 10, waving his hat and posing for photographers.

Any Government on the brink of war has to take precautions, and it would be unfair to suspect Hoare, the Home Secretary, of ulterior motives; but undoubtedly the crowd's reception of Chamberlain was stimulated by the news that morning that thirty-eight million gas masks were ready for distribution, and that the Home

Office had asked local authorities to begin digging air raid trenches immediately. Within a few days of these announcements, London shops had run out of cellophane, used for making windows splinter-proof; stationers had sold out their supply of will forms; the price of petrol in some London suburbs was rising from just under a dollar to fifteen dollars for a two-gallon tin; and when a waitress dropped a tray in a tea shop, everybody jumped.

Behind the scenes, Lord Gort, Chief of the Imperial General Staff, sent for Ironside, told him he was to go immediately as Commander-in-Chief of the Middle East, and said, "You will be cut off from us and will have military charge of the whole Middle East. We shall expect you to win the war for us out there."

Members of a Territorial battalion called up on September 26, and sent to defend one of the Navy's main ammunition dumps near Chatham against low-flying aircraft, found themselves with 1914-18 Lewis guns they had never fired, without mountings to fire them from, and with no rations except a lorryload of bread bought from a civilian baker.

Sir Kingsley Wood, the Air Minister, learned that he had no reserves of fighters or bombers.

The flap was on.

The Inner Cabinet met at 3:30 P.M. and, according to Hoare, at once decided that Hitler's Godesberg terms were unacceptable. Cadogan, who was also present, recorded in his diary a very different story: "P.M. made his report to us. I was completely horrified—he was quite calmly for total surrender. More horrified still to find that Hitler has evidently hypnotized him to a point. Still more horrified to find that P.M. has hypnotized Halifax who capitulates totally. P.M. took nearly an hour to make his report, and there was practically no discussion."

Chamberlain then went for a short rest before presiding over a meeting of the full Cabinet in the evening. He again gave his account of the Godesberg negotiations and according to Hore-Belisha "seemed convinced that there is no other chance of getting a settlement on peaceful lines." Four or five members of the Cabinet were once again brought to the point of contemplating resignation, but the only one who got beyond contemplation was Duff Cooper, the First Lord of the Admiralty, who offered his resignation to Chamberlain on the following day, and was asked by the Prime Minister to withdraw it. For the time being, he did so.

During the night, however, there was a startling change in the attitude of Halifax. After Saturday evening's Cabinet, Cadogan drove the Foreign Secretary home and gave him "a bit of my mind," apparently without shaking him. But in the still watches of the night, God joined His voice to that of the Permanent Under-Secretary of State for Foreign Affairs, and the combination was irresistible.

When the Cabinet met on Sunday morning, Halifax, in low tones and speaking with some emotion, said that up to this point he had been in complete agreement with the Prime Minister's views, but now there was some divergence between them. Britain could not advise the Czechoslovaks to accept the Godesberg ultimatum, and if in consequence France went to their help, Britain should go to the help of France.

Chamberlain, tired and under intense strain, was desperately shaken. Halifax had meant to see him before the meeting, to warn him of his overnight change of mind, but Chamberlain had arrived at the meeting late, and so had had no intimation of what was to come. In a private exchange of notes during the meeting he hinted at his own resignation: "Your complete change of view since I saw you last night is a horrible blow to me . . . It remains to see what the French say. If they say they will go in, thereby dragging us in, I do not think I could accept responsibility for the decision." And again, "What D.C. [Duff Cooper] and O.S. [Oliver Stanley, President of the Board of Trade] want us to do is to encourage French and Czechs to resist and promise them our help. That I will not myself consent to."

But it came very close to Masaryk's hope of a Government crisis. By the end of the meeting, according to Duff Cooper, nine or ten members of the Cabinet were in favour of rejecting the Godesberg terms, ten were in favour of supporting them, and two members sat on the fence.

Lord Hailsham, the Lord Chancellor, who was certainly no firebrand, believed that Chamberlain would never get the Godesberg ultimatum past the House of Commons, and Duff Cooper thought that if he tried to do so, he would be swept out of office.

But the House of Commons was not in session, and in Cabinet, Chamberlain succeeded in keeping his options open. It adjourned without any decision, in order to see what the French would say.

It was at about this time that the Prime Minister, walking up and down the garden at Number 10, was overheard saying to himself, "It can't be right. Even if it were to fail, I should still say that it was right to attempt it."

As the crisis in Europe mounted towards its climax, the United States had its own preoccupations. A 100-mile-an-hour hurricane struck New England, killing nearly 500 people. The Dies Committee unearthed sinister Communist influence on the W.P.A. Federal Writer's Project, and the trial of Tammany district leader James J. Hines revealed the sinister influence on New York municipal affairs of the gangster Dutch Schultz. Europe and its problems seemed very far away. "I can't for the life of me understand why anybody should want to go to war to save the Czechs," Joseph Kennedy, the American Ambassador to Britain, had proposed to say on behalf of his fellow-countrymen in a speech he was to make at Aberdeen. Only Roosevelt's direct intervention persuaded Kennedy to strike the sentence out.

On that Saturday morning, France awoke to the fact of mobilization. Shortly before six o'clock, gendarmes bicycled from point to point, putting up the official black and white mobilization posters which called a million men to the colours, and men reading them on their way to work returned home, packed their necessities, kissed wives or sweethearts, and tramped stoically off to report for duty. Now that the unthinkable had happened, there were few protests. Even the building workers, it was reported, had patriotically called off a strike.

In the higher reaches of politics, however, there was less stoicism. Pierre Flandin, a former Prime Minister, "spontaneously" called on the British Ambassador to tell him that the peasants were against war, and although in case of necessity they would march, their hearts would not be in it. If there were initial reverses and heavy air bombardments, they would agitate for early peace.

Communist leaders, Phipps reported, "who are the most active in egging on war, are already telling their men that if there were these heavy air bombardments, they should rise up, declare that France had been betrayed by her Government, and set up a Communist regime."

A number of well-publicized delegations began to call on Bonnet at the Foreign Ministry, leaving resolutions in favour of peace.

On the other hand, Mandel and Reynaud had at last resigned from the French Government; or at any rate Reynaud said they did, though they agreed to hold their resignations in suspense as a patriotic duty during the crisis. According to the unreliable de Monzie, Daladier gave a rather different account of this episode. "If they had offered me their resignation," he is said to have told de Monzie, "I should have accepted it." As it was, he had "shown the touts the door."

On Saturday afternoon, Phipps sent to London a shattering telegram of what he described as his purely personal impressions:

"Unless German aggressions were so brutal, bloody and prolonged (through gallantry of Czechoslovak resistance) as to infuriate French public opinion to the extent of making it lose its reason, war now would be most unpopular in France.

"I think therefore that His Majesty's Government should realize extreme danger of even appearing to encourage small but noisy and corrupt war group here.

"All that is best in France is against war, *almost* at any price (hence the really deep and pathetic gratitude shown to our Prime Minister). Unless we are sure of considerable initial successes we shall find all that is best in France, as well as all that is worst, turn against us and accuse us of egging France on to fight what must have seemed from the outset a losing battle."

Asked sharply by Cadogan on the following day to define his reference to "small but noisy and corrupt war group," Phipps replied that he meant the Communists, who were paid by Moscow and had been working for war for months. "A well-known French Minister has also been advocating a preventative war for many months." He was told to go and find out the views of a number of people, including Weygand, Pétain and Laval. No record has been published of any reply, but one can perhaps imagine what would have been said by those architects of French surrender in 1940.

By the afternoon of September 26, Phipps had changed his opinion about the temper of France, which, he said, had altered completely as the result of publication of the Godesberg demands. The public had responded admirably to the Government's emergency measures, and was showing calm and resolution. But by the time this revised view was received in Downing Street, much damage had been done. A great deal of use had been made of Phipps' earlier telegram as an indication of French unreliability. At 2:30 P.M. on Sunday, September 25, the French Council of Ministers met to consider the Godesberg memorandum before Daladier and Bonnet left to meet Chamberlain in London. Owing to an unfortunate delay on the part of the Ministry of Foreign Affairs, the French ministers did not have very much time to acquaint themselves with the memorandum itself. It was handed by the British to the Foreign Ministry at twenty minutes past ten on Saturday night, but did not emerge from the Ministry until half-past ten on the following morning, when there was no chance of it "leaking" to Sunday morning newspapers. According to de Monzie, unreliable but writing at the time, no clear-cut decision was reached by the French Council of Ministers, but Daladier and Bonnet were instructed to act for the best when they met the British Ministers in London. De Monzie, however, is flatly contradicted by Daladier, who is sure that there was a clear and unanimous decision to reject the Godesberg memorandum, without any qualifications.

The French ministers reached Downing Street at nine o'clock on Sunday evening, and by nine twenty-five were in conference with a formidable British team: Chamberlain himself, Halifax, Simon and Hoare, supported by Vansittart, Wilson, Cadogan, Edward Bridges, Secretary to the Cabinet, and other officials.

There cannot be much doubt that Chamberlain deliberately set out at this meeting to batter the French into surrender; though perhaps they did not take much battering. He had, however, a subsidiary purpose, which was to put back squarely on French shoulders the responsibility which they had been so successfully transferring to the British.

The conference followed lines which had now taken on almost the stately formality of a minuet. Chamberlain gave a dramatic account of his negotiations at Godesberg, emphasizing how close they had been to war. Daladier spoke in beautifully modulated tones about honour and duty. Then Chamberlain, allowing some traces of animosity to show in his manner, asked what the French proposed to do next.

Each of us, said Daladier, would do what was incumbent upon him.

No doubt, replied Chamberlain, but in the case of France, what exactly did that mean? He would ask Sir John Simon to put certain points to Daladier which had troubled the British ministers a great deal in the past.

The same points had troubled Daladier also, but he stood up with a better grace than might have been expected to the detailed cross-examination to which Simon now subjected him.

Simon had been very bellicose while Chamberlain was in Godesberg, extremely pacific upon Chamberlain's return. He was tall, egg-headed, a noted cross-examiner in his days at the bar. He did not wish, he explained with becoming modesty, to pose as a strategist, for he was only an ordinary public man. But when the French troops had been called up to do their duty, was that duty just to man the Maginot Line and remain there without any declaration of war, or was it the intention of the French Government to declare war and take active measures with their land forces?

That, said Daladier, would depend upon many things.

Second question, said counsel for the prosecution: did the French Government intend to use their air forces over Germany? If so, would not that constitute an attack on Germany? And if France attacked Germany, though Sir John Simon carefully did not say it, would that not excuse the British from any obligation under the Treaty of Locarno?

Daladier replied that it would be ridiculous to mobilize an army only to leave it under arms doing nothing in its fortifications, and equally ridiculous to do nothing in the air. But he wanted to speak more about the moral obligations of France than of war and strategy.

Simon assured Daladier on behalf of the British ministers how deeply and truly sensible they were of the profound considerations which he had so eloquently put forward. But did the French propose to fight, and if so, how?

Daladier, bursting into another oration, became so visibly restive that Chamberlain passed a note across to Hoare, possessor of a noted bedside manner, asking him to utter a few soothing words. Hoare did so, saying how fully he understood M. Daladier's feelings, and hoping he would not think anyone present liked the German proposals. He went on to discuss a suggestion by Daladier that an international commission should be sent out to the Sudetenland to make inquiries quickly, and so enable Hitler to take possession of many areas in the near future—a suggestion which, he thought, was worthy of consideration. However, it was not considered. Hoare's intervention had calmed Daladier, and Chamberlain immediately resumed the cross-examination: Daladier had said the French plan was to attack the Siegfried Line and bomb German factories and military centers. What did he propose to do that with? The British had received disturbing accounts of the state of the French air force. What would happen if a rain of bombs descended on Paris, on French industrial districts, military centers and aerodromes? Could France defend herself, and was she in a position to make an effective reply? It would be a poor consolation if, in fulfillment of her obligations, France tried to come to the assistance of Czechoslovakia but found herself unable to keep up her resistance and collapsed.

Daladier said that he was glad to reply to these questions, and failed to do so at considerable length. He has since claimed that he was not prepared to discuss French military plans in front of so many people. He did offer, however, to ask General Gamelin, the French Commander-in-Chief, to fly to London on the following morning to satisfy Chamberlain's burning curiosity about French strategy.

About what happened next there is that conflict of evidence between British and French sources which seems so wearily inevitable at every stage of Anglo-French contact throughout the crisis.

Either that evening, according to Hoare, or on the following morning, according to Cadogan, Chamberlain took another of his lightning and unilateral decisions, which were like those of a man who snuggles under the blankets on a frosty morning and steels himself to jump out of bed when he has counted ten. According to these British sources, Chamberlain gave Daladier a promise which was a complete reversal of British policy until that date. Hoare describes this as "the specific pledge of a British Expeditionary Force to France if France went to war with Germany." Cadogan calls it a promise "to be with them [the French] at once if they are 'engaged in active hostilities' as a result of a German invasion of Czechoslovakia."

In the account of this meeting which M. Daladier has given me, he makes no mention of any such pledge, although the question I specifically asked him was whether one had been given. There is this to be said in his support: if Chamberlain did give such a pledge, he does not seem to have mentioned it to his War Minister, either at a brief meeting of the full British Cabinet on that Sunday night or subsequently, and indeed it would have been difficult at that time to find a British Expeditionary Force to send to France.

According to Daladier's account of what happened that night, the Anglo-French meeting adjourned for a short time while Chamberlain presided over a meeting of his own ministers. When the British Prime Minister returned, it was nearly midnight. He proposed to Daladier that the Anglo-French conference should adjourn until the morning. He would then, he said, like to have a short talk with Daladier alone, when he would put to him a proposition suggested by the British Cabinet during its short meeting.

It was not, in fact, the British Cabinet which had suggested this plan, but Chamberlain who had told his Cabinet that he was going to put it into execution. He proposed, he said, to make one last effort to avert war by sending Sir Horace Wilson with a personal letter to Hitler. The letter would ask the Fuehrer to delay his timetable and to accept a joint commission including German, Czechoslovak and British representatives, to negotiate the handover of Sudeten territory. If Hitler refused, Wilson was to be authorized to say that if France went to war, Britain would stand by France.

Here again there is a conflict of evidence. Chamberlain apparently told his Cabinet that this was to be a verbal warning. Daladier, however, claims that on Monday morning, September 26, Chamberlain showed him a written note which Wilson was to give to Hitler and which was in two paragraphs, the second containing the warning. The point becomes of importance later.

Shortly after nine o'clock on that morning, as Wilson was preparing to leave for Berlin, General Gamelin, dapper as ever, reported to the French Embassy in London for a preliminary briefing. Gamelin, in Ironside's memorable phrase, was a nice little man, in a well-cut pair of breeches. On this occasion, he wore civilian clothes. He was told at the French Embassy that the British felt they were scarcely ready to go into action, either on land or in the air, and that they wanted to gain time. It was his job, he was instructed, to put some heart into them. He was also told that Daladier did not want Bonnet to be present at the Commander-in-Chief's talk with Chamberlain, because "it was he who discouraged everybody." It had been arranged, therefore, that Bonnet was to be carried off by Halifax while Gamelin joined Daladier and Chamberlain, who were already talking together at Number 10.

Gamelin, according to his own account, gave Chamberlain an encouraging report on the situation. France had five million men, about a hundred divisions to start with, a system of fortifications which allowed them freedom to maneuver, but an inferior air force. Germany had an uncertain high command, an unfinished system of fortifications, important shortages of trained officers, N.C.O.'s and reserves, and a shortage of raw materials, particularly oil. She had a superior air force. "We shall suffer from that," Gamelin said, "especially as regards the civilian population; but so long as morale holds out, that will not prevent a happy outcome for our arms."

The appreciation reads ironically now, in the light of what happened in 1940, but to a Prime Minister unversed in strategy, the survey no doubt sounded impressive. Gamelin does genuinely seem to have put heart into Chamberlain, who for a few hours became, if not bellicose, then at least resigned to the need for bellicosity in others.

Gamelin was less successful, however, at a later meeting with the British Service ministers and Chiefs of Staff, which was held under the chairmanship of Sir Thomas Inskip, Minister of Defence. Gamelin himself noted of this meeting, quite fairly, that the British Army and Air Force representatives seemed reluctant to go to war. The British for their part, cross-examining Gamelin about French plans, thought they discovered a French intention to mount an attack on the Siegfried Line at the beginning of war which would be just strong enough to ensure that the British came in. After that, the French would withdraw to the Maginot Line and do nothing for six months until they had assembled their reserves.

The British were almost certainly right in their suspicion. When a French military delegation came to London in March, 1939, to coordinate Franco-British strategy, they revealed that the official French plan of operations was, first to ensure the security of French territory, then to remain on the defensive, while maintaining an economic blockade of Germany, until sufficient resources for an offensive had been built up. In September, 1939, when war broke out over Poland, this is what the French did. There is no reason to suppose that they would have done anything different in September, 1938.

Moreover, Gamelin was less reassuring to the Service ministers than he had been to Chamberlain about the strength of Czechoslovak resistance. He had told Chamberlain that if the Czechoslovaks could hold out to the north and south of Moravia, they might be able to save their army at the cost of abandoning territory. He was asked twice at the Services meeting how long he thought the Czechoslovaks could hold out. The first time he ducked the question. The second time he answered, "Were I a politician and not a soldier, I would be able to give a figure, but as it is I am only prepared to say that Czechoslovakia could hold out certainly for a few weeks, but perhaps not for a few months. The whole question in fact depends on the attitude of Poland. I think that Yugo-slav and Rumanian help could be counted upon in the event of action by Hungary."

This answer by Gamelin, taken together with British suspicions about a French offensive, meant that the Czechoslovaks might hold out for several weeks, but that they would not be able to count on any effective French help for several months. Chamber-lain was back to the appreciation he had drawn up in March: "We could not help Czechoslovakia—she would simply be a pre-text for going to war with Germany. That we could not think of unless we had a reasonable prospect of being able to beat her to her knees in a reasonable time, and of that I see no sign." Only the Royal Navy was remotely ready for war. Lindbergh, invited to London by Joseph Kennedy, the American Ambassador, had been spreading terrifying accounts of German air superiority. Prague would be wiped out, Paris, London—and none of it would save Czechoslovakia.

The impression left by Gamelin on the Services meeting did not percolate to Chamberlain until the following day, September 27, but when it did, it was probably decisive. The first reaction was to draft a message to the French Government, asking them to keep the British informed of any offensive action they intended to take against Germany. This was originally meant as a spur to the French to attack the Siegfried Line and keep on attacking it. But by the time the telegram left the Foreign Office at half-past eight on that Tuesday evening, it could be, and was, justifiably read as a British brake on French offensive action. Bonnet enthusiastically welcomed it: "It behooves us both to be extremely prudent and to count our probable and even possible enemies before embark-ing on any offensive action whatever."

So much for General Gamelin's heartening mission.

This, however, was still in the future. The impression on Sep-tember 26 was all of confident, resolute action. At a short Cabinet meeting after the French had gone home, the War Minister was instructed to call up anti-aircraft reserves, and there was a pre-liminary decision to mobilize the Fleet if the speech Hitler was to deliver in Berlin that night was not reassuring.

Churchill, making one of his periodical forays into Downing Street, left with the impression that the French had been brave and solid, that Gamelin had restored confidence, and that the Cabinet were united in feeling how brave, how strong, how resolute they had always been.

The Godesberg terms had been published. "Hitler's gone too bloody far this time, he needs teaching a lesson and I'm prepared to give it him!" was a confident assertion heard among the crowds waiting in Whitehall. And a patient policeman, moving on demonstrators with their banners proclaiming "Stand by Czechoslovakia," said, "Yes, I know, lady, there's lots could have done better than Mr. Chamberlain, that's what they all say. They ought to have a try. Now move on, will you, please?"

CHAPTER 21

Up to the Czechs

IN CZECHOSLOVAKIA, a brilliant Indian summer. That superb reporter G.E.R. Gedye recorded: "As the fields hardened under the sun into fine tank tracks and the moon lit up every corner of Prague, we prayed for rain and mists."

On the evening of September 23, while Chamberlain waited tensely at Godesberg for the Fuehrer's ultimatum that was only a memorandum, Harry Hochfelder, a young student in Prague, went to bed early. He was awakened soon after midnight by the excited housekeeper in his block of flats: "We're at war with Germany!"

He switched on the light, and there was a shout from the street to turn it off. When he went outside, Prague was in darkness.

Rumours proliferated: the Luftwaffe was already on its way, every target pinpointed; September mist hung about in the hollows—how could one tell it from German gas? Those who had them carried grey gas-mask canisters slung from their shoulders.

Although the streets were crowded with people, there was no panic. The whole of Prague seemed to be on the move. At last the demonstrations of the past two days had stiffened the Government to resist. Czechoslovakia was mobilizing.

When the call-up proclamation came over the radios in crowded cafés, people ran out into the streets cheering. Theaters and cinemas broke off their performances, hotel waiters stopped serving in the middle of meals, printers went straight from their composing rooms to report for duty. Within ten minutes, not a taxi was to be had in the center of Prague. In the suburbs, motorists cruised in search of reservists wanting lifts. By morning, scarcely an able-bodied man was to be seen, unless he was in uniform.

According to Hochfelder, "There had been a grim determination about this operation. I think people would have welcomed the bombs. It would have been interpreted as an indication that the point of no return had been reached."

Perhaps fortunately, the Syrovy Government failed to live up to the heroic expectations of those who had put it into office. The Government accepted mobilization reluctantly, as the one faint hope of dissuading Hitler from marching into Prague as he had marched into Vienna. They took care, however, to apologize in advance for what they were doing.

At eight o'clock on the evening of September 23, half an hour before formal promulgation of the mobilization order, Hencke, the German chargé d'affaires, was asked to call upon Dr. Cermak of the Czechoslovak Foreign Ministry at his home.

Hencke, unlike his superior, Eisenlohr, was a tough and whole-hearted supporter of Hitler. Cermak, as a "well-known partisan of the German point of view," explained to him that Benes and the Syrovy Government were ready to accept any dictated settlement if Germany would allow the Czechs to live as an independent state in their own territory. Only the Communists wanted war, said Dr. Cermak. The Sudetenland could be evacuated in a few days. But would the Fuehrer please tell his people to stop making trouble. The Czech authorities had been ordered to exercise the greatest restraint, but they could not be told to allow themselves to be shot defenselessly; although, Dr. Cermak added obligingly, in isolated cases they had done just that.

The impression the President of the Republic gave to those who saw him at this time was that of an agonizingly tired and increasingly desperate man, who still could not bring himself to believe that the diplomacy which had been his weapon for twenty years was now of no avail. He held long telephone conversations with Masaryk in London, Osusky in Paris, Fierlinger in Moscow. He presided over meetings of the small executive which included Syrovy, Krejci, now Commander-in-Chief, Krofta, the Foreign Minister, and members of Hodza's former Inner Cabinet. From these meetings, agreed decisions were taken by Syrovy, Krofta, or Benes himself, for rubber-stamping by the nominal Government.

Benes had written a personal appeal to the Polish President, offering a settlement over the coal-mining areas of Teschen in return for Polish neutrality. According to Ripka, he hoped that negotiations with Hitler over the Anglo-French terms could be prolonged for several weeks, during which he could come to an agreement with Poland. If that could be achieved, the General Staff held out the hope that they might be able to put up a fight against Germany.

One must beg leave to doubt whether Benes had any such serious hope. He went on doing these things because he did not know how to fight in any other way.

An English translation of the Godesberg ultimatum was handed over to Krofta at six o'clock on the evening of September 24, some sixteen hours after Chamberlain's talk with Hitler had ended. Very late that night, the British military attaché in Berlin, Colonel Mason-Macfarlane, arrived with the memorandum in German, a map showing the areas to be occupied, and the timetable. Mason-Macfarlane had driven from Berlin to the Czechoslovak frontier, walked several miles through the frontier defenses, and driven on again to Prague, which he reached shortly before midnight.

The Godesberg memorandum, whether in English or German, can have left Benes no hope that he was going to be given time for negotiations with the Poles or anybody else. It could only be accepted or rejected.

The events which followed its reception reflect a growing uncertainty and confusion. On Sunday, September 25, the Ministry for Foreign Affairs in Prague told Newton that no reply to the memorandum would be available until the following day, Monday, and the Czechoslovak Government was still considering a British invitation to send a representative to London to discuss it.

On the same afternoon, Masaryk in London delivered to the British Foreign Office a ringing rejection: "Against these new and cruel demands my Government feel bound to make their utmost resistance and we shall do so, God willing. The nation of St. Wenceslas, John Hus and Thomas Masaryk will not be a nation of slaves."

The British Foreign Office, since they had been told that no reply would be available until Monday, queried this rejection with the British Legation in Prague. The Legation rang the Czechoslovak Foreign Ministry, which explained after some delay that this was indeed the Government's reply, but that an explanatory memorandum was being prepared, and that it was this which would be available on Monday.

In fact, the Syrovy Cabinet does not seem to have considered the Godesberg memorandum until the evening of September 26, when the discussion was not entirely in the spirit of Masaryk's invocation of St. Wenceslas, John Hus, and his own famous father.

But either on September 25 or 26, Masaryk had an extremely indiscreet telephone conversation with Benes over lines that ran through Germany. Masaryk was understandably overwrought, and seems to have believed that speaking in Czech would be enough protection against telephone tapping. The conversation was, however, recorded in Germany, and selected extracts from the transcript were read to Henderson and Horace Wilson on September 26. According to these extracts, Masaryk had urged Benes not to give an inch and to play for time, promising that in the meanwhile British opinion could be mobilized, and Chamberlain forced out of office. Hitler, who may be allowed to be a good judge in the matter of invective, told Wilson primly that Masaryk used language about Chamberlain and Wilson which could not be repeated in a drawing room. Of greater importance, Masaryk's conversation confirmed the German belief that London, Paris and Prague were not as firm in private as they appeared to be in public.

It seems possible that the Godesberg memorandum was never rejected by the Czechoslovak Government, only by Masaryk, acting without authority. But his telephoned insistence that Chamberlain could be brought down seems to have put some heart into Benes, and for two or three days the Prague press and radio continued to give an impression that the Syrovy Government was standing firm, and that help could be expected from France, Russia and Britain.

No doubt much of this was propaganda, designed to keep the Prague crowds quiet and stave off the Communist coup which some Czechoslovak party leaders feared rather more than they feared Hitler. Certainly no attempt was made to prepare public opinion for a surrender which, when it came, left a lasting mood of cynicism and indifference among those who had cheered and demonstrated during the nights of heroism.

Meanwhile Czechoslovakia, like Britain, France and Germany, prepared for war. At night, the intense darkness of the blackout turned familiar streets into unknown country. The muzzles of anti-aircraft guns, their positions changed every evening, pointed towards the sky. On the long frontier with Germany, roads were blocked and mined. Newly called-up reservists sweated through the hot summer days digging anti-tank ditches, or watched apprehensively from the slots of pillboxes, wondering what the first German invaders would look like, and how they themselves would stand up under attack.

In Egerland, sporadic machine-gun and rifle fire marked the progress of Henlein's Freikorps and their German allies, who by September 27 were in firm control of Asch. On that day, representatives of Himmler's S.S. were authorized to go to Asch "to take advance measures regarding organization falling within the province of the police." South of Bratislava, two barge-loads of Jewish refugees from Austria waited in the middle of the Danube, without food or water, for permission to land in Czechoslovakia. The Czechoslovak Government hesitated for several days to give permission, lest they provoke Germany.

In Hradcany Castle, the President of the Republic played his lonely game of diplomatic chess, contemplating the pieces as he had been accustomed to do for so long: Russian castle and Polish knight; Rumanian, Yugoslav, Hungarian pawns; pale French king and jet-black German queen.

But this time it was not chess, it was war, and on him lay the burden of deciding whether the people of Prague should have their patriotism subjected to the test of maimed children and burning homes.

CHAPTER 22

Knight's Move

ON THE MORNING of Monday, September 26, Sir Horace Wilson, Chamberlain's adviser, left London for Berlin on one of many occasions in the next twelve months which were to be described as "a last effort for peace."

Wilson, with his neat dark suit, tie slightly askew, carefully rolled umbrella, did not look the kind of man likely to convey to a barbarian chieftain the full force of the warning he carried. But he had a dogged persistence, and his outstanding characteristic, apart from the discretion to be expected of a senior civil servant, was an absolute and very moving loyalty to his much-abused master, coupled with an unrepentant belief that in the circumstances of the times Chamberlain could have done no other than he did. This characteristic, one may perhaps assume, is why he, and no one else, was chosen for this difficult and delicate mission. Wilson could be absolutely relied upon to do what he was told, neither more nor less.

The letter Wilson carried to Hitler began with the information that the Czechoslovak Government, while honouring its predecessor's acceptance of the Anglo-French terms, had rejected the Godesberg memorandum. The letter went on to repeat Chamberlain's previous warning that if, in those circumstances, Germany tried to occupy the Sudetenland by force, the Czechoslovaks would resist, with a probable effect upon public opinion in Britain, France and throughout the world. It proposed an immediate meeting between Czechoslovak and German representatives, to negotiate an orderly hand-over of the territory the Czechoslovaks had agreed to cede. There was also an offer to appoint a British representative to attend these negotiations, as a guarantee that the British Government accepted responsibility for seeing that the Anglo-French terms were carried out by Czechoslovakia.

There was no mention in the letter of any stronger warning, but Wilson was to convey one verbally if Hitler turned down Chamberlain's proposals.

Shortly after four o'clock, Wilson's instructions were strengthened by a telephone message from Chamberlain to the Berlin Embassy: "Since you left, French have definitely stated their intention of supporting Czechoslovakia by offensive measures if latter is attacked. This would bring us in: and it should be made plain to Chancellor that this is inevitable alternative to a peaceful solution."

At about half-past three that afternoon, Churchill descended upon Downing Street. He found Chamberlain and Halifax together in the Cabinet Room, still under the stimulation of the morning's dose of Gamelin tonic.

Churchill urged upon them the desirability of issuing some public warning to Hitler before he spoke that evening at the Sportpalast in Berlin.

In a postwar letter written by Churchill to Halifax, there is a pleasing evocation of the scene, "I no doubt making suggestions, especially about Russia." Churchill claims that a communiqué was discussed, and that he, Halifax and Chamberlain seemed to be much of a mind.

Halifax, in his reply to Churchill's letter, denies that an actual communiqué was discussed, but agrees that the three of them were at that point of one mind. Halifax's letter continues: "But that evening at the F[oreign] O[ffice] Rex Leeper, who was then Head of the Press Department, brought me in the communiqué for approval. I approved it, without reference to Neville, because I thought it was completely in accord with his thought and with what I imagined we had all been saying to each other at our meeting. But, greatly to my surprise, Neville was much put out when the communiqué appeared, and reproved me with not having submitted it to him before publication. I never understood then, and I don't understand now, why he should have been vexed—unless it was that he thought it 'provocative' and not fully consistent with his desire to make further conciliatory appeal to Hitler."

The communiqué, issued to the world that evening, contained the sentence, "The German claim to the transfer of the Sudeten areas has already been conceded by the French, British and Czechoslovak Governments, but if in spite of all efforts made by the British Prime Minister, a German attack is made upon Czechoslovakia, the immediate result must be that France will be bound to come to her assistance, and Great Britain and Russia will certainly stand by France."

On the face of it, there does not seem much doubt about what had happened to make Chamberlain change his mind between his afternoon meeting with Churchill and the evening issue of the communiqué. It was the receipt, at about quarter-past seven that night, of two short messages from Wilson describing his interview with Hitler: "Very violent hour. He is clearly determined to make great passionate speech tonight and was most impatient. On hearing translation of second part of letter he got up to walk out and it was only with difficulty he was persuaded to listen any more and then only with insane interruptions... In view of intense emotion and frequent references to tonight's speech it seemed better not to deliver special message and I am to see him again tomorrow morning."

However encouraging he may have found Gamelin, it is clear that Chamberlain still hoped for peace. Wilson had found the Fuehrer so violent that he had not dared deliver a private warning. And the communiqué uttered publicly the warning that Wilson had thought it inadvisable to give.

The consequences were unfortunate. The Russian Government had said publicly on a number of occasions that they would honour their obligations to Czechoslovakia if the French honoured theirs. One may suspect that the Russian attitude was not quite as straightforward as it appeared, but that is only conjecture. Certainly any Russian intervention was being actively discouraged by Chamberlain, and the Russians had not been consulted about the communiqué before it was issued. It said no more, however, than the Russians had said themselves. The Russian Government now purported to detect in the communiqué a maneuver designed to direct German attention eastward, and indignantly dissociated themselves from it.

Bonnet also dissociated himself. According to his own account, when he confronted Phipps with the communiqué, Phipps explained that it had been *machinée* by Churchill and Vansittart and could be ignored. Bonnet not only ignored the communiqué, but took elaborate steps to suppress or discredit it in the French press, to the indignation of French correspondents in London and Leeper at the British Foreign Office.

Chamberlain himself weakened its effect by a much less firm statement later that night.

Once again, at a moment when the need was for Hitler to see his opponents standing firm and united, they had publicly and unnecessarily thrown themselves into disarray.

With this background in mind, one may follow the fortunes of Sir Horace Wilson as he flew into a Berlin excited to the point of hysteria, streets thronged with devoted Nazis gathering for that night's orgasm in the Sportpalast, marching bands playing patriotic airs, radios blaring sensational stories of new Czech atrocities against defenseless Sudeten Germans.

Shortly before five o'clock, Wilson drove to the Chancellery with Henderson, and Kirkpatrick as interpreter and notetaker. Hitler was working himself up for his Sportpalast speech, and in no mood to listen patiently to anything. The first explosion came when Wilson, explaining the background to Chamberlain's letter, said that the Godesberg memorandum had profoundly shocked British opinion.

"In that case," Hitler interrupted, "it's no use talking any more."

Wilson doggedly asked the Fuehrer to listen to his remarks. Hitler impatiently did so, scarcely able to sit still. When Schmidt translated the paragraph of Chamberlain's letter stating that the Czechoslovak Government had rejected the Godesberg terms, Hitler shouted, *"Es hat keinen Sinn weiter zu verhandeln!"* "There's no point in negotiating any more!" and stamped towards the door.

According to Schmidt, this was the first and only time in the interpreter's presence that Hitler completely lost his nerve. One may suggest, however, that the explanation for the violence of this outburst was not loss of nerve, but quite the opposite. Hitler had with him the transcript of Masaryk's telephone conversation with Benes, from which he may have known that it was Masaryk in London, not Benes in Prague, who was resisting the terms, and he may have assumed that somebody, somewhere, was trying to bluff him. He returned to the subject of the Czechoslovak rejection later, asking carefully whether he could publish the fact that the Czechoslovaks had rejected the memorandum. No, said Wilson and Henderson, the rejection was confidential "because we still hoped to move the Czechs in the direction of a settlement."

Hitler got as far as the door and then, according to Schmidt, seemed to realize how impossible his behaviour was. He came back like a defiant boy, but continued to interrupt the reading of Chamberlain's letter with exclamations: "Incredible! Amazing!"

When the reading was finished, he said roughly that the Czechoslovaks could send a representative to Berlin if they liked, but on the clear understanding that the territory should be handed over on October 1.

"If I don't know for certain that the Czechs accept in the course of the next two or three days," he said threateningly, "the territory may well be cleared of Czechs before October first."

Then he reflected briefly and added, "They must agree within two days, this is to say, by Wednesday."

"Midnight, Wednesday?" Henderson asked hopefully.

"No," retorted the Fuehrer. "By two P.M."

This did not seem to Wilson a happy moment for countering Hitler's ultimatum with another one. Whether he was right or wrong must depend upon an assessment of Hitler's mind at that moment. If the Fuehrer was bluffing, then Wilson was clearly wrong. But on the previous day, Ciano had noted in his diary: "Hitler still believes France and England will not march. But should they do so, he is ready for the conflict. He even adds that the military and political situation is so favourable to the Axis that it might be better to play now a game which will inevitably have to be played one day. Ribbentrop even more extremist in this direction." If Hitler was still hesitating between the choice of war now or war later, then Wilson was clearly right not to take the risk of precipitating war. Daladier, however, continues to believe that the warning should have been given, since it might have stopped Hitler from committing himself publicly in his speech at the Sportpalast that night to occupation of the ceded areas by October 1. It is also possible—this is only my personal conjecture—that Daladier suspects there was never any intention to give the warning at all.

The Berlin Sportpalast that evening was packed with twenty thousand of the party faithful when, among the flags and the floodlights, Hitler rose to speak. The British politician Leo Amery described the speech as "the most horrible thing I have ever heard, more like the snarling of a wild animal than the utterance of a human being." But a British observer at the Sportpalast, Ian Colvin, thought Hitler hesitant and uncertain of himself. The speech heartily abused Benes: "This Czech State began with a single lie, and the father of this lie was named Benes . . . There is no such thing as a Czechoslovak nation." The Fuehrer was careful, however, to leave some escape routes open. The Czechoslovak Government, he pointed out, had already agreed to the cession of territory. The only new demand he had put forward at Godesberg, he insidiously suggested, was the occupation date of October 1, designed to ensure that Benes should be stopped from wriggling out of his promises. Was it really worth going to war, he urged, over such a detail?

There is no doubt that in the British Prime Minister he found one listener eager to be converted to this point of view. The speech brought an immediate reply from Chamberlain. The British Government, he said, regarded itself as morally responsible for seeing that the Czechoslovak promises were carried out, provided that Hitler would negotiate and not go to war. Chamberlain also softened his instructions to Wilson, who was now told that, although he must not leave Berlin without delivering the verbal warning, he should give it more in sorrow than in anger. One may perhaps guess that, whether in sorrow or in anger, the warning would not have been given to Hitler at all if it had not already been shown to Daladier.

Wilson's second meeting with Hitler began with an exchange of civilities about the Fuehrer's speech of the previous evening. Then

Wilson said he was leaving for London immediately. Had the Fuehrer any message for the Prime Minister?

"The Prague Government," answered Hitler, "have only the choice between two solutions. They can accept the German memorandum or reject it."

Wilson said he would report this to Chamberlain. Then he took the plunge. There was, he went on, one more thing to say, and he would try to say it in the tone of the Prime Minister himself. "We are now faced with two alternatives. If the Czechs accept the memorandum, well and good. If they reject it, the question arises where the conflict will end."

"The first end will be the total destruction of Czechoslovakia," remarked the Fuehrer.

Wilson ploughed doggedly on. In that case, he said, the French would fulfill their treaty obligations. "If that means the forces of France become actively engaged against Germany . . ."

"That means if France attacks," Hitler interrupted, "since I have no intention of attacking France."

". . . the British Government would feel obliged to support her," finished Wilson; and metaphorically, no doubt, wiped his brow.

But the expected explosion was delayed for several minutes. Hitler repeated quietly: "I don't intend to attack France. It therefore means that France will attack Germany; and England, too, will attack Germany."

Wilson repeated his careful formula: "The French Prime Minister had not said that France would attack Germany; he merely talked of their fulfilling their obligations. We did not know exactly in what form the French would decide to fulfill their obligations, but if in the fulfillment of these obligations France decided that her forces must become actively engaged, then for reasons and grounds which would be clear to Herr Hitler and to all students of the international situation, Great Britain must be obliged to support her."

"What it all boils down to," retorted Hitler, "is that if France attacks Germany, Britain will support France, and we shall all be at war in six days simply because Czechoslovakia refuses a proposal which means the execution of obligations she has already undertaken."

His voice rose, and he began to shout, *"Ich werde die Tschechen zerschlagen,"* which Schmidt faithfully translated as "I will smash-sh-sh the Czechs." Bombs would fall on Prague. The Czech army would be routed, and Benes forced to ignominious flight.

Wilson tried to break into this tirade, but Henderson tugged at his arm to come away. Just before Wilson left the room, alone with the Fuehrer, he said, "I will try to make those Czechos sensible."

"I would welcome that," answered the Fuehrer. But just in case, Hitler gave the order for his seven assault divisions to move up to their start-lines, at twenty-four hours' notice to mount Operation Green at any time after September 30. Or, of course, to occupy a sensibly-ceded Sudetenland.

In London, a huddle of ministers, with the Chiefs of Staff, sat glumly contemplating the mess into which their chosen role of benevolent and disinterested mediators had led them. They had before them a gloomy assessment of Czechoslovak army morale from Mason-Macfarlane, the Service chiefs' assessment of Gamelin's intentions, and a report from Malcolm MacDonald, the Dominions Secretary, that Canada, Australia and South Africa were not prepared to go to war over Czechoslovakia. To this discouraging picture was added Wilson's brief report, telephoned from the Berlin Embassy: Hitler would not move an inch from the Godesberg memorandum, "and to avoid what we feared, we should bring pressure upon Czechs to accept. The alternatives were clear and there were only two."

War, or pressure upon the Czechs. "What pressure *can* we put on the Czechs," Chamberlain had written to Halifax during the Foreign Secretary's brief mutiny, "except the negative one of saying that we are not coming in unless the French are in it?" They had said that. What more could be done? They set to work drafting yet another compromise: German troops should be allowed to enter the Egerland and Asch—which was already in German hands—on October 1. On October 3, German and Czechoslovak plenipotentiaries would begin negotiating transfer of the remaining territory, and on October 10 German troops would advance to the line agreed by that date.

Late in the afternoon, Wilson himself returned to London with the full story of his stormy reception, and another telegram was drafted to be sent by Chamberlain to Benes:

"I feel bound to tell you and Czechoslovak Government that the information His Majesty's Government now have from Berlin makes it clear that German forces will have orders to cross Czechoslovak frontier almost immediately, unless by 2 P.M. tomorrow Czechoslovak Government have accepted German terms. That must result in Bohemia being overrun and nothing that any other Power can do will prevent this fate for your own country and people, and this remains true whatever may be the ultimate issue of a possible world war."

But supposing Benes still would not face these realities? A question, answered by a single faint nod from the Prime Minister, authorized the last talisman, the conjuration to the aid of these unhappy men of the spirits of Drake, Nelson, Hood, Rodney, Beatty—Chamberlain authorized the mobilization of the Fleet.

Duff Cooper, the First Lord of the Admiralty, was not present at the meeting, but upon Chamberlain's nod, the First Sea Lord, Sir Roger Backhouse, shot out of his chair and telephoned the authority to the Admiralty before there could be any more changes of mind.

Daylight faded across the park, and the huddle went on. At half-past seven they were cleared out of the Cabinet Room by British Broadcasting Corporation engineers, come to rig a microphone for the Prime Minister's broadcast at eight o'clock.

He had wanted to broadcast also to the United States, but Roosevelt had wisely vetoed the proposal. Chamberlain was exhausted. He said, "I'm wobbling about all over the place." Exhaustion was reflected in the tired, grey voice uttering grey words: "How horrible, how fantastic, how incredible it is that we should be digging trenches and trying on gas masks because of a quarrel in a faraway country between people of whom we know nothing!"

Although he had said he would announce that the Fleet was mobilizing, he did not do so. That news was not made public until shortly before midnight.

In Prague, at a few minutes before seven o'clock, Newton—with what shame and distaste—entered Hradcany Castle once more to read to Benes Chamberlain's cold message.

When it was done, Benes said he would immediately call his Cabinet to take a decision.

He added: "My conscience is clear. Mistakes may have been made, but none which could justify such a penalty."

The first-class civil servants, the constitutional lawyers and party politicians who formed the Czechoslovak Government met at half-past nine. Much of an hour-long meeting was spent discussing whether the Czechoslovak people should be told that Germany was mobilizing. They decided—or rather, Benes decided for them —that the people should not be told. They took no other decision.

In Berlin, the Fuehrer stood on the balcony of the Chancellery, watching a military parade. The marching men, the guns, the tanks, took three hours to pass. Berliners ducked into subways, refusing to look, and in the working class districts the marching men were met with clenched fist Communist salutes.

After he had watched for some time, Hitler went inside and turned upon Goebbels, the man responsible for psychologically preparing the German people for war. "It's impossible for me to make war with a people like this!" he complained.

At midnight, Weizsaecker took Chamberlain's new compromise plan to Hitler and Ribbentrop at the Chancellery. The impression he carried away was that they were still determined to force war upon Czechoslovakia.

CHAPTER 23

Black Wednesday

WEDNESDAY, SEPTEMBER 28, 1938, has gone down in history as Black Wednesday, a day of surrender and shame. It was certainly a day of diplomatic and political hysteria, with ambassadors running in and out of the Berlin Chancellery like outraged husbands in a Feydeau farce. But the surrendering had been done, the shame already earned.

By the early morning of September 28, Hitler had ample evidence that if he went any further, he would be faced with war. The British Fleet was mobilizing. France expected to have sixty-five divisions on the German frontier by the sixth day of mobilization. Appeals and warnings showered upon Berlin. The pro-German King of Sweden told Hitler that if the time limit of October 1 was not postponed until October 10, world war would certainly break out, Germany would be branded as the aggressor and would lose the war. Roosevelt had appealed to Hitler—as well as to Benes, in case such an appeal was needed in that quarter—to continue negotiations. "Should you agree to a solution in this peaceful manner," wrote the American President, "I am convinced that hundreds of millions throughout the world would recognize your action as an outstanding historic service to all humanity." The Fuehrer was probably less concerned about his outstanding historic service to all humanity than about a warning from the German Ambassador in Washington: "The American Government . . . are doing everything to suppress the existing but decreasing isolationist tendency among the American people, so that, when the moment comes, the whole weight of the United States can be thrown into the scale on the side of Britain." There is no doubt that Roosevelt was doing his best in this direction, but as *The New York Times* publicly underlined in a front page diplomatic story on the morning of September 28, he was almost helpless. If war broke out, the *Times* forecast, Roosevelt would automatically have to apply the Neutrality Acts, which banned the export of munitions to any of the belligerents. The President's only alternative was to risk a resounding defeat by bringing special legislation before Congress. Since Britain and France had placed large arms orders in the United States, and Germany had not, the effect of the Neutrality Acts was inevitably pro-German. In such circumstances, Roosevelt could do little but go on urging negotiations. "It can't do any harm," he privately remarked to Cordell Hull. "It's safe to urge peace until the last moment."

A more striking warning to Hitler than anything from across the Atlantic came from General Franco in Spain. Sustained though he was by German and Italian arms, Franco gave notice that, in the event of war, he would declare his neutrality.

Hitler was under intense pressure from his Service chiefs, Goering, Raeder, Brauchitsch, not to invade Czechoslovakia. Only Ribbentrop, in the face of this avalanche of pacific advice, maintained his stand in favour of war while the going was good.

The frenzied diplomatic activities of the day began at four o'clock in the morning, with a telephone call from Paris to François-Poncet, the French Ambassador in Berlin. François-Poncet was instructed to seek the earliest possible interview with Hitler and present him with yet one more set of compromise proposals which went further than those of the British Government and had not, unlike Chamberlain's, been shown even cursorily to the Czechoslovaks.

The French plan, according to Weizsaecker, offered German occupation of "all four sides of the Bohemian quadrilateral," including the fortifications, which would, however, continue to be guarded by Czechoslovak troops. Hitler was to be asked if this offer was acceptable. If it was, "the French Government would demand acceptance from the Czech Government. If Czechoslovakia refused, conclusions could be drawn which he [François-Poncet] did not need to define more closely."

By half-past eight, François-Poncet was on the telephone to Weizsaecker, outlining these proposals and asking for an interview with the Fuehrer. He had received no reply by ten o'clock and telephoned Henderson, telling him that "he feared the worst." Just over an hour later, however, he was in the Fuehrer's presence, unrolling a map he had had drawn up on which the territories to be ceded stood out enticingly in bright red, to show the magnitude of the French offer.

Scarcely had he spread his map on the table before an aide-de-camp in S.S. uniform appeared, summoning Hitler to an even more urgent interview with another ambassador. To explain the presence of the latter, it is necessary to journey to Rome, through which the main British initiative of the day was being directed.

On the evening of September 27, Lord Perth, the British Ambassador in Rome, had asked the Foreign Office for permission to invoke Mussolini's influence in favour of peace, and had been instructed to seek an interview at the earliest possible moment on the following day. At half-past nine, Perth was on the telephone to Ciano, who described subsequent events with a high sense of drama and of his own importance, which in fact was that of a not particularly effective telephone orderly:

"September 28. 10 A.M. Four hours to go before the outbreak of hostilities, when Perth telephones to ask for an interview. I receive him at once. He says, with much emotion, that Chamberlain appeals to the Duce for his friendly intervention in these hours, which he considers the last in which something can be done to save peace and civilization . . . I ask Perth whether I am to regard his demarche as an official invitation to the Duce to assume the role of mediator. Yes. In that case there is no time to lose—the offer deserves to be given consideration. I tell Perth to wait for me at the Palazzo Chigi. I go to the Duce."

There was never any question, one may observe in passing, of hostilities breaking out at 2 P.M., but Ciano told Perth that there was, and Perth passed this information on to London, adding to the consternation there.

Mussolini, who had received no very satisfactory answers to his requests for information from Hitler during the previous weeks, swelled with self-importance to find himself suddenly invited to advance to the center of the stage. According to Ciano, the Duce instructed him to telephone Attolico, the Italian Ambassador in Berlin, but it seems that the Duce first told Ciano to telephone Ribbentrop. Ciano tried to reach Ribbentrop at the Foreign Ministry, but was told he was with Hitler at the Chancellery. He tried the Chancellery, and was told that Ribbentrop could not be disturbed. Only then did he get on to Attolico, and as soon as he had the Ambassador on the line, the Duce took the telephone from him.

"Go to the Fuehrer," commanded the Duce. "Say that in any eventuality I shall be at his side. But tell him that I recommend that the commencement of hostilities should be delayed for twenty-four hours. Meanwhile I undertake to study what can be done to solve the problem."

Ciano returned to the Palazzo Chigi to give this information to the waiting Lord Perth. "I inform Perth that hostilities are to begin today and confirm that our place is beside Germany. His face quivers and his eyes are red. When I add nevertheless the Duce has accepted Chamberlain's request and has proposed a delay of twenty-four hours, he bursts into a sobbing laugh and rushes off to his Embassy." Lord Perth, a diplomat of nearly forty years' experience, was perhaps not much given to sobbing laughs, but his official dispatch otherwise confirms the gist of Ciano's account.

One may now follow the fortunes of Ambassador Bernardo Attolico as he raced with his life-and-death message to the Fuehrer. It was Attolico, it may be remembered, who had made miserable the life of the head of Protocol at Nuremberg with his extravagant demands upon the slender resources of the diplomatic train. Attolico transcribed the Duce's telephone message, and without waiting for his hat, rushed out to the ambassadorial car. The car was there, but not the chauffeur. The chauffeur could not be found, and the hatless Ambassador with his desperate message spent some time running about looking for a taxi. When he reached the Chancellery, at about half-past eleven, "he seemed utterly out of breath," noted Paul Schmidt, "and his face was red with emotion. His little intelligent eyes continually darted about behind his thick spectacles."

The Chancellery was in a state of turmoil. Everywhere were

aides-de-camp, men with private axes to grind, party members, soldiers, Foreign Ministry officials, who had come with their generals or ministers to see Hitler.

The Fuehrer himself moved from room to room, talking now with one person, now with another. "No one could utter the slightest word," Schmidt recorded, "since Hitler treated each of them, whether he liked it or not, to a long speech on the way in which he himself saw the situation. That morning he made a whole series of little speeches of the Sportpalast kind. It was only with Ribbentrop, Goering or some soldier, generally Keitel, that he went back into his office for a longer talk. Indeed, that day the Chancellery was more like the camp of an army in the field than the center of an organized government."

Among the excitements of the morning had been a schoolboy quarrel between Goering and Ribbentrop. Goering, arguing for peace, seems to have been taunted by Ribbentrop about his personal courage. He in his turn called Ribbentrop, the advocate of war, a "criminal fool," and loudly protested that if the Fuehrer told him to march, he would go himself in the leading aeroplane, on the sole condition that Ribbentrop was in the seat next to him.

When Attolico arrived upon this scene of the government of a great and civilized nation, Hitler was closeted with François-Poncet. There was a "leak" from the British Embassy in Rome during this period, and it is not beyond the bounds of possibility that Perth's cable to London of the day before had been read in Rome, the British approach expected, and Hitler prepared to receive Attolico. At any rate, as soon as his Italian visitor was announced, Hitler left François-Poncet with his brightly coloured map and went off to Attolico in another room.

Attolico, seeing Hitler approach, began to shout: "Fuehrer! I have an urgent communication for you from the Duce!" Then more calmly, he put forward Mussolini's assurance of support and offer of mediation. There was a long silence. Then Hitler said: "Tell the Duce that I accept his proposal."

Paul Schmidt, who was with Hitler throughout the morning, is convinced that this was the moment of decision, the moment when Hitler made up his mind not to march.

Having dismissed Attolico, the Fuehrer returned to François-

Poncet, to whom he merely said, "Mussolini is asking me to postpone things, too," without revealing that he had agreed to do so.
That revelation was reserved for the British.

His next visitor was Henderson, carrying another letter from
that indefatigable correspondent, the British Prime Minister, sent
off from the British Foreign Office at half-past eleven that morning.

"After reading your letter," Chamberlain wrote, "I feel certain
that you can get all essentials without war and without delay. I
am ready to come to Berlin myself at once to discuss arrangements for transfer with you and representatives of the Czech
Government, together with representatives of France and Italy
if you desire. I feel convinced we could reach agreement in a
week. However much you distrust Prague Government's intentions, you cannot doubt power of British and French Governments
to see that promises are carried out fairly and fully and forthwith.
As you know I have stated publicly that we are prepared to undertake that they shall be so carried out. I cannot believe that you
will take responsibility of starting a world war which may end
civilization for the sake of a few days' delay in settling this long-
standing problem."

Hitler's first words to Henderson were: "At the request of my
great friend and ally, Signor Mussolini, I have postponed mobilizing my troops for twenty-four hours."

When Chamberlain's message was read to him, he said that
he must consult Mussolini before answering. But Henderson's
interview was interrupted by a second arrival of Attolico, who
now came with Mussolini's advice to accept the Chamberlain
proposal of a five-power conference, which had been telephoned
to Rome as well as to Berlin.

Attolico that morning paid four visits to the Chancellery in
three hours. One hopes he had by this time found his chauffeur,
or at any rate kept the taxi. There were so many telephone calls
from Rome to Berlin that the lady telephonist in Rome who put
them through received a bonus of 2,000 lire from Mussolini in
appreciation of her services.

The first news that Hitler had agreed to postpone mobilization
for twenty-four hours reached London in a telephone call from
Rome at one o'clock. At the same time came another message,

saying that Mussolini was recommending a five-power conference to Hitler, and would ask to be represented himself.

At 2:35 P.M., a message from Henderson: "Issue is still in the balance. I need not urge importance of appealing to House of Commons not to aggravate the situation by attacks on Herr Hitler and National Socialism."

The Commons even then was waiting on its packed benches to hear the Prime Minister's speech. Outside the House, noted Harold Nicolson, "there is a large, shuffling shambling crowd and people putting fresh flowers at the base of the Cenotaph. Crowd very silent and anxious. They stare at us with dumb inquisitive eyes."

Soon after half-past two, Henderson telephoned Cadogan with confirmation of the Rome message that Hitler had agreed to postpone mobilization. But "with reference to the suggestion made by the Prime Minister this morning that he would be prepared to make another visit to Germany, the Fuehrer does not think it likely that there will be any necessity for such a visit." Henderson also said that Hitler seemed to be objecting to the timetable of the overnight British proposals, which appeared to leave a loophole for further Czech evasions.

Cadogan retorted that Henderson ought to make it plain that the time was past for talking about Czech evasions; Britain was guaranteeing the timetable. In that case, said Henderson, it was essential to obtain immediate Czech assent to the timetable, and Cadogan gave instructions that Prague should be asked for an immediate reply.

Then he waited, looking out across the park, where mounds of raw clay marked the sites of the air raid trenches.

Between a quarter-past and half-past three came Henderson's second telephone call: "Herr Hitler invites the Prime Minister to meet him at Munich tomorrow. He has also invited Signor Mussolini, who will arrive at ten A.M., and M. Daladier."

He had not invited M. Benes.

When the message had been typed, Cadogan ran with it across to the House of Commons. Unlike Attolico, he did not forget his hat, or his rolled umbrella.

The House of Commons had its half-hour of hysteria which

everyone present except Harold Nicolson would probably prefer to forget.

The Czechoslovak Government met at half-past four, under Benes's guidance. There were thirty people present at this meeting, including Syrovy, Hodza, the Social Democrat Rudolf Bechyne, who had been Hodza's deputy Prime Minister, and the Agrarian Rudolf Beran, strongly pro-German and anti-Communist, who was to become Prime Minister in December, 1938.

"There was utter confusion on all sides," Beran afterwards recalled. "The Government seemed to take both the suggestions and the ultimatums for granted, without considering the constitution or anything else . . . The situation and the mood of those present was at this time extremely pessimistic."

According to the published minutes of the meeting, Benes began by pointing out that the choice lay between implementing the plan put forward by Chamberlain on the previous evening, and invasion. In the event of a world conflict, he said, Czechoslovakia could not recover her present frontiers.

Krofta, the Foreign Minister, supported Benes, saying that the new British plan could not be rejected. They could simply say that certain conditions were unacceptable, while in the case of others, particularly those which were dangerous, reservations must be made.

Benes spoke again to recommend "the integral execution of the Franco-British plan and its guarantee, the rejection of a plebiscite in Czech territory, and the fixing of the frontiers before evacuation by an international committee in order to prevent the rest of the country coming entirely under German influence."

There was a last spark of opposition to these proposals, and renewed suggestions that Parliament should be recalled.

"If we were to bring the matter before Parliament now, there would be terrible chaos," Benes said, reminding the intransigents that they had only twenty-four hours' grace in which to reach a decision.

"We have a war-minded party in the Republic," the Social Democrat Bechyne observed, "which hopes for war because they think this is perhaps what Russia wants. This party would act in Parliament in such a way as to produce the opposite of unity . . . What must not be allowed are fiery speeches in Parliament. A war party is of use only in wartime."

Benes reported that the negotiations with Poland, about which he had previously been optimistic, had now all gone wrong. The Poles were making demands and threats, with dates and deadlines which would have to be refused.

Benes afterwards told Sir Lewis Namier that the Polish ultimatum, received on September 30, "provided me with the last and decisive reason for the fact that, in spite of the insistence of Moscow, I did not provoke war with Germany in 1938." It may be so; but reluctant though one is to judge a man in an intolerable situation, the record tells a different story. There were too many scapegoats, the French, the British, the Russians, the Poles, the fear of revolution and civil war; never the soft center of the crisis, the President of the Republic of Czechoslovakia.

The Government meeting ended at seven o'clock, and at half-past seven Benes telephoned Newton with an appeal to the Prime Minister to do nothing at Munich which could put Czechoslovakia in a worse situation than under the original Anglo-French proposals.

"We are determined to put the proposals into force, honestly and without useless delay," he said, "but we must have time and help. Poland is now beginning to deliver threats and has given a kind of ultimatum to take effect next Friday. The people will be driven desperate by such treatment. I ask Mr. Chamberlain very earnestly for help because it is our real desire to contribute to peace."

Newton pressed for a reply to the new British plan and timetable. Benes said it was being drafted. At 10:40 P.M. he telephoned a preliminary acceptance, subject to reservations. A long list of these followed in the small hours of next morning. The principal one was that there could be no evacuation of territory or demobilization until the new frontiers had been fixed and internationally guaranteed, a proposal which met with short shrift from the Fuehrer at Munich.

A British request for a Czechoslovak representative to be available at Munich on the following day resulted in more confusion.

The German Foreign Ministry was informed that Jan Masaryk would be coming, on Chamberlain's invitation, as an observer. Masaryk refused to go unless, as the representative of Czechoslovakia, he could attend the conference itself. Chamberlain would not—dared not—make this a condition of attending the conference himself. In Masaryk's place, the Czechoslovak Government appointed the more amenable Dr. Mastny, from Berlin, who was joined by Hubert Masaryk of the Prague Ministry and Lisicky from the London Legation. None of them reached Munich in time for the start of the conference at a quarter to one. Perhaps this was deliberate. In any event, it did not matter. The Fuehrer was in no mood to take any notice of a Government that claimed to have more than a million men under arms and no will to use them.

At six o'clock, Mussolini and his entourage left Rome by train for Munich. Now that war seemed to be safely postponed, the Duce had become belligerent. "As you see," he told Ciano, "I am only moderately happy because, though perhaps at a heavy price, we could have liquidated France and Great Britain for ever. We now have overwhelming proof of this." The "we" is a pleasing touch.

The Duce was in high good humour on the journey, enlivening his travelling companions with sparkling *mots*. Of the British, he remarked that "in a country where animals are adored to the point of making cemeteries and hospitals and houses for them, and legacies are bequeathed to parrots, you can be sure that decadence has set in," and "Four million surplus women! Four million sexually unsatisfied women artificially creating a host of problems in order to excite or sublimate their desires! Not being able to embrace one man, they embrace humanity."

Before he left Rome, Mussolini had received a memorandum drawn up in Berlin that evening by the peacemakers Weizsaecker, Neurath and Goering. They sought to forestall any troublemaking from Ribbentrop by providing Mussolini with a compromise solution which he could put forward at Munich as his own. Goering had taken the precaution of first showing it to Hitler who, after a quick look, was kind enough to say, "Well, perhaps it might be acceptable."

The Fuehrer himself, in his special train, met Mussolini at Kuf-
stein, on the former frontier between Austria and Germany, and
gave him a further briefing. There was to be no nonsense at
Munich: either he got what he wanted out of the conference
quickly, or he marched.

"Besides," Hitler continued, "the time will come when we shall
have to fight side by side against France and England: it would
be just as well if this were to come about at a time when the Duce
and myself are at the head of our two countries, still young and
full of vigour."

Mussolini does not seem to have grasped at the chance thus
offered to liquidate France and Great Britain forever. Indeed,
after this warning, no one was more anxious for the success of
the Munich Conference than the Duce.

As the train pulled on in the morning light through the wooded
Bavarian countryside, people beside the track waved and cheered.
"It makes one realize their joy," Ciano observed sententiously, "at
the event which is in the air."

There was one group of Germans who, one must assume, felt
no joy. These were the conspirators for whom the order to march
against Czechoslovakia was to be the signal to strike for freedom.
Their movements on this day, as described by three of their number, Hans Bernd Gisevius, Erich Kordt and Fabian von Schlabrendorff, might be musically entitled the "Enigma Variations."

When General Halder, who had patriotically taken Beck's
place as Chief of the Army Staff, received Hitler's order to mobilize, "tears of indignation ran down his cheeks . . . He was amazed
that Hitler could have played him so false as not to inform him of
his real plans."

Witzleben, organizer of the Berlin end of the coup, dispatched
Halder to express some of this indignation to Brauchitsch, the
Commander-in-Chief. Brauchitsch in his turn set out to add to
the chaos at the Chancellery by demanding an explanation from
Hitler. Witzleben then returned to his own headquarters to await
the telephone call from Brauchitsch and Halder which would
mean action.

Shortly after eleven o'clock that morning, there was a knock
on the outer door of Erich Kordt's office at the Foreign Ministry.

This was another conspirator, Schulenberg, Deputy Chief of the Berlin Police.

"He was no less excited than myself," Kordt has recorded. " 'Brauchitsch is said to be willing to cooperate. I have come to ascertain whether the international situation is unchanged,' he said in haste.

" 'The great war may start at any moment,' I replied. 'Immediate action is necessary before our plot is discovered. Don't wait till the afternoon or even tomorrow,' I begged him."

Kordt assured Schulenberg that no security precautions had been taken at the Chancellery, adding, "I can get you into the Reich Chancellery. If several of us are inside, we may be able to open the great door behind the guard and let an advance detachment into the Chancellery."

If the situation at the Chancellery that morning was indeed as described by Schmidt and Henderson, one likes to think of that advance detachment filing in, no doubt suitably disguised as ambassadors of foreign powers.

Then, according to Kordt, came that dramatic telephone call from Ciano in Rome. The Italians were intervening, the crisis was over.

Brauchitsch was saved the necessity of another unpleasant interview with the Fuehrer. Before he got to the Chancellery, he too heard that new mediation efforts, requested by Britain, were under way.

Witzleben and Schulenberg waited in vain for their telephone calls.

When Major-General Telford Taylor, the chief United States prosecutor at Nuremberg, asked Halder why the *Putsch* had been abandoned, Halder answered simply, "The purpose of the *Putsch* was to prevent war; the announcement of the Munich Conference made it clear there was to be no war; therefore there was no longer any reason for the *Putsch.*"

It was, of course, all Chamberlain's fault.

CHAPTER 24

Munich

MUNICH, ONCE THE CAPITAL of the proud and independent kingdom of Bavaria, still has the civilized air of a capital city, with its opera houses, theaters, concert halls, centers of government. The patrician towers of rococo churches contrast pleasantly with the elaborate bourgeois decorations and noisy jollity of the city's celebrated beer halls where Hitler found his first political following. Munich is as yet a city, bearing the marks of its princely past, and with a blunt, tangy character of its own. It has not yet sprawled into one more provincial parking lot for commuters' motor cars.

The taxi drivers of Munich now speak English with an American accent because of a war which the Munich Agreement delayed but had no hope of averting. There is still an American military presence discreetly outside Munich, but the sight of an American uniform in the center of the city is almost as rare now as it was in 1938, when the principal representatives of Britain's successor as a world power were its foreign correspondents, driving from hotel to lush hotel to read in a casual phrase of Goering, an unguarded look from Daladier, the chances of war or peace.

The city swarmed with journalists, with photographers and newsreel camera teams jostling outside the discreet Hotel Regina for a shot of Chamberlain, all teeth and starched wing collar, or of Goering entering the Vier Jahreszeiten in one of a changing series of dazzling uniforms which, Daladier noted censoriously, emphasized the General's fatness.

The delegations, indeed, could be divided into the uniformed and the non-uniformed. The Italian diplomats with Mussolini outshone the gold-braided brilliance of the soldiers. The Duce himself, chest thrown out, wore a uniform which seemed, to the lounge-suited Daladier, rather too small for his well-developed figure. Even the Fuehrer was dressed in khaki tunic, swastika armband, long black trousers reaching down to rather old black shoes. The representatives of democracy looked like black beetles among these butterflies. Daladier, in François-Poncet's phrase, "a broad-shouldered, sunburnt man with his head sunk on his shoulders, his forehead furrowed with lines"; Chamberlain, like an elderly English lawyer, "greying, bowed, with thick eyebrows and protruding teeth, a blotchy face and his hands reddened by rheumatism."

These notables drove in big official Mercedes cars through streets decorated with swastikas and flags of the four nations—but not of a fifth; Czechoslovakia officially did not exist—and streamers proclaiming *"Willkommen."* They were cheered, the same hopeful cheers which had greeted Daladier at Le Bourget, where women held up their babies and shouted, "Long live Daladier! Long live peace!" and which Chamberlain had heard at Heston, where his entire Cabinet had assembled to smile at the cameras and ostentatiously display their solidarity. Resign? Such a thought had obviously never occurred to any one of that confident, happy group of servants in the popular cause of peace.

Léon Blum in the Socialist *Populaire* had spoken for everyone that morning: "The news of the Munich meeting has aroused an immense wave of faith and hope . . . It would indeed be a crime against humanity to break off the negotiations or make them impossible. The Munich meeting is an armful of wood thrown on to the sacred hearth just at a time when the flame was dying down and in danger of going out."

In Britain, just in case anybody forgot what was going to happen if the flame went out, copies of a Home Office pamphlet, "The Protection of Your Home Against Air Raids," came plopping through suburban letter-boxes.

The most memorable thing about the Munich Conference was its confusion. With less than twenty-four hours for preparation, the logistics broke down at every point. The British delegation found it quicker to send a message by car from the conference room to their hotel than to telephone. There were no arrangements for a formal note of the proceedings to be taken, no chairman, only the most sketchy agenda. The truth is that the Fuehrer was not interested in arrangements. In his opening remarks, he made quite clear to his guests what was expected of them.

"In my speech at the Sportpalast," he said, "I stated that whatever happened I should enter Czechoslovakia on October first at the latest. The objection was raised that this act would have a violent character. Very well, let us take advantage of the fact that we are gathered here to remove this character from it. But it must be done quickly!"

Nobody felt in a position to dispute this statement.

The conference was held in the Fuehrerhaus, a new building on the great open square of the Koenigsplatz, which had a Greek façade superimposed upon a squat Teutonic body. It belonged to the Nazi Party, not to the German nation, but none of the older and civilized halls in Munich were big enough to accommodate the expected throng of diplomats, soldiers, journalists and hangers-on. The principal feature of the Fuehrerhaus was a central hall a hundred feet wide, sixty-five feet high, from which an imposing stone staircase led to suites of rooms above. In one of these rooms, a buffet had been laid out, served by footmen in knee-breeches and silver-buckled shoes. Chamberlain was the first to arrive at the Fuehrerhaus. Then came Daladier, who, such was the state of distrust that now existed between the British and French, had had no previous consultation with Chamberlain. Mussolini made a delayed entrance at the head of a train of uniforms, and was ostentatiously greeted on the great staircase by the Fuehrer in person, although they had parted only a short time before. Mussolini's handshakes for Daladier and Chamberlain were pointedly brief and cold. "There is a vague sense of embarrassment," noted Ciano, "particularly on the part of the French. I talk to Daladier, then François-Poncet about trivial things. Then to Chamberlain, who says he wants to talk to the Duce. The Duce, coldly, does not take advantage of the opening, and the conversation peters out."

The Fuehrer left his guests little time to eat, drink and chat, but shepherded them firmly into a big, rectangular room set with a round table, some armchairs, and a sofa. Schmidt, who had to take a note of the proceedings, complained that, as usual at the Fuehrer's conferences, the table and chairs were too low for him to write comfortably. The Fuehrer, however, liked low chairs, and it was his conference. Without waiting for his guests, he slumped into the first chair he came to, on the left of the door, leaving the rest to seat themselves where they liked. Schmidt sat down on the Fuehrer's right. Chamberlain sat next to Schmidt, with Wilson on his other side. Mussolini and Ciano, crumpling their uniforms, lounged on a sofa. Daladier and Alexis Léger of the French Foreign Ministry sat facing the Fuehrer.

When they had settled themselves, the Fuehrer expressed a few perfunctory thanks to his guests for their presence. Then he launched into the familiar tirade, voice raised, clenched fist punching into open palm: distress and misery of Sudeten German population . . . barbaric persecution . . . no end to flood of refugees . . . unbearable situation . . . immediate decision . . .

Mr. Chamberlain, Wilson noted primly, replied suitably, as did M. Daladier and Signor Mussolini. But of course they did not reply suitably, although Daladier made some show of standing up for the Czechoslovaks and, according to his own account, threatened to walk out, as everybody did on their first encounter with the Fuehrer.

"I should like the Chancellor's intentions to be made perfectly clear," Daladier said. "If, as I understood him, he means to destroy Czechoslovakia as an independent state and purely and simply join it to the Reich—to annex it—I know what remains for me to do. There is nothing left but for me to return to France."

That was not the Chancellor's present intention, and Mussolini quickly intervened: "No, no, there's a misunderstanding. That isn't what the Fuehrer meant to say. On the contrary, he has dwelt on the fact that apart from the Sudeten districts, Germany doesn't claim any part of Czech territory."

Mussolini spoke French, as well as German and English; Hitler, German only. During this exchange, Hitler never took his eyes off Mussolini. When the translation had been made, he himself broke in: "No, Monsieur Daladier, I have expressed myself badly. I don't want any Czechs. If you offered me the lot, I wouldn't accept a single one."

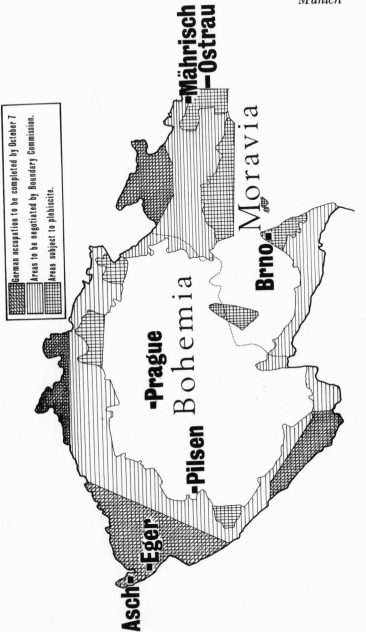

At Godesberg, Hitler demanded immediate German occupation of all those areas not subject to plebiscite. The Munich compromise allowed German occupation of the four cross-hatched areas to begin on October 1. No plebiscites were held, the Boundary Commission deciding most disputes in Germany's favour.

As a matter of cold fact, 800,000 Czechs came under German rule as a result of German interpretation of the Munich Agreement. But for the moment there were sighs of relief, the Fuehrer was springing no surprises in the manner of Godesberg, nobody was going to have to walk out with consequences too appalling to contemplate.

These preliminaries out of the way, Mussolini produced a little thing he happened to have in his pocket, the memorandum drafted for him by Weizsaecker, Goering and Neurath, "a short compromise proposal," as he modestly described it.

The Anglo-French terms accepted by the Czechoslovak Government involved the transfer to Germany of areas in which more than half the inhabitants were Sudeten Germans, with an adjustment of the frontier to be carried out by an international body including a Czechoslovak representative, and an international guarantee of the new boundaries. The areas to be transferred included most of the Czechoslovak fortifications, but no time limit was set for the transfer.

At Godesberg, Hitler added a time limit, October 1, for the transfer of the area which included the bulk of the fortifications. This area was to be handed over with all its installations, communications, and goods intact. A second area was to be subject to plebiscite and subsequent adjustment by a German-Czech or international boundary commission.

The British compromise proposal put to Hitler on September 28 offered occupation by October 1 of Asch, and those parts of the Egerland which were on the German side of the fortifications; an immediate meeting of an Anglo-German-Czech boundary commission; and the handover on October 10 of further areas to which that commission had agreed.

The compromise Mussolini now produced required the evacuation of the largest area, including the fortifications, to begin on October 1, with a guarantee from Britain, France and Italy that the handover would be completed by October 10 without destruction of any of the installations. This first handover would be followed by a plebiscite under international supervision and an international commission to determine the final frontiers.

The key to all this, of course, was the fortifications. Once those were surrendered, the Czechoslovaks had no chance in a fight even if they had the will. It was Colonel Moravec's complaint against the Czechoslovak politicians that they would not defend the fortifications, and they were too afraid of public opinion to reach an agreement with Germany. So it was left to Chamberlain and Daladier to do it for them at Munich. It cannot be claimed that these defenders of democracy behaved very heroically, but they should not be left to bear the odium alone.

When Mussolini's compromise had been produced, discussion of it rambled on for some time. Chamberlain was concerned about the guarantee. How could Britain, France and Italy give a guarantee, he asked, if there were no Czechoslovak representatives present to accept it on behalf of their Government?

Hitler was standing no nonsense of that kind: "If we have to ask the Czechs for their consent to every detail we shall still be at it in a fortnight's time. In the present state of tension the slightest delay would be terribly dangerous."

Always the unspoken threat over their heads: "I shall march in, and then what will you do?"

Chamberlain nevertheless stubbornly insisted that there must be no guarantee. The British, he said, regarded the word "guarantee" as meaning a great deal.

On this point—it was about the only one—he eventually got his way. Britain, France and Italy did not have to guarantee that the Czechoslovaks would evacuate the territory by October 10 without destroying anything. They agreed that it should be done, and held the Czechoslovak Government responsible for doing it.

Chamberlain turned to another point: what was the meaning of the regulation in the German memorandum stating that no cattle should be taken out of the evacuated territory? Did this mean that the farmers would be expelled but that their cattle would be retained?

Chamberlain has of course been ridiculed for talking about cattle at such a time. Nevertheless, farmers are more interested in their cows, shopkeepers are more interested in their stock-in-trade, and householders are more interested in their furniture than any of them are in fortifications. Perhaps this is wrong, but it is so.

The Fuehrer agreed with Chamberlain's critics. He swept these insignificant people and their cattle out of his way: "Our time is too valuable for us to waste it over trifles of this kind."

This was the man speaking who could contemplate the Final Solution, the extermination of the Jewish race; the great Romantic of the Berlin bunker, making his own splendidly defiant ending without regard to its effect upon unimportant people who bother about cattle. It is comforting to recall that, so far, the farmers and their cattle have always won in the end.

At three o'clock the conference adjourned to consider in their separate groups the Italian proposals. Hitler left the Fuehrerhaus first, looking straight in front of him, driving off alone to his flat in Prinzregentenstrasse. Daladier followed, and almost got into Mussolini's car by mistake. When he found his own, Goering climbed in beside him, and they drove off together, Goering laughing heartily.

When a French journalist asked Daladier during this adjournment what were his impressions, he answered carefully: "I have no impression . . . When I say that I have no impression, it must be understood that I do not say I have a bad impression. On the contrary, the mere fact that we are all four here is in itself a good sign, as I see it."

It was about the best that could be said.

The British had arranged for a conference with the French at a quarter-to-four to formulate a joint approach to the Italian memorandum. The French did not appear. They were, according to Ivone Kirkpatrick of the British delegation, resolved to reach agreement at any cost. It seems more probable that, with Gallic logic, they saw no point in quibbling about cows when Chamberlain was clearly bent on surrendering the fortifications, without which, Gamelin had told Daladier, Czechoslovakia would "cease to be an effective military asset."

The four delegations met again at a quarter-to-six, and there followed hours of chaos, with small multilingual working-parties drafting clauses which then got lost and had to be laboriously agreed upon again. The Italian Ciano found it agreeable: "This allowed a more intimate way of thinking, and it broke the conversational ice." Hitler showed his opinion of these proceedings by sitting moodily apart, from time to time glancing ominously at his watch. He crossed and uncrossed his legs, folded his arms, and glared round the room, wriggling on his sofa. At intervals, with an obvious effort, he joined in a conversation, only to relapse quickly into silence. On one of these conversational forays, he angled for an invitation to Paris from Daladier, with whom he talked "as between two ex-soldiers." Daladier claims to have been surprised and to have thought of the Parisians' expressions if he returned with Hitler and Goering in his plane. Unsatisfactory as the British were as allies, however, he does not seem to have contemplated swapping horses yet again.

Mussolini was bored by the vaguely parliamentary atmosphere. He strode up and down, up and down, hands in pockets, or allowed himself to be buttonholed by Chamberlain for what Wilson described as "some useful conversation." But Mussolini, like Daladier, remained steadfast to his ally.

A banquet had been arranged at the Fuehrerhaus for eight o'clock. Chamberlain and Daladier had been invited, but preferred to dine at their hotels. There was, they explained, so much still to do, and colleagues in London and Paris had to be consulted by telephone. Without these skeletons at their feast, the Germans and Italians were able to enjoy themselves. Mussolini became expansive on the subject of democracies: "The fools! If they had simply extended their sanctions to cover oil, in a week they would have made it impossible for me to conquer Abyssinia!" It was perhaps fortunate that he did not know the British Mediterranean Fleet, upon which enforcement of oil sanctions would have depended, had only enough ammunition at the time to fire for fifteen minutes.

While the banquet proceeded, wild rumours circulated among the assembled journalists. There was a last-minute hitch, Chamberlain was flying back to London to consult his Cabinet, this would certainly mean war. Goebbels' representative at Munich stilled the rumours, however, by announcing rather prematurely that agreement had been reached on all the main points. Only one difficulty had arisen: how the terms of the agreement were to be transmitted to the Czechoslovaks.

It was still five weary hours before the legal experts had finished their drafting. A little before two o'clock on the morning of September 30, the Munich Agreement was ready to be signed. It followed closely the Italian proposals: evacuation of the ceded areas was to begin on October 1 and be completed by October 10. The conditions governing the evacuation would be laid down by an international commission consisting of representatives of Germany, Britain, France, Italy and Czechoslovakia. This commission would also determine the areas in which a plebiscite was to be held, and the final frontier lines. An annex repeated the Anglo-French offer to join in an international guarantee of what remained of Czechoslovakia. The German and Italian Governments agreed to join the guarantee "when the question of the Polish and Hungarian minorities has been settled."

François-Poncet glanced through the agreement, flushed, and said aloud: "That is how France treats the only allies who have remained faithful to her." Mussolini congratulated a stone-faced Daladier: "You'll be cheered when you get back to France." Hitler looked glum. Perhaps he was thinking how much better it would have been to squash these democratic black beetles once and for all.

The four statesmen lined up to append their signatures to this document. The photographers filed respectfully in. The newsreel men set up their cameras and switched on their lights. It was then found that the imposing inkwell provided was as empty of ink as the conference had been of conferring.

Ink was fortunately procured, and the agreement signed. Frederick T. Birchall of *The New York Times* was in consequence able to tell the world that "all four seem to have worked together with a thoroughness of purpose and speed in execution that restore to the practice of conferences some of its lost prestige."

There then arose, as Wilson delicately put it, the question, "What to do about the Czechs?" A British suggestion that Daladier, as Prime Minister of Czechoslovakia's ally, should personally take the agreement to Prague was turned down by that statesman. The British were now determined, however, that there should be no more shuffling off of French responsibilities on to British shoulders, and it was decided that Daladier and Chamberlain together should see Dr. Mastny, the Czechoslovak Government's official representative, and hand over the document to him. This meeting took place, according to Wilson, in the Prime Minister's room in the Hotel Regina at about quarter-past two in the morning.

"I gave M. Daladier the prepared copy (with map) so that he might hand it to M. Mastny," Wilson recorded pointedly.

Mastny read the document, and asked a number of questions. "He was given a pretty broad hint," wrote Wilson, "that—having regard to the seriousness of the alternative—the best course was for his Government to accept what was clearly a considerable improvement upon the German Memorandum."

Accustomed though he was to being given pretty broad hints by Goering, Ribbentrop and every other bully, Mastny could not keep back his tears. François-Poncet consoled him: "Believe me, all this is not final. It is only a moment in a piece of history that is beginning and in which everything will soon be called into question once again." One would like to believe that François-Poncet did say it, and did not simply invent it for his memoirs.

Daladier was brusque and embarrassed. Chamberlain could not hide his yawns. He was, he said, tired, but pleasantly tired. He had, after all, achieved what he had set out to achieve, which was to prevent war.

The French and British Prime Ministers got away from the weeping Mastny as quickly as they decently could. Perhaps rather more quickly.

A telegram was soon on its way to the British Minister in Prague: "You should at once see President and on behalf of His Majesty's Government urge acceptance of plan that has been worked out today after prolonged discussion with a view of avoiding conflict. You will appreciate that there is no time for argument; it must be a plain acceptance."

At half-past six that morning, Hencke, the German chargé d'affaires in Prague, wakened Krofta, the Czechoslovak Foreign Minister, with a telephoned summary of the Agreement and with an invitation to send representatives to the first meeting of the international boundary commission. This was to be in Berlin at five o'clock that afternoon. Benes was being made to pay dearly for May 21 and September 13.

At nine o'clock, Mastny reached Prague with the full text and took it straight to Benes. At half-past nine, Benes telephoned Alexandrovsky, the Russian Ambassador. He said the great powers had sacrificed Czechoslovakia to Hitler in the most shameful way, and for their advantage. The final settlement of formalities had been left to Czechoslovakia. This meant that Czechoslovakia was faced with a choice. Either she could start a war with Germany, in which Britain and France would be against her, or at least their Governments would try to influence public opinion by representing Czechoslovakia as the cause of war. Or she could capitulate. Benes said he did not know what the attitude of Parliament and the political parties would be, but he inquired about the attitude of Russia either to fighting or to capitulation. He asked for a reply by six or seven o'clock that evening.

This was a dying kick, if indeed it was a kick at all, and not just something Benes wanted written into the record. He had a very good idea what the attitude of the political parties was likely to be, since, if Beran is to be believed, he had been telephoning the leaders during the night, giving them a military assessment of the situation produced by Husarek, the new Chief of Staff. According to Beran, Husarek's appreciation was that on the outbreak of war, Germany, Poland and Hungary would attack, Bohemia and Moravia would be quickly cut off from Slovakia, and "despite heroic efforts from the army, they would be thrown on their own resources and not be in a position to resist for long. Therefore, to go to war would be almost synonymous with suicide."

Communications between Prague and Moscow were such that Alexandrovsky was told he could not get a telephone call through until five o'clock that evening. He therefore telegraphed Benes's inquiry, then went up to Hradcany Castle to find out what he could about the situation.

At the castle, two meetings were going on simultaneously. The first was attended by Benes, members of the former Hodza Government, and the party leaders. The second involved General Syrovy and his ministers, the nominal Government, which Syrovy opened with the pronouncement that they were faced with a choice between being murdered or committing suicide.

Krofta followed Syrovy with a report on the Munich terms.

Theoretically, he said, it would be possible to reject them, but then there would be a German invasion and a war in which no one would be on their side. Poland would also attack. It was doubtful whether Russia would help, or if she did, whether her help would be of any use. On the other hand, they could accept the agreement, and perhaps avert the worst by negotiations.

One member of the Government, Zenkl, the Lord Mayor of Prague, asked for the recall of Parliament, but was silenced by the customary argument: Parliament could not be recalled in time, there must be an immediate decision, it was a matter of acceptance or rejection.

At half-past eleven this meeting adjourned, assembling again a quarter of an hour later to hear the President of the Republic. Minister Zenkl caused some concern by ostentatiously absenting himself from this second meeting. As one of his colleagues remarked, nobody should be allowed to break the unity they had maintained until now, or to oppose the Government at such a critical time. In short, if there was to be another Defenestration of Prague, Minister Zenkl should be prepared to be thrown out of the windows with the rest of them.

Benes made his report: he had no other course but to propose acceptance of the ultimatum. If they did not accept it, they would, of course, fight an honourable war, but they would lose their independence and people would be exterminated. The leaders of the political parties saw matters in that light. If the Cabinet were now to agree with them, then there would be complete unanimity.

One by one, these unhappy men made their little speeches. If they accepted, said the first, it must be firmly insisted upon that the Germans should not use force. The President of the Republic, said another, must restrain the Communists. If the Commander-in-Chief assured them that no defense was possible, said a third, he had no option but to agree to the Munich terms.

The President of the Republic said he would regard these statements as agreement. He solemnly called on Government, State and People to rise above this crisis. History, he said, would judge.

At midday, Alexandrovsky, waiting in the office of the President's principal secretary, was told that in deference to the decision of the Government, no answer to Benes's inquiry was now required from Moscow.

It is, of course, impossible to reconcile this statement to Alexandrovsky with the record of how the question of Russian help was put to the Government by Krofta, or of the manner in which the Government reached its agreement. But Benes and his colleagues were men under almost intolerable strain.

The news of surrender was kept from the people of Czechoslovakia until five o'clock that evening, and came at the end of a broadcast by Syrovy. When they heard it, some wept, some got drunk, a few shot or gassed themselves. The rest, thanks to Benes and Chamberlain, went on living.

CHAPTER 25

Peace for Our Time

MANY A YOUNGER MAN than Chamberlain would have been exhausted by the strain of the past twenty-four hours, but the British Prime Minister never wearied in well-doing, and with the tiresome problem of Czechoslovakia out of the way, he passed at once to the next business.

On that Friday morning, only a few hours after the agreement had been signed, William Strang of the British Foreign Office, who had accompanied the Prime Minister on all his flights, was awakened in his hotel room at Munich by a message from Chamberlain, asking him to draft a short statement on Anglo-German relations.

Strang composed three paragraphs, of which Chamberlain rewrote the second and made some minor changes in the other two. The final document read:

"We, the German Fuehrer and Chancellor and the British Prime Minister, have had a further meeting today and are agreed in recognizing that the question of Anglo-German relations is of the first importance for the two countries and for Europe.

"We regard the agreement last night and the Anglo-German Naval Agreement as symbolic of the desire of our two peoples never to go to war with one another again.

"We are resolved that the method of consultation shall be the method adopted to deal with any other questions that may concern our two countries, and we are determined to continue our efforts to remove possible sources of difference and thus to contribute to assure the peace of Europe."

The Anglo-German Naval Agreement, signed in 1935, limited German naval tonnage to 35 percent of that of Britain. But as Germany had previously been forbidden any navy at all, and as the British had signed the agreement without consulting the French, it amounted to a private British condonation of another breach of the Treaty of Versailles. Strang protested to Chamberlain that this agreement was not a thing to be proud of. Chamberlain said that, on the contrary, it was just the kind of agreement Britain should try to reach with Germany. Strang suggested that Chamberlain should tell Daladier what he was doing. Chamberlain refused.

During the choas of the previous day, Chamberlain had arranged a meeting with Hitler for eleven o'clock that morning. As he was about to leave the Hotel Regina for this interview, he asked Strang, "What's that noise?"

Strang looked out of the window. Maximiliansplatz, in which the Hotel Regina stands, is a wide street divided by an island down the middle, and looking from the window, Strang saw that the whole of this space was packed with people.

"They want to see you," he told Chamberlain, and suggested that the Prime Minister should step out on to the balcony for a few moments.

There followed an ovation for the peacemaker, cheer upon cheer, handclapping and singing.

The same kind of demonstration had been going on outside Daladier's hotel in Maximilianstrasse since eight o'clock that morning. Daladier was more fortunate than Chamberlain; he had, not a Foreign Office official, but a pretty secretary from the French Consulate to consult about the meaning of this phenomenon.

She said, "They have a big fear. They only know one thing. They won't have to fight."

The shifting crowds went on shouting and singing for hour after hour: "Be kind, dear little Daladier, and show yourself at your little window; otherwise we shall go home." Dear little Daladier obliged, though not without misgivings that the demonstration had been arranged by Goebbels. He was reassured, however, by the black looks of Goering, staying at the same hotel.

"He's very put out that they're not cheering him," remarked the French Consulate's pretty secretary.

Hitler, according to Paul Schmidt, was also very put out. "Instead of rejoicing at the prospect of grappling with the enemy, weapons in hand," Schmidt afterwards wrote, "the inhabitants of Berlin and Munich had, in a manner that left no room for doubt, shown their aversion from war and their delight at seeing peace saved." This may be so; but one cannot help wondering if Hitler was not now gripped by doubt as to whether Ribbentrop had been right after all. It had been so easy, the French and British had so obviously been terrified. Should he have signed the agreement? Should he not have provoked the Czechs into war and gone on to Prague? Many years afterwards, with all the advantages of hindsight, he told his deputy, Martin Bormann, that he ought to have kept the initiative in 1938. He returned to the same theme two or three times in various forms: the critical moment was when Chamberlain and Daladier returned home from Munich, both of them should have seen very clearly that the first thing to do was to dissolve their parliaments. If Daladier had organized an election, the fire-eaters would have been routed. "In similar cases," he remarked on one occasion, "I've always made arrangements for a plebiscite to be held. It produces an excellent effect, both at home and abroad."

For a few fleeting moments, in the early days of that October, Hitler seems to have thought of scrapping the agreement he had just signed and ordering his troops on to Prague. A series of questions went out from Schmundt, the Fuehrer's adjutant, to Keitel's headquarters: what reinforcements would be needed to break any Czechoslovak resistance in Bohemia and Moravia? How much time would be needed for regrouping and moving the reinforcements up? How much time would be required to achieve the state of readiness of October 1? But he did not go on.

Whether it was for this reason, or that given by Schmidt, or because he was exhausted from the strain he had been under, the Fuehrer was pale and bad-tempered when Chamberlain arrived, though he was, Schmidt thought, secretly flattered that the British Prime Minister should, yet again, be waiting upon him.

The discussion which took place rambled over a number of points: Spain, limitation of armaments, trading relations in Southeast Europe. Chamberlain made the running. Hitler answered distractedly. Then, saying that he must not keep Herr Hitler any longer, Chamberlain produced his draft. He suggested that it would be helpful to both countries and to the world in general if they could issue some statement which showed they agreed on the desirability of better Anglo-German relations. The statement was translated by Schmidt, and at each pause Hitler ejaculated: "*Ja! Ja!*"

When the translation was over, Hitler said he would certainly agree to sign this document. When would the Prime Minister like him to do so?

"Immediately," said Chamberlain.

"Then let us sign," said the Fuehrer cordially.

"I've got it," Chamberlain said to Strang when he returned to the Hotel Regina, complacently tapping his pocket. And to assembled journalists he said, "As a consequence of the conversation we had this morning, Chancellor Hitler and myself have together decided to publish an important communiqué that will be given you very shortly."

Just after half-past five on that Friday afternoon, the Prime Minister's plane touched down at Heston on his return from Munich.

British opinion had swung about wildly during the crisis, but had come down at last where it had begun, firmly on the side of Chamberlain. Ten percent had been against him after his first flight, 40 after his second, 10 after his third. In this post-Munich poll, 20 percent of the men were anti-Chamberlain, only 4 percent of the women. A Lancashire Labour M.P. reported that the men in his constituency had been prepared to stand up to Hitler, but the women were frightened out of their wits: "I'd sooner see the kids dead than see them bombed like they are in some places."

For two hours before the Prime Minister's plane arrived, roads leading to the airport were made almost impassable by parked cars. People drove as near as they could get, abandoned their cars, and walked on. Inside the airport gate, the road was lined on either side by a hundred and twenty top-hatted boys from Eton. Hundreds of children waved flags. Among the notables assembled on the tarmac were the Lord Mayor of London, members of the Cabinet, a number of diplomats, not including Jan Masaryk.

A shower of rain fell just before the Lockheed Electra descended out of grey skies. When the door of the plane opened, the Prime Minister appeared at the top of the gangway, triumphantly holding up and flourishing a single sheet of paper. Presently he was reading it before the microphones: "This morning I had another talk with the German Chancellor, Herr Hitler, and here is the paper which bears his name upon it as well as mine. Some of you perhaps have already heard what it contains, and I would just like to read it to you."

When he came to the words, "the desire of our two peoples never to go to war with one another again," the cheers from the crowd became deafening, though one can detect on the sound track of the newsreel film a single dissenting "Boo!"

Chamberlain was cheered into his car, and when he was in, crowds broke through the police cordon and tried to open the doors to shake his hand.

Halifax, driving with Chamberlain towards London through these cheering crowds, thought it advisable to get in first with a word on a subject about which he expected the Prime Minister to come under considerable pressure: an immediate General Election. Halifax said Chamberlain would be given this advice, but he hoped he would reject it and instead foster national unity by inviting Churchill, Eden, and the Labour and Liberal leaders into a coalition Government.

Chamberlain swept aside the idea of an immediate election.

"All this will be over in two or three months," he said, gesturing at the crowds. He made no comment on the suggestion of a coalition. Churchill's activities had not endeared themselves to him, and his contempt for the Labour Party was certainly greater than its distrust of him.

Chamberlain had been asked by the King to drive straight to Buckingham Palace. The great open space in front of the palace forecourt was packed with people, and shortly before the Prime Minister's car arrived, some of them were convinced that they had seen a rainbow.

When he appeared on the palace balcony with the King and Queen, the cheers broke out, shouts of "Good old Chamberlain!", singing of "For he's a jolly good fellow."

The people who had guessed wrongly, and gone to Downing Street and Whitehall, waited somewhat glumly in the rain, unwilling to give up their good places, but wishing the Prime Minister would come. A flag-seller walked among them, shouting encouragingly, "Don't forget your wave," and photographs of the Prime Minister were on sale. Business was poor.

By seven o'clock, there were five thousand people in and around Downing Street, and enthusiasm was rising. The crowds began to sing, "O God, our help in ages past," and then, a little reedily, the great, crashing statement of imperial self-confidence, "Land of Hope and Glory":

> "Wider still and wider
> Shall thy bounds be set;
> God Who made thee mighty,
> Make thee mightier yet."

One undergraduate in the crowd said to another, "I know we've let them down like hell, but then we're always swines, aren't we?" The British were in the process of manufacturing that guilt-complex about Munich which has haunted them ever since.

A car driving into Downing Street was mobbed. When it was found to contain only Sir Kingsley Wood, the Air Minister, a young workman said magnanimously, "Well, they all deserve a cheer."

At seventeen minutes past seven Chamberlain's car turned into Downing Street. There was a tremendous burst of cheering, broken by a few boos. People waved their arms, hats, newspapers and, appropriately, umbrellas.

Chamberlain, with a set, tired smile, posed for photographers, and went inside Number 10. The door closed behind him. The crowd went on cheering and chanting, "We—want—Chamberlain!"

Inside Number 10, an exhausted man on the verge of a breakdown was urged by his colleagues to go out to them.

"What can I say?" he asked.

"Say that you've come back with peace with honour, and go on the balcony where Disraeli said it before," one of his staff told him.

At 7:27 P.M., Chamberlain appeared on the balcony with Mrs. Chamberlain. He stretched out his arm for silence, and some people in the crowd, an irreverent observer noted, took this gesture for a Hitler salute, returning it in kind.

There were shouts of "Speech, speech," and then the fatal words came out:

"My good friends, this is the second time in our history that there has come back from Germany to Downing Street peace with honour." For some time he was not able to go on because of the cheering. When he could continue, he said, "I believe it is peace for our time. We thank you from the bottom of our hearts."

"*We* thank *you*," shouted the crowd, and "God bless you."

"And now," said Chamberlain, "I recommend you to go home and sleep quietly in your beds."

He went inside. The crowd sang "For he's a jolly good fellow" and the National Anthem, and raggedly dispersed.

"The Downing Street statement made me shiver when I heard it," Halifax wrote long afterwards, and Chamberlain himself tried to explain it away to the Commons a few days later: "I hope hon. Members will not be disposed to read words used in a moment of some emotion, after a long and exhausting day, after I had driven through miles of excited, enthusiastic, cheering people—I hope they will not read into those words more than they were intended to mean."

What, then, were they intended to mean? There is plenty of evidence for the genuineness of Chamberlain's belief that he had brought back lasting peace. To Lord Swinton, a few days later, he said, "But don't you understand? I've brought back peace," and Sir John Wheeler-Bennett quotes an unnamed Cabinet colleague to whom the Prime Minister said, "You see, my dear fellow, this time it's different; this time he has made the promises to me."

These could be explained as the remarks of a man who, knowing that his policy was splitting his party, was trying to rally support. The opinion of one close to Chamberlain at the time is that "he hoped but was not deluded. He deliberately gave publicity to the document he brought back from Munich, first because he thought it might help Hitler to keep his word, and secondly because if he broke it, the public here and in America would see clearly the kind of man he was."

This is an interesting line of argument. So tremendous was the buildup for Hitler's promise of peace that the letdown, when it came, was proportionately great. Ribbentrop seems to have been furious when he heard that Hitler had signed the document, even daring to reproach him: "How could you do this when there are all those other outstanding things to be settled?" Ribbentrop, of course, had his suspicions about British Government war propaganda working on a pacific people. Hitler convinced himself in the course of time that Chamberlain had come to his flat only "in order to trick and cheat him." It could certainly be claimed that, whereas the British people would have gone to war in 1938 reluctant and divided, in 1939 they were still reluctant, but on the whole not divided. To this result, Chamberlain's scrap of paper may have contributed. Whether the Prime Minister deliberately willed it must remain a matter of opinion.

On that night in September, 1938, the words to most people meant what they seemed to mean: peace in our time, no bombing of our home tomorrow, take the strips of brown paper off the windows, put the gas masks in the attic, go away for the weekend with thankful hearts and relieved minds. A number of them, who had stocked up canned groceries against a war, tried to get their money back from the shops and were indignant when they were refused.

Poems, gifts of flowers, umbrellas and fishing rods showered in on Downing Street. Fifty letters to *The Times* proposed a National Fund in Chamberlain's honour. The Nobel Peace Prize was suggested. In Brussels, a medal was struck to the "apostle of peace," and from Greece came a request for a fragment of his umbrella to make a relic in an ikon. He was created an honourary citizen of Versailles, and the Avenue de la Paix in Strasbourg, which was to have been evacuated in the event of war, was renamed Avenue Neville Chamberlain.

The French paper *Paris-Soir* suggested that the Prime Minister should be offered a corner of French soil: "A simple house—for his tastes are simple; beside a river—since he likes to fish; with a field around it—since there could be no more faithful image of peace, of his labours, and his gentleness."

Nobody offered a corner of English soil to that tough political realist Daladier, nor a corner of French soil for that matter, but he too had his few hours of triumph. He left Munich before Chamberlain, and brought back no scrap of paper, though Bonnet hastily tried to get one when he heard about it. During the return flight to Le Bourget, Daladier remained gloomy and preoccupied. He had no illusions about peace in his time. As the plane lost height above the aerodrome, he saw a huge crowd waiting. "They've come to boo me," he said to one of his staff. "Tell the pilot to circle for a few minutes. I haven't had time to think about the little speech I should like to make, nor about the face I ought to put on it."

But when the plane did land, it was cheers Daladier heard, cheers all the way from half a million people lining the roads from the airport to the center of Paris. Bonnet had taken care that Daladier's route should be known, but not even he could have organized such a reception. In the city itself, shop girls stood on the balcony of the Galeries Lafayette, waving tricolor flags. Below them, a street sweeper irreverently mimicked them with a handkerchief tied to his broom.

Daladier drove in a small open car, looking red and bewildered, but he put a cheerful face on it, and as crowds brought the car to a halt, gave orders to his police escort to let them do as they liked. Roses and gladioli piled up in the car, showers of torn-up paper descended from office buildings, women flung their arms round the Prime Minister's neck and kissed him.

Only the members of Daladier's staff in the car are said to have heard him mutter, "The idiots! If they knew what they were cheering!"

Bonnet, it was observed, was weeping. "He no longer knew himself," de Monzie acidly recorded in his diary, "nor, I must observe, did he any longer know his friends—we who had so vigorously supported him that we had seemed to be hustling him along."

From the Brenner Pass to Rome, Ciano lyrically recorded, from King to peasants, Mussolini received a welcome such as his Foreign Secretary and son-in-law had never seen.

King Victor Emmanuel drove in person to the railway station at Florence from his country estate to congratulate the Duce. As the train pulled into Rome, the crowds chanted the familiar "Duce! Duce!" but mingled with it were less familiar shouts for the Angel of Peace. In the Via Nazionale, an arch of laurel leaves had been built. At sight of it, Mussolini exploded with anger: "Who's responsible for this carnival?" But he, too, had to submit temporarily to being the Angel of Peace, not the God of War. From the famous balcony of the Palazzo Venezia he told the cheering crowds, "You have lived memorable hours. In Munich we have worked for peace with justice. Is this not the ideal of the Italian people?"

Privately, he remarked that what the Italian people needed was a good punch in the stomach.

The Fuehrer re-entered Berlin as a conquering hero. Almost a million people lined the mile-long route from the Anhalter Station to the Chancellery. When the special train pulled in, there was a fanfare of trumpets and the bells of the city's churches rang a triumphant peal. Two little girls in Sudeten German peasant dress presented the Fuehrer with bouquets, which he accepted graciously.

The thought still seems to have been haunting him, however, that the bouquets should have been presented in another place.

"That fellow Chamberlain's spoiled my entry into Prague," he said, scowling, to his S.S. entourage as he drove slowly through the cheering crowd.

A few seconds before two o'clock on the afternoon of Saturday, October 1, Sergeant Juehner, of General Ritter von Leeb's 12th Army, clicked his heels, saluted and reported, "Men on right flank in position, Sir."

Sergeant Juehner's officer returned his salute, shook hands with him for the benefit of the newsreel cameras, and gave the signal to advance. Five columns of troops moved forward on a twenty-mile front: armoured cars, lorries filled with infantry, horse-drawn light artillery.

Enthusiastic Henleinists had built laurel arches across the roads at the frontier, and through these arches the columns moved, while Sudeten German villagers cheered and threw flowers to the soldiers.

The Czechoslovak troops retired for about a mile in front of the advancing Germans. There was no contact between them. The formal handover was left to customs officers and gendarmes.

In a few places, Czechoslovak officers were found who said they would rather fight, and here and there they did so, but the main danger to life and limb came from the fact that the Germans drove on the right-hand side of the road, the Czechoslovaks on the left.

In Berlin, those stout warriors Henderson and Mastny did what they could to influence the German members of the International Boundary Commission, but by October 10, according to Henderson, direct cooperation and negotiation between Czechs and Germans was sufficiently advanced for the political section of the Commission to dissolve itself. Or to put it another way, as Halifax was later honest enough to do, "In applying the Agreement, every contentious point was decided in Germany's favour."

The German security police moved in smoothly behind the German forces, and some 20,000 Sudeten German Social Democrats were rounded up and sent to concentration camps.

When a known Socialist not thought worth arrest went into a Sudetenland café, the Henleinists present greeted him with a massed chorus of "*Sieg Heils!*" which continued for several minutes. Then the band would be requested to play the Egerland March and similar patriotic tunes which had been adopted by the Henleinists, followed by more "*Sieg Heils!*"

It was not malicious, noted one recipient of this treatment, it was a triumphant, schoolboy, "Yah, we've won!" Most of the Sudeten Germans, like most of their neighbours across what had been the frontier, were quite decent fellows. When their sons began to be killed in Hitler's war, some became very anti-Nazi. At the end of the war thousands of them were massacred by Left Wing Czech partisans, and over two millions were deported to West Germany, whence they will no doubt seek an opportunity some day to return to what they consider their homeland.

When that day comes, we shall see who has learned what from history, and whether a later generation is any more adept than Chamberlain at securing peace under the shadow of the knockout blow.

CHAPTER 26

The Summing Up

SOME MONTHS AFTER the Munich Agreement had been signed, and when the reaction against it and against Chamberlain was gaining momentum, a twenty-three-year-old Harvard graduate, expanding his senior thesis into a book, had the courage to return a verdict of "Not guilty."

"People in America," John Fitzgerald Kennedy wrote in *Why England Slept*, "filled with the myth of Britain's invincibility through the centuries, could not understand Chamberlain's desperate efforts to avert a war. They felt, and many still do feel, that Hitler in 1938 was merely bluffing. 'Just show him some strength and he will back down quickly enough.' Many in England shared this belief, even in August, 1939. These people felt Chamberlain was badly taken in, but I think a study of the position of the two countries will show that Chamberlain could not have fought, even if he had wanted to . . . I feel that Munich was inevitable on the grounds of lack of armaments alone."

John Kennedy was no doubt influenced in these views by his father, the isolationist American Ambassador in London, but one cannot, more than a quarter of a century later, find much to quarrel with in his assessment. Chamberlain was wrong to become involved in the affairs of Czechoslovakia in the first place. He was wrong to try to negotiate from weakness. He was certainly wrong, whatever his reasons, to express public belief in "peace for our time." But in the circumstances in which he had placed himself, he was right to sign the Munich Agreement, though he did so for all the wrong reasons.

To argue otherwise presupposes that Hitler was bluffing and that he would have abandoned his designs on "aircraft carrier Czechoslovakia" if Chamberlain had confronted him at Obersalzberg with the ultimatum he evidently expected. In support of this argument, historians have made much of Keitel's evidence at Nuremberg that the Wehrmacht was not ready for war. Too much weight, in my view, should not be attached to this evidence. The German generals who opposed the invasion of Czechoslovakia also opposed the German offensive against France in 1940, and were so astonished when Guderian did what he said he was going to do that they stopped him in his tracks, allowing the British Expeditionary Force and a substantial portion of the French northern armies to escape through Dunkirk. The French were beaten in 1940 not by weight of men and armour or even by air superiority, but by an attitude of mind. Like the senior German generals, like Churchill, they did not understand the tactics of the *Blitzkrieg*. They would have been beaten as easily in 1938 or 1939 as they were in 1940. In 1938 and 1939 Britain lacked the radar cover and the fighter planes which enabled her to survive in the late summer of 1940, when General Douhet's knockout blow from the air was at last proved to be a myth.

Did Hitler understand this, and was he prepared to precipitate war with France? I think he understood it, and that for a few days, between his meeting with Chamberlain at Obersalzberg and the first day's meeting at Godesberg, he was genuinely listening to Ribbentrop's advice. He then lost his nerve and decided to play for safety, reverting to those "chemical dissolution" tactics which led, in a matter of a few months after Munich, to the peaceful elimination of aircraft carrier Czechoslovakia. The Poles and Hungarians took their cut of the dismembered state, and the final agents of destruction were the Slovaks who, stimulated from Berlin, forcefully claimed their independence. Benes's successor as President of Czechoslovakia was a mild, elderly lawyer, Emil Hacha, who, summoned to Hitler's presence, was so terrified by threats that Prague would be bombed that he fainted. When he had been revived with an injection, he signed a document announcing that, in order to preserve "calm, order and peace," he had "placed the destiny of the Czech people and country with

confidence in the hands of the Fuehrer of the German Reich."
On the following day, March 16, 1939, Hitler made the delayed
entry into Prague which "that fellow Chamberlain" had so inconsiderately spoiled in the previous October. As in the case of
Austria, this was not an invasion, but negotiation, Hitler style.
The French and British Governments did not feel called upon
to fulfill the guarantee of the dismembered state which they had
promised in return for Benes's acceptance of the Anglo-French
terms.

But by his march into Prague, Hitler signed his own eventual
death warrant. He finally convinced Chamberlain, and the British
people, that he could not be dealt with peacefully. It then became a question of when Britain would be ready to fight.

For some months after Munich, in the face of universal dis-
couragement which would have daunted a less obstinate man,
Chamberlain pursued his policy of appeasement. The Germans
were advised from Number 10 Downing Street to ignore pronouncements by the British Foreign Office—the Foreign Secretary could be relied upon to speak with his master's voice, but
only Chamberlain himself expressed official policy. Hitler was
promised trade concessions, an enormous loan, perhaps even the
return of Germany's African colonies, if only he would be good.
There was no response from the Fuehrer. "This fellow Chamberlain shook with fear when I uttered the word 'war,'" he declared
after Munich. "Don't tell me *he* is dangerous."

At home, Chamberlain's prediction among the cheering crowds
that "all this will be over in two or three months" was fulfilled.
In December, he faced a revolt by his junior ministers. Robert
Hudson, junior at the Board of Trade, their spokesman, told him
that "in our view, his policy of appeasement was the correct one
but that we and many people in the country thought that certain
members of his Government were not contributing as fast as we
should like to see to the essential corollary of appeasement, namely
rearmament." Hudson named Runciman, who had joined the
Government after Munich; Winterton, Chancellor of the Duchy
of Lancaster; Sir Thomas Inskip, Minister of Defence; and Hore-
Belisha, Secretary of State for War, as ministers who should be
sacked. Lord Gort, Hore-Belisha's own choice as Chief of the

Imperial General Staff, joined in the attack on his chief, telling Inskip that Hore-Belisha was unfit for his job, was lazy, took no interest in the War Office, and that the only things he was interested in were matters which he thought would redound to his own personal credit. The Government was not a happy ship.

Nor was the country. At some point before November, 1940, Chamberlain had to face a General Election. The Conservative Central Office began routine preparations towards the end of January, 1939, but some at least of its professionals regarded the prospect without confidence. Dame Marjorie Maxse, then Chief Organisation Officer, tells me that "Munich split the Conservative Party from top to toe with a bitterness that was unparalleled . . . At the best, an election would have lessened our majority considerably. We might easily have lost it."

Still Chamberlain plodded doggedly on. What kept him going? I believe the answer may be found in a remark he made to the Labour leaders after his Obersalzberg meeting with Hitler, recorded by Lord Citrine: "If we accept the challenge now, it means war. If we delay a decision, something might happen. Hitler might die."

The events following Hitler's entry into Prague are charged with that tragic irony which underlies the whole of this story. Chamberlain took one of those count-ten-and-leap-out-of-bed decisions which so disconcerted his advisers. He allowed himself to be persuaded by Mr. Ian Colvin, the *News Chronicle* correspondent in Berlin, who had arranged Ewald von Kleist's visit to Britain, that a German attack on Poland was imminent. On March 30, with his own hand, he wrote an unconditional guarantee against any threat to Polish independence "which the Polish Government accordingly felt obliged to resist with their national forces."

The French were dismayed. It was they who had insisted, for their own safety, on dragging Britain into Europe. They now found themselves being dragged by the British and the Poles into what they regarded as a pointless war. The Polish Government became increasingly haughty in their attitude to Germany. No craven Benes surrender for them—after all, they had the finest cavalry in Europe. A little under five months after the

British guarantee to Poland had been announced, Hitler signed a pact with Russia which took the innocent British completely by surprise and rendered their guarantee to Poland even more useless than it had been in the first place.

On August 25, Hitler gave the order for the Wehrmacht to advance on the Polish frontier. As he had anticipated, the French and British at once began to show signs of crumpling. That evening, he halted the Wehrmacht and waited confidently for the new Munich which his misjudgment of the *Schlappschwanz* led him to anticipate. It did not happen. Poland was invaded, Warsaw bombed. On the morning of September 3, 1939, Paul Schmidt brought to Hitler and Ribbentrop at the Berlin Chancellery a British ultimatum. The Fuehrer was given two hours to announce the withdrawal of German forces from Poland.

"Hitler was sitting at his desk," Schmidt has written, "and Ribbentrop stood by the window. Both looked up expectantly as I came in. I stopped at some distance from Hitler's desk, and then slowly translated the British Government's ultimatum. When I finished, there was complete silence. . . .

"After an interval, which seemed an age, he turned to Ribbentrop, who had remained standing by the window. 'What now?' asked Hitler with a savage look, as though implying that his Foreign Minister had misled him about England's possible reaction."

A war had begun which lasted six years and cost some 30 million lives.

The Polish part of it lasted three weeks. The country was then partitioned between Russia and Germany, but Polish partisans kept up a constant guerilla struggle against their conquerors, and the sufferings of the Polish people for the next six years were appalling. The Czechs had not fought in the first place, and there was little partisan activity in Czechoslovakia. It would be unfair to say that the Czechs had a good war—nobody did—but on the whole they had a better war than most of Europe.

One may follow briefly the wartime fortunes of the principal characters in this drama.

After the British declaration of war, the British Cabinet met and agreed to prepare for a struggle lasting three years. Chamberlain laid his forehead on the table and kept it there for nearly ten minutes. When he looked up, his face was ghastly. He was not a wartime Prime Minister, and he knew it, but he continued in office until a British disaster in Norway led to his downfall. Just over a year after the declaration of war he died of cancer, the seeds of which may well have been within him throughout his negotiations with Hitler.

The Fuehrer outlasted him by four and a half years. Then on Monday, April 30, 1945, with Russian troops in the suburbs of Berlin, and after dictating a grandiloquent message to the German people, the Fuehrer shot himself "to escape the disgrace of deposition or capitulation." What happened to the German people thereafter was no concern of the Great Romantic.

Five days after Hitler's suicide, troops of the American 1st Infantry Division of General Patton's Third Army, brought half across the world to finish Secretary of State Lansing's unfinished business of a quarter of a century before, were advancing in the neighbourhood of Eger.

A prisoner of war reported to them that Konrad Henlein and Dr. Robert Ley, head of the German Labour Front, had been seen in Eger two days previously. They were causing adverse comment by doing a lot of drinking and having a big party. "Civilians were mad about it because they didn't think it was the proper thing for them to do at this time."

On May 8, Brigadier-General Thomas L. Harrold of the American 9th Armored Division was inspecting road blocks and screening points established for the control of captured German troops, when he recognized the Fuehrer's Viceroy among a crowd of civilians. "This person," as the official report calls Henlein, was detained and sent over with his secretary to the 1st Infantry Division. He was interrogated, telling his captors, "I've always been a man of high honour." They told him he would be handed back to the Czechs. In his prisoner-of-war cage he opened the veins of his wrist with a razor blade concealed under a patch of adhesive tape on his cigarette case.

Henlein's former lieutenant, Karl Hermann Frank, had far outshone his leader under the Nazi regime, becoming head of the S.S. and the police, and State Secretary to the Protector of

Bohemia-Moravia. In 1945, with the Russians on one side of him and the Americans on the other, he tried to stage a grandstand exit even more glorious than the Fuehrer's, with a devastated Prague to provide his funeral pyre. This romantic notion was stopped by the German commander, General Toussaint, and Frank, too, fell into the hands of the American Army. This time they took care that there were no concealed razor blades and handed him back to the Czechs, who with great satisfaction publicly hanged him in Prague on May 22, 1946, after trial by a People's Court.

Benes resigned the presidency of the Czechoslovak Republic on October 5, 1938, and spent the next few months in America. When war broke out, he became President of the Czechoslovak National Committee in London, and returned to a Russian-occupied Prague in May, 1945. Benes continued to negotiate hopefully with the Russians and with the Czechoslovak Communists, who seized power in the spring of 1948, but they, like Hitler, were too much for him. He resigned as President for a second time, and died shortly afterwards, on September 3, 1948.

Daladier, very clear-headed at eighty-three, and Bonnet, aged seventy-seven, are at the time of writing the only distinguished participants in these events who are still alive.

> I tell the tale that I heard told.
> Mithridates, he died old.

Appendix

SIR NEVILE HENDERSON'S MEMORANDUM ON BRITISH POLICY TOWARDS GERMANY

This 13-page memorandum, dated May 10, 1937, had been written before Henderson took up his appointment in Berlin at the end of April in that year, but it was not until August that he sent it privately to Sir Orme Sargent, Assistant Under-Secretary at the Foreign Office. The Foreign Office, in forwarding a copy to Halifax before his visit to Germany in November, noted that "we gather that it still substantially represents his views."

The important paragraphs are these:

"The obstacles to an Anglo-German understanding are, it is true, extraordinarily formidable. Quite apart from Germany herself, the Nazi régime, her traditional mentality and character and her inevitable urge towards unity and expansion, it is not to the interest—for obvious reasons—either of Italy or of Russia to witness its consummation. And, though it is difficult not to feel convinced that it would be to her ultimate interest, it will be exceedingly hard to obtain the co-operation of France, who has her own ideas as to what is her own best national policy. Yet can we go forward without France? It would seem therefore that the first objective must be to convince France that she must and can rely on us to guarantee her security as part of an understanding with Germany ... The alternative, however disagreeable and only as a last resort, would then be a direct Anglo-German understanding based on French security and integrity but including some guarantee of neutrality in the event of a Russo-German conflict . . .

"Expansion in the East is an elastic term. If the national integrity and independence of her [Germany's] neighbours were safeguarded, His Majesty's Government would not be justified in actively objecting to a political and economic predominance which the German armies and German industry and population will in any case ensure of their own volition.

"As regards Austria, it is conceivable that sooner or later she will wish of her own free will to be reunited [sic] to Germany. Even today she would never take sides against Germany in a world struggle. She may be anti-Nazi, but she is assuredly German . . . If the movement for union were to come from within Austria herself and not from pressure from without—as it well might eventually if, for instance, Schuschnigg were to disappear and Nazism become more tolerant—His Majesty's Government would find it morally impossible to contest the right of Austria as a nation to dispose of her own fate. In the end we may well be faced there with a 'fait accompli' which we could not prevent and which we would be regarded as having opposed in vain. Danzig is likely to revert to Germany in much the same way, and ultimately Memel.

"As regards the Sudeten deutsche and the other numerous German minorities in Europe, the best prospect for a peaceful solution lies firstly in a greater political wisdom than the Czechs themselves have hitherto displayed and in more energetic action than the League of Nations has yet shown in respect of the effective protection of minorities. Only so can we hope to ensure the maintenance of the promise which . . . might today, but possibly not tomorrow, be extracted by us from Hitler.

"In any case, whatever may have been possible yesterday, it is most improbable that any attempt to achieve an understanding with Germany has today even a faint chance of success except on the following minimum basis:

"(a) an undertaking that if and when—but only when—Austria herself honestly and spontaneously desires it, we shall not oppose the Anschluss;

"(b) the recognition in principle of Germany's right to own colonies and an eventual arrangement whereby some part of say West Africa is allotted to her;

"(c) an assurance that His Majesty's Government has in principle no jealous objection to German economic and even political predominance in Eastern Europe provided Hitler undertakes to abide by his public assurances of May 21, 1935 [that he would seek peaceful revision of the Treaty of Versailles]. In return for these concessions and economic assistance, we could ask Hitler to implement the proposals which he made at the time of the remilitarisation of the Rhineland as contained in the German memorandum of March 7th, 1936, including Germany's return to a reformed League of Nations. Perhaps we should try to make this last desideratum our real starting point.

"Whether an advance on these lines commends itself or not to His Majesty's Government or is compatible with British international moral and legal conceptions, it would still be highly unwise to allow the present system of drift to continue . . . The conviction that Britain is barring the way to Germany in every direction, however legitimate, is deepening. More and more Germans are beginning to feel that, since conciliation has failed, war with Great Britain will again have to be faced if Germany is to realise her destiny . . .

"If Germany is blocked from any Western adventure—and Mr. Eden's definite public declaration that Great Britain would regard as a casus belli in future any aggression not only against Belgium but against France and Holland has made the position crystal clear in this respect—have we the right to oppose German *peaceful* expansion and evolution in the East? . . .

"Surely our right course is to be prepared to submit, provided we secure peace in the West, without too great discomfort to the surge and swell of restless Pan-Germanism in Central and Eastern Europe. It is true that the idea of leaving a comparatively free hand to Germany eastwards will alarm and dissatisfy a section of public opinion both informed and uniformed [sic] in England. Yet what other practical course is open to us if we are to avoid the insane fatalistic folly of setting our course for another war? Even if we beat Germany again the result, after another period of chaos, would be the same as today. Unlike Great Britain and France, or even Italy since 1914, Germany as a political entity is still incomplete. Nothing we can do or say can make black white. The restlessness of Germany in the 20th century is inevitable and will make itself intensely disagreeable, particularly to Russia and Italy, as well as to the smaller States, but not necessarily to Great Britain, in spite of the out-of-date premiss as regards British opposition to any predominant Power in Europe . . .

"Is not the present limit-of-what-is-possible an agreement with Germany which, while going far in the direction of her aspirations (and some must legitimately be conceded to her), still binds her to respect vital principles? . . . We have at long last realised ourselves that the League of Nations, collective security and Treaty engagements constitute no reliable substitute for a Navy and Air Force capable both of defending Great Britain from invasion or attack and of making her due influence felt in the world. Would it not be equally wise to admit at once, without further delay, that Germany is now too powerful to be persuaded or compelled to enter into an Eastern Pact, that a certain German predominance eastward is inevitable, and that peace in the West must not be sacrificed to a theoretically laudable but practically mistaken idealism in the East . . . To put it quite bluntly, Eastern Europe emphatically is neither definitely settled for all time nor is it a vital British interest and the German is certainly more civilised than the Slav, and in the end, if properly handled, also less potentially dangerous to British interests—one might even go so far as to assert that it is not even just to endeavour to prevent Germany from completing her unity or from being prepared for war against the Slav provided her preparations are such as to reassure the British Empire that they are not simultaneously designed against it . . ."

The Foreign Office, in a note dated October 13, 1937, sharply repudiated Henderson's views:

"Whether or not we believe that territorial expansion by Germany is in any event inevitable, we should, by making any such intimation to the German Government, run the gravest risks of disturbing the stability of Europe, and bringing about hurriedly and out of season developments which should preferably take place, if they must, in their own good time, when the hour is ripe. Europe is in a tense and potentially unstable condition. What keeps it from immediate collapse more than anything else is the closeness of the Anglo-French connection, the published programme of British rearmament, and a lingering doubt in the minds of some Governments whether, in fact, Great Britain would refrain from armed intervention if trouble arose. Austria and Czechoslovakia occupy a special position in Europe and they are regarded by the world at large as tests or symbols of the direction in which the world is likely to move. Any intimation on the part of His Majesty's Government to Germany of her possible acquiescence in territorial changes to Germany's benefit would almost certainly at once become public property and would set up reactions in the minds of European Governments which might bring the European card-castle tumbling down . . .

"The position so far as we are concerned is as follows: (1) any territorial change in Central and Eastern Europe, even if it comes slowly and in good order, is certain to have political effects in Europe which it is not possible to assess, but which might well be to our disadvantage; (2) we are not (though we do not publicly say so) prepared to intervene by force of arms to prevent it; (3) the object of our policy is to keep the situation as steady as we can, without bringing ourselves face to face with war. The situation is therefore one of great delicacy, in which the resources of diplomacy are, thanks to our backwardness in rearmament, our chief instrument—unless it be our fortunately still powerful prestige. The problem is one for the most delicate handling, and it is unlikely that anything but confusion could result from any sudden plunge into a new policy of open undertakings to make concessions to Germany . . ."

Throughout the Munich Crisis and beyond, the British Government balanced uneasily between the advice given by Henderson and that of the Foreign Office. Henderson, Sir Robert Vansittart's choice as Ambassador to Germany, never ceased privately to voice the views expressed in his memorandum, and though he was occasionally rebuked, he was neither recalled nor repudiated. One wonders how much of the British Ambassador's memorandum "leaked" to Russian eyes, and whether it affected Soviet policy in the years ahead.

Notes on Unpublished Sources
Not Attributed in the Text

CHAPTER 1. p. 8. The microphone in the Commons. The Librarian of the British Broadcasting Corporation informs me that "We can find in our records no evidence of any intention to broadcast the Prime Minister's speech." Sir Charles Harris, at the time private secretary to the Government Chief Whip, writes, "I have no recollection of any intention to broadcast Mr. Chamberlain's speech . . . The purpose of the microphone was to enable the overflow of Peers to hear the Prime Minister's speech live in a room of the House of Lords."

p. 9. Sir Alexander Cadogan has given me this account of how the last-minute invitation to Munich reached the House of Commons.

CHAPTER 2. p. 22. According to some German writers, Christie was a member of the British Intelligence Service. Group Captain Christie tells me that "I have never been a member of the British Intelligence Service. My visits to Henlein and my dealings with him throughout were entirely at my own expense. At first they were wholly on my own initiative, but later I informed my friend, Robert Vansittart, who encouraged me to pursue this friendly contact . . . I only saw and collaborated with Vansittart."

CHAPTER 3. p. 36. Ribbentrop's earlier, and more interesting, report (No. A5522) is described as "Not found" in *Documents on German Foreign Policy*, Series D, Vol. I, page 162. It is now available in the British Foreign Office Library and, no doubt, elsewhere.

CHAPTER 9. p. 95. I must emphasize that this is Dr. Brand's recollection of what was said to him by Vansittart. No report of this meeting by Vansittart has been published.

CHAPTER 12. p. 117. The possibility of Czech and Sudeten-German access to official British telegrams was mentioned to me by Sir John Troutbeck.

p. 128. Stopford's account of this and other incidents appears in a lecture on the Sudeten crisis which he delivered at Frankfurt on June 7, 1962.

CHAPTER 18. p. 179. Prchala's account of his interview with Benes was published in *Dr. Beneš o vojně pred válkou i za ní* (*Dr. Benes about Warfare, before the War and After*) by a Right-wing anti-Benes member of the Czechoslovak Parliament, Frantisek Schwarz. It has been supplemented for me by Mr. J. Kosina, to whom Prchala told the story in Poland in 1939, with the additional information that he had intended to assassinate Benes if the President turned down his ultimatum.

CHAPTER 21. p. 213. Masaryk's telephone conversation with Benes is referred to in *Documents on British Foreign Policy 1919-1399,* Third Series, Vol. II, Nos. 1118 and 1126. No. 1201 contains denials from Krofta and Masaryk that Masaryk had said what the Germans alleged he had said. A member of Masaryk's staff at the time tells me that Masaryk did have such a telephone conversation with Benes, during which he was excessively indiscreet.

CHAPTER 22. p. 216. Letters from Churchill to Halifax of July 23, 1947, and from Halifax to Churchill of July 24, 1947. Hickleton Papers, Nos. A4.410.19.2/3.

CHAPTER 26. p. 265. Revolt by junior ministers. Memorandum by R.S. Hudson, 1st Viscount Hudson. Hickleton Papers, A4. 410. 22A.

Principal Published Sources

Benes, Eduard, *Memoirs: From Munich to New War and New Victory*, Verry, 1954.

Birkenhead, Earl of (Frederick W. F. Smith), *Halifax: The Life of Lord Halifax*, Houghton, Boston, 1966.

Bonnet, Georges, *Défense de la Paix*, C. Bourquin, Geneva, 1948.

Brand, Walter, *Die Sudetendeutsche Tragedie*, Rudolf Zitzman-Verlag, Lauf bei Nürnberg, 1949.

Bullock, Alan L., *Hitler, A Study in Tyranny*, Harper, New York, 1964.

Carr, E. H., *German-Soviet Relations Between the Two World Wars, 1919–1939*, Johns Hopkins, Baltimore, 1951.

Ciano, Count Galeazzo, *The Ciano Diaries, 1937–1938*, Doubleday, New York, 1946.

Citrine, Lord, *Men and Work*, Hutchinson, London, 1964.

Collier, Basil, *The Defence of the United Kingdom*, Her Majesty's Stationery Office, London, 1957.

Colvin, Ian, *None So Blind*, Harcourt, New York, 1965.

Cooper, A. Duff, *Old Men Forget*, Dutton, New York, 1954.

Dalton, Hugh, *Memoirs, 1931–1945: The Fateful Years*, Muller, London, 1957.

Davies, Joseph E., *Mission to Moscow*, Simon & Schuster, New York, 1941.

Documents and Materials Relating to the Eve of the Second War, Vol. II, *The Dirksen Papers, 1938–1939*, Foreign Languages Publishing House, Moscow, 1948.

Documents on British Foreign Policy, Third Series, Vols. I, II and III, Her Majesty's Stationery Office, London, 1949–.

Documents on German Foreign Policy, 1918–1945, Series D, Vols. I and II, Her Majesty's Stationery Office, London, 1949–.

Dolezal, Jiri and Kren, Jan, *Czechoslovakia's Fight*, 1938–45, Czechoslovak Academy of Sciences, Prague, 1964.

Douhet, Giulio, *The Command of the Air*, Coward-McCann, New York, 1942.

Duranty, Walter, *U.S.S.R.*, Lippincott, New York, 1944.

Feiling, Sir Keith, *The Life of Neville Chamberlain*, Macmillan, New York, 1946.

Gajan, Koloman and Kvacek, Robert, *Germany and Czechoslovakia, 1918–1945*, Orbis, Prague, 1965.

Gamelin, General Maurice, *Servir*, Vol. II, *Le Prologue du Drame*, Plon, Paris, 1946.

Gedye, G. E. R., *Betrayal in Europe; Austria and Czechoslovakia: The Fallen Bastions*, Harper, New York, 1939.

Gisevius, Hans Bernd, *To the Bitter End*, Houghton, Boston, 1947.

Guderian, General Heinz, *Panzer Leader*, Dutton, New York, 1952.

Haldane, J. B. S., *A.R.P.*, Gollancz, London, 1938.

Henderson, Alexander, *Eyewitness in Czechoslovakia*, Harrap, London, 1939.

Henderson, Sir Nevile, *Failure of a Mission*, Putnam, New York, 1940.

Hesse, Fritz, *Hitler and the English*, Wingate, London, 1954.

Hitler, Adolf, *Hitler's Secret Conversations*, Farrar, Straus & Giroux, New York, 1953.

Ironside, Field-Marshal Lord, *Time Unguarded: The Ironside Diaries, 1937–1940*, McKay, New York, 1963.

Jaksch, Wenzel, *Europe's Road to Potsdam*, Praeger, New York, 1963.

Kirkpatrick, Ivone, *The Inner Circle*, Macmillan, London, 1959.

Korbel, Josef, *Communist Subversion in Czechoslovakia, 1938–1948*, Princeton, Princeton, N.J., 1959.

Lockhart, Sir Robert Bruce, *Came the Reckoning*, Putnam, New York, 1947.

Mass-Observation, *Britain*, Penguin, London, 1939.

Minney, R. J., *The Private Papers of Hore-Belisha*, Doubleday, New York, 1960.

Moravec, Emanuel, *Das Ende der Benesch-Republik*, Orbis, Prague, 1941.

Namier, Sir Lewis, *Diplomatic Prelude*, Macmillan, New York, 1948.

———. *Europe in Decay—1936–1940*, Macmillan, New York, 1950.

———. *In the Nazi Era*, St. Martins, New York, 1952.

Neue Dokumente zur Gesichte des Muenchener Abkommens, Orbis, Prague, 1959.

Nicolson, Nigel, *Harold Nicolson: Diaries and Letters 1930–1939,* Atheneum, New York, 1966.

Noguères, Henri, *Munich: "Peace for Our Time,"* McGraw-Hill, New York, 1965.

O'Brien, T. H., *Civil Defence,* Her Majesty's Stationery Office, London, 1955.

Postan, M. M., *British War Production,* Her Majesty's Stationery Office, London, 1952.

Rabl, Kurt, "Neue Dokumente zur Sudeten Krisis 1938," *Bohemia,* Vol. I, Year Book of the Collegium Carolinum, Munich, 1960.

Reynaud, Paul, *In the Thick of the Fight,* Simon & Schuster, New York, 1955.

Ripka, Hubert, *Munich: Before and After,* Gollancz, London, 1939.

Robertson, E. M., *Hitler's Pre-War Policy and Military Plans,* Citadel, New York, 1965.

Schellenberg, Walter, *Labyrinth: Memoirs of Hitler's Secret Service Chief,* Harper, New York, 1957.

Schlabrendorff, Fabian von, *The Secret War Against Hitler,* Pitman, New York, 1965.

Schmidt, Paul, *Hitler's Interpreter,* Macmillan, New York, 1951.

Schwarz, Frantisek, *Dr. Beneš o vojně pred válkou i za ní,* St. Clements Press, London, 1940.

Shirer, William L., *Berlin Diary: The Journal of a Foreign Correspondent, 1934–1941,* Knopf, New York, 1941.

Strang, Lord, *Home and Abroad,* Deutsch, London, 1956.

Taylor, A. J. P., *The Origins of the Second World War,* Atheneum, New York, 1962.

Taylor, Telford, *Sword and Swastika,* Simon & Schuster, New York, 1952.

Templewood, Viscount, *Nine Troubled Years,* Collins, London, 1954.

Vansittart, Lord, *The Mist Procession,* Hutchinson, London, 1958.

Webster, Sir Charles, and Noble Frankland, *The Strategic Air Offensive Against Germany,* Vol. I, *Preparation,* Her Majesty's Stationery Office, London, 1961.

Weizsaecker, Ernst von, *Memoirs,* Regnery, Chicago, 1951.

Whalen, Richard J., *The Founding Father,* New American Library, New York, 1964.

Wheeler-Bennett, Sir John W., *Munich: Prologue to Tragedy,* Meredith (Duell), New York, 1963.

INDEX